The
Urban
Voter

The Politics of Race and Ethnicity

Series Editors
Rodney E. Hero, University of Notre Dame
Katherine Tate, University of California, Irvine

Politics of Race and Ethnicity is premised on the view that understanding race and ethnicity is integral to a fuller, more complete understanding of the American political system. The series' thematic emphasis welcomes work employing various theoretical perspectives and methodological approaches. The goal is to provide the scholarly community at all levels with accessible texts that will introduce them to, and stimulate their thinking on, fundamental questions in this field. The editors also invite projects that offer original and informative perspectives for the general public on social issues related to the politics of race and ethnicity. We are interested in books that creatively examine the meaning of American democracy for racial and ethnic groups and, conversely, what racial and ethnic groups mean and have meant for American democracy.

The Urban Voter: Group Conflict and Mayoral Voting Behavior in American Cities Karen M. Kaufmann

The
Urban
Voter

Group Conflict and
Mayoral Voting Behavior
in American Cities

Karen M. Kaufmann

The University of Michigan Press
Ann Arbor

To Gadi

Copyright © by the University of Michigan 2004
All rights reserved
Published in the United States of America by
The University of Michigan Press
Manufactured in the United States of America
♾ Printed on acid-free paper

2007   2006   2005   2004   4   3   2   1

A CIP catalog record for this book is available from the British Library.

Library of Congress Cataloging-in-Publication Data

Kaufmann, Karen M., 1959–
The urban voter : group conflict and mayoral voting behavior in
American cities / Karen M. Kaufmann.
p.   cm. — (The politics of race and ethnicity)
Includes bibliographical references and index.
ISBN 0-472-09857-8 (Cloth : alk. paper) —
ISBN 0-472-06857-1 (Paper : alk. paper)
1. Local elections—United States.   2. Elections—California—Los
Angeles.   3. Elections—New York (State)—New York.   4. Mayors—United
States—Election.   5. Mayors—California—Los Angeles—Election.
6. Mayors—New York (State)—New York—Election.   7. United States—Race
relations—Political aspects.   8. Los Angeles (Calif.)—Race
relations—Political aspects.   9. New York (N.Y.)—Race
relations—Political aspects.   I. Title.   II. Series.

JS395 .K38 2004
324.973'092'091732—dc22   2003016346

Contents

Acknowledgments

This book would not have been possible without the help and support of many people. I owe enormous gratitude to my graduate school professors at UCLA. In particular, I want to thank Frank Gilliam for his commitment to this project and for the numerous hours he invested in reading its earliest incarnations. He is a wonderful mentor, and his many insights and sometimes brutal red pen were invaluable to me. I am also tremendously grateful to John Petrocik for teaching me the "nuts and bolts" of political science research and for continuing to be a source of information, inspiration, and great friendship.

While at UCLA, I was fortunate to work with several scholars whose research profoundly shaped this work. In particular, Larry Bobo was a major influence on my thinking about group conflict as it relates to city politics. I am indebted to Larry for his generous encouragement at every stage of this project. I also owe considerable thanks to David Sears for his thoughtful feedback and positive support. In addition, I want to thank Raphael Sonenshein, John Mollenkopf, and David Halle for their encouragement during the early stages of this research.

Many of my colleagues at the University of Maryland have consistently gone above and beyond the call of duty in helping with this book. I am particularly indebted to Jim Gimpel, Irwin Morris, Ric Uslaner, Mark Lichbach, and Christian Davenport. My Maryland colleagues, beyond advising me on the substance of the book, provided invaluable help in navigating the murky waters of academic publishing. I cannot thank them enough.

I am also grateful to Bob Stein, Rodney Hero, Katherine Tate, and several anonymous reviewers for taking the time to read earlier versions of this manuscript and for providing a wealth of helpful suggestions. Jeremy Shine from the University of Michigan Press, while no longer my editor, was nonetheless a constant source of support, and my gratitude to him is enormous. I also owe considerable thanks to Daron Shaw, Kristen Williams, Julie Shapiro, Brian Shapiro, Donna Farkas, Richard Farkas, Laurie Content, and Sam Ross for their good humor and friendship.

Finally, I owe the greatest debt to my family—to my parents, Marilyn and Marvin Malmuth, for nurturing my love of politics, and especially to my husband, Gadi, and my wonderful daughters, Katie and Amy. There is no way to quantify the many sacrifices they have made on my behalf. My love and appreciation for them, however, are infinite.

Introduction

In 1993 Richard Riordan, a white Republican from Los Angeles's affluent Westside, beat his Democratic opponent, Michael Woo, to become the first Republican mayor of Los Angeles in over thirty years. Woo, an incumbent city councilman from the liberal West Hollywood district, was expected to win. In a city where Democrats outnumber Republicans by a two to one margin, and where nearly two-thirds of its residents are racial and ethnic minorities, it seemed inconceivable that a white, Republican multimillionaire would succeed Tom Bradley as the mayor of Los Angeles. A short five months later Republican Rudolph Giuliani defeated Democrat David Dinkins to become the mayor of New York City, a metropolis like Los Angeles where Democrats represent the vast majority of voters.

New York and Los Angeles had long been viewed as liberal cities where Democrats dominate the local politics. The ascendance of these two Republican mayors caught many in the media and in the academy off guard. How could presumably liberal cities with large minority populations elect Republican mayors? Why did large numbers of white Democrats abandon their long-standing party identifications in support of these Republican candidates? What did these victories mean for the future of city politics and the minority empowerment that had come to characterize many urban regimes?

Jack White, a senior correspondent for *Time* magazine, contended that "the revolution in America's city halls" (1993, 28) that began with Carl Stokes's 1967 election in Cleveland was ending, that this new breed of urban mayors was focusing on efficiency and fiscal responsibility in the same fervent voice they once used to call for racial and ethnic equality. In a similar vein, political observer Jim Sleeper (1993) argued that the pattern of urban election returns in the early 1990s—Republican Brett Schundler's 1991 victory in Jersey City, Republican Giuliani's 1993 victory in New York, and Richard Riordan's victory in Los Angeles—represented a fundamental shift in voter preferences away from the Jesse Jackson–style rainbow politics that had been so prevalent in the prior decades.

Much was made of these electoral outcomes, yet in this same time period when cities such as New York and Los Angeles were rejecting Democratic, minority, and liberal mayoral candidates, other cities such as Seattle, Minneapolis, Cleveland, Dallas, Denver, and San Francisco were newly electing and reelecting black mayors. Even Houston, the largest American city that had never been run by a minority mayor, elected its first in 1997. And more recently yet, Los Angeles, after eight years of Republican rule, reverted to its Democratic tradition by electing Democrat James Hahn to succeed Richard Riordan in 2001. Given the enormous inconsistency in mayoral election choices over the past ten years, the proposition that conservative outcomes in Los Angeles and New York signified a sweeping trend across American cities seems somewhat inflated. There were several instances of conservative victories in reputedly liberal cities, just as there were noteworthy liberal and minority victories in cities with less progressive traditions (Keiser 2000).

Conventional theories of voting cannot explain the variability of urban political behavior over the past ten years. Partisanship, a consistently profound influence in national elections, is an apparently less reliable factor in local politics. Within the realm of local elections, there are many examples where Democrats and Republicans behave like loyal partisans but there are also many others where traditional political alliances explain relatively little about how people vote. There are times when minority candidates evoke enormous opposition and stimulate enhanced political participation among all groups. There are other circumstances when the race, gender, ethnicity, or religion of a candidate makes little difference to the vote. If we are to comprehend the factors that motivate voting behavior in urban elections, we must first understand when race matters and when it does not, as well as when partisan identities are important to voting and when they are likely to be abandoned in favor of other more salient group identities.

The theoretical perspective I develop in this book argues that relative levels of perceived intergroup conflict, within cities and between them, can help guide our expectations about the political behavior of voters. Cities with palpable levels of interracial conflict are likely to experience racially polarized voting. In the absence of such conflict, or when conflict subsides, voters will rely on traditional political identities—partisanship and ideology—to guide their choices at the polls. In cities that experience persistent interracial discord, racially polarized voting is typical. In cities where perceived conflict is periodic and transitory, voter behavior adjusts to the changes in political context— racially polarized in one case, notably more partisan in another. From this perspective, I argue that heightened perceptions of racial conflict make racial group interests politically salient. And as such, I refer to this framework as the group interest theory of local voting behavior.

A central idea in this book is that local politics differ from national politics in important ways. For example, party identification, so important to presidential and congressional voting, is not always salient in local elections. Presumably this is because, unlike in national politics, the candidates and issues that surround local elections do not necessarily emphasize traditional partisan cleavages. Group interests—apart from normal partisan or ideological leanings—can be quite stark at the level of local politics. Will the new park be located in my neighborhood or yours? Will additional police be patrolling my streets or yours? Will the new police chief be sensitive to the needs of my immediate community? Will new resources be directed to the public schools in my neighborhood or will they continue to flow to the other side of town?

These kinds of issues are the mother's milk of local politics. They are, in a relative sense, more immediate and more tangible than much of the national rhetoric about social security "lock boxes," economic stimulus packages, campaign finance reform, and the like. In the short run, they may also appear more consequential. At a minimum, people's local wants and needs are fairly simple to identify and pretty easy to understand. They can also be extraordinarily contentious issues that elicit heightened conflict in communities.

In my own experience as a homeowner in Los Angeles, I recall a public meeting on the topic of using our local public school as a site for Saturday soccer games. As the parent of a second grader who would likely get to play on this site, I happily attended the public meeting, albeit somewhat curious about what the source of opposition to such an innocuous activity might be. I was shocked, however, to find hundreds of local residents attending this meeting. Parents of school-age children crowded on one side of the room, while empty nesters and otherwise child-free adults crowded to the other side. Clearly there was more at stake here than I had originally anticipated. "Hoards of unwanted spectators would descend on the neighborhood every Saturday," we were warned. (Not to sound skeptical, but only immediate relatives attend these Saturday games and usually under duress.) "Children may jump out into the street and be killed." "Second grade soccer could pose a fire hazard. . . . What if fire trucks can't get through?" And the arguments went on and on. Had this conflict occurred during an election season, it very well may have become a divisive political issue, with supporters of the soccer games on one side of the political divide and opponents on the other. Were this the case, normal political considerations, such as party identification, probably would have been trumped by a more personal set of interests and a more relevant set of identities. Once the issue was resolved, however, it is unlikely that these salient group identities—soccer sympathizers versus others—would continue to retain their electoral relevance. It was, after all, the conflict that made these identities salient in the first place, and it is reasonable to expect that, when the battle receded, other more proximate identities would inform future political decisions.

The preceding example illustrates the central proposition in this book—that group conflict affects the basis upon which individuals make electoral decisions. In particular, group interest theory maintains that heightened levels of group animosity within a community turn group-related attitudes into salient voting considerations. This perspective treats intergroup attitudes such as stereotypes and resentments as a set of relatively stable predispositions similar to other political and social attitudes. *Group conflict is important, then, because it*

*influences the relative weights that voters apply to these sets of attitudes
in the context of electoral choice.*

The focus of this book, however, is not on soccer moms and the
attendant problems they face in modern suburbia. Rather this work
centers on the role of racial group conflict in the politics of contemporary American cities with the objective to shed some light on the
various patterns of electoral behavior that have characterized urban
voters over the past thirty-five years. Levels of perceived group
conflict vary within cities and between them. Some cities do experience persistent racial hostility, and in these cities racial interests and
racial identities are typically consistent predictors of voting behavior.
In other cities, racial discord is more variable. When elections take
place in a conflictual environment, voting behavior will likely reflect
the temporal salience of these interests. However, when racial conflict
recedes, voting behavior will likely revert to more "normal" political
considerations such as party identification or political ideology. Thus
the group interest theory is a contextual theory of local voting behavior that accords substantial theoretical weight to the presence or
absence of intergroup conflict generally and interracial conflict more
specifically.

This book explores group conflict and political behavior at two levels. The primary analyses in this work concentrate on individual-level
political behavior and how changes in the degree of group conflict
affect voting decisions. The general argument is that heightened levels of perceived interracial conflict make racial interests and racial attitudes salient voting cues. On a macrolevel, this work also addresses
the question of what triggers intergroup hostility in cities. In particular, I explore a number of possible correlates to group conflict,
including social diversity and rapid demographic change, historical
group relations, local economic conditions, as well as the kind of
political candidates and issues that characterize local politics. Thus
the aim of this work is to provide insight into both the macrolevel and
individual-level processes that influence voting behavior and correspond with racial polarization in contemporary American city politics.

The empirical focus is on the mayoral politics of Los Angeles and
New York over the past thirty-five years. These two largest American

cities exemplify social processes that happen in most large cities, especially those with growing racial and ethnic diversity. New York represents an East Coast city with a long history of ethnic politics, machine-like governing institutions, and racially polarized voting. Los Angeles exemplifies the archetypal reform city with a weak mayor, nonpartisan elections, and sporadic evidence of racially motivated political behavior.[1] Los Angeles, in 1973, was the first major U.S. city without a majority black population to elect a black mayor. Mayor Tom Bradley was reelected four times without so much as a runoff election. By contrast, New York elected its first black mayor in 1989, and then only by the slimmest of electoral margins. By 1993, however, both cities were run by Republican mayors. These electoral outcomes were not, as has been argued by others, indicative of a growing conservatism among city electorates across the country. Nor were they evidence that the civil rights movement had come to a screeching halt. Rather, this book argues that increasing perceptions of group conflict in Los Angeles made racial cues salient to voters in the 1990s and that, when levels of group conflict in Los Angeles were comparable to those in New York, their electoral politics were strikingly similar as well.

Outline of the Book

The chapters in the book explore the behavioral effects of group conflict on the electoral choices of urban voters. Chapter 1 elaborates on the factors that at times distinguish local politics from national politics and explores the applicability of traditional partisan theories of voting to the unique case of local elections. Chapter 2 explains the logic behind the group interest theory and the expectations that are derived from this perspective.

Chapter 3 explores the mayoral politics of Los Angeles in 1969 and 1973. The dramatic and conflictual backdrop to the 1969 election (i.e., race riots and Vietnam War protests throughout the country)

---

1. The Los Angeles Charter Reform proposal, which passed in 1998, considerably strengthened mayoral authority in appointments and oversight. Nonetheless, given the fairly small number of government jobs controlled by the mayor and the continued clout wielded by the elected city council, Los Angeles would still be characterized as a "weak mayor" city.

coupled with an overtly racial campaign by Bradley's opponent, Sam Yorty, are credited for Bradley's defeat. Four years later, however, these same two candidates met in a rematch, with Bradley as the victor. Using public opinion data from this period, I illustrate how the basis for mayoral voting behavior changed in concert with the change in political context from 1969 to 1973.

Chapter 4 turns to Los Angeles mayoral politics in the post-Bradley era. Nearly twenty years of a biracial governing coalition and relatively peaceful race relations ended with riots in 1992. With a deep economic recession and civil unrest as the setting, the mayoral contest between Richard Riordan and Michael Woo was unlike its predecessors. Analyses using public opinion data illustrate the powerful relationship between negative racial attitudes and the voting behavior of whites. The findings from this case are particularly interesting given that racial attitudes play a central role in voting behavior in an election where neither candidate was black.

Chapter 5 moves to New York City and its politics. Using historical records, voting returns, and public opinion surveys, this chapter examines New York mayoral elections from the 1960s through 1993, with particular attention paid to the victory and subsequent defeat of New York City's first black mayor, David Dinkins. The main claim is that, unlike in Los Angeles, racial group conflict has been a persistent feature of New York City politics since the 1960s. Circumstances surrounding the 1989 election—a strong economy, fatigue with Koch's racial divisiveness, and an inexperienced challenger—opened the door for Dinkins. The subsequent decline in the local economy, the continuing escalation of racial discord, and accusations of racial favoritism on the part of the mayor contributed to his defeat in 1993.

Chapter 6 describes Riordan's and Giuliani's successful reelection campaigns in 1997 and in particular explores the nature of retrospective voting in a racially combative political context. While traditional theories of retrospective voting would place individual-level assessments of the incumbent at the center of any voting calculus, the analyses presented in this chapter clearly illustrate the continuing significance of racial interests—above and beyond opinion regarding the mayor and his job performance.

Chapter 7 explores the most recent mayoral elections in New York

and Los Angeles—two cases that powerfully illustrate the role that
changing political context plays in voter decision making. Faced with
a buoyant economy and a favorable racial climate, voters in Los Angeles overwhelmingly supported two liberal Democrats in the nonpartisan open primary. Furthermore, racial resentments that were such
potent predictors of voting behavior in the preceding elections were
considerably less influential in this contest. As much as any other
example, Los Angeles voting behavior in 2001 provides stark confir-
mation for many of the main tenets of group interest theory. New
Yorkers in 2001, unlike their Los Angeles counterparts, rejected the
Democratic candidate for mayor, Mark Green, in favor of the political newcomer, Republican billionaire Michael Bloomberg. And while
the terror attacks on New York City most certainly influenced the
politics of this mayoral election, intergroup conflict—in this case
between racial minorities and the white Democratic candidate—also
played a pivotal role in its outcome.

Finally, chapter 8 looks to the future of urban electoral politics at
the start of a new century. In particular, I discuss the increasing racial
and ethnic diversity of American cities and speculate as to the challenges that these changes pose for the people and the politics of urban
America. As large American cities continue to become more diverse,
and as the growth in Latino populations in many cities outpaces that
of both non-Latino whites and previously empowered African-American communities, group dynamics will inevitably change. New coalitions will be formed and new sources of conflict will most certainly
arise. If we have learned anything from big city politics over the past
three decades, it is that change is inevitable.

As for the soccer field, the parents prevailed in this exchange, but-
tressed by the support of Mayor Riordan. With the exception of a few
skinned knees and bruised egos over the course of the season, no serious impediments to life, liberty, and the pursuit of happiness have
been realized.

1 Constructing a Theory of Local Voting Behavior

The most commonly accepted theories of voting—at the level of presidential, gubernatorial, Senate, and House elections—point to the importance of party identification to voter choice. In most forms of American electoral politics, partisanship is a major force (Stein 1990; Kahn and Kenney 1999; Bartels 2000; Jacobson 2001). Yet local politics often represent an interesting exception to this general rule. Sometimes local elections are predictably partisan affairs. In many cases, however, party allegiances are distinctly *unimportant* to the choices that voters make in their local elections. In place of partisanship, alternate group identities and group interests tend to shape local choices. In particular, racial and ethnic group identities often subsume partisan ones as important voting cues, especially when the political context in a given election is characterized by relatively high levels of intergroup conflict. With this in mind, the central goal of this work is to identify the contextual factors that tend to trigger racially and ethnically polarized voting within the domain of local elections and to use these insights to construct a theory of local voting behavior.

The theoretical perspective I develop and explore in this book—the group interest theory—represents an extension of the group influence model proposed by Angus Campbell, Philip Converse, Warren Miller, and Donald Stokes in their 1960 work, *The American Voter*. From *The American Voter*'s perspective, individuals identify with political parties in much the same way as they identify with ethnic groups, racial groups, religious groups, and other social groups.

9

Political identities are nonetheless more important, they argue, because they are more proximate and salient to voting. Group interest theory, however, suggests that in the case of local politics partisan identities are not always the most proximate or salient and that other group identities may supersede partisan leanings in their electoral importance. Unlike the typical case in national politics, local political issues do not necessarily have a partisan focus. The essential questions that dominate many local elections revolve around the allocation of goods and services, and it is this emphasis on the distribution of benefits that often imbues local politics with a tangible competition over resources. Groups that are small by the standards of a state or the nation can be both numerically large and influential within the context of a city. As such, local politics offer an important stepping stone to minority incorporation, as previously excluded groups seeking representation in the larger democracy have found their greatest opportunities close to home. Minority challenges to majority-controlled regimes can result in powerful countermobilization and polarized voting, but not always. Group interest theory represents a contextual framework that links characteristics of the political and social context to expected patterns in individual-level voting behavior.

My central proposition is that heightened perceptions of group conflict affect the basis upon which individuals make electoral decisions. Past research on group conflict has focused on the relationship between intergroup competition and racial prejudice. Findings suggest that out-group hostilities such as ethnocentrism and discrimination arise from perceived competition between different racial and ethnic groups (Blumer 1958; Giles and Evans 1986; Bobo 1988; Olzak 1992; Quillian 1995; Bobo and Hutchings 1996). Group interest theory applies this research on interracial conflict to the study of individual political behavior and suggests that the heightened salience of intergroup hostilities makes racial identities and racial group interests important to voting.[1]

---

1. The terms "racial" and "ethnic" are used interchangeably throughout this work. Both refer to the perceived distinctiveness of racial and ethnic groups in terms of culture and self-identity. I also presume that such perceived differences are socially constructed rather than primordial and that the social inequalities and racial hierarchies that characterize most American cities perpetuate these common notions of race and racial group differences (Jennings 1994; Valle and Torres 2000).

Three important themes recur in this work. First, I make a case that group-based conflict over power and material resources is more common in the domain of local politics than it is in the national realm. Interests—whether personal or group interests—can be more difficult to ascertain and quantify at the level of national politics. As a result, party identification is a rational decision-making shortcut that many voters use to identify those candidates and policies most congruent with their own personal and political values. By contrast, questions of "who gets what" are the essence of local politics and are often zero-sum. The outputs of local government—police and fire protection, garbage collection, parks and recreational facilities, the quality of roads and public schools—are also more proximate to the lives of ordinary citizens. As such, individual and group interests may be more accessible to political choices in the realm of local politics.

A second important idea is that social identities and group interests often bear heavily on electoral choices in local elections. Individuals comprise multiple group identities (Turner 1987). The extent to which racial or ethnic identities become politically salient vis-à-vis other political identities is a function of the political context. When the political context is fraught with intergroup tensions, electoral cleavages are likely to form around these rivalries. In the absence or diminution of such discord, traditional partisan and ideological identities are likely to be salient and highly related to local vote choice.

Finally, I challenge the notion that social diversity—especially the rapid demographic changes that many large American cities have undergone over the past thirty years—automatically elicits heightened tensions between different racial and ethnic groups. There is no doubt that relative levels of social diversity influence the attitudes and political preferences of white and nonwhite voters (Kinder and Mendelberg 1995; Hero and Tolbert 1996; Hood and Morris 1997; Hero 1998; Taylor 1998). Nonetheless, social diversity is not an automatic precursor to interracial strife. It is but one factor in a complex process. The nature of governing institutions, the size of local bureaucracies, the presence of grass roots political organizations, the character of local leadership, the economic structure of a given community, its fiscal health and prosperity, and levels of minority incorporation all contribute to the larger social and political milieu. The extent to which social diversity leads to escalating group discord can be either exacerbated or constrained by these and other factors.

Relative to the body of research conducted on other types of electoral politics, it is safe to say that we have a relatively meager understanding of why people vote the way they do in local elections. Research conducted on national elections has produced a variety of theories and sophisticated models to explain political choice. To date, however, there are no comparable theories that treat local political behavior as distinctive from other forms of voting.[2] Theoretical development, by definition, involves weaving separate spheres of research into an integrated whole. In the case of this work, a number of different social science disciplines inform an integrated perspective. The following concepts emerge as critical to a theory of local political behavior: groups and group identities, individual decision-making processes, intergroup competition, and political context. What features of local politics are unique from other levels of politics, and in these differences do we find explanations for the distinctive political behavior of local electorates? How do local elections fit into extant political behavior paradigms? Is there a way to apply existing theories of voting behavior to the case of local politics, or must we alter some of the basic assumptions for a more satisfying fit? Do the competitive relations among subgroups within a given city structure political behavior, and do periods of intense intergroup conflict correspond with disproportionately high levels of partisan defection? These are but a few of the questions that motivate this work.

The primary focus of this research is on explaining how individuals make voting decisions in local elections. In particular, I argue that

---

2. In the body of research on local voting behavior, only a few studies explore individual determinants of the vote (Jennings and Ziegler 1966; Hahn and Almy 1971; Sears and Kinder 1971; Jeffries and Ransford 1972; Halley, Acock, and Greene 1976; Murray and Vedlitz 1978; Bullock 1984; Lieske and Hillard 1984; and Lieske 1989). By and large, these studies focus on the phenomena of racial voting, offer little in the way of theoretical development, and in general are methodologically restricted to correlational analyses between a small number of socioeconomic factors and the vote. Given the relatively large body of theoretically driven research conducted on presidential elections, not to mention the sophisticated causal modeling in work such as Page and Jones 1979, Markus and Converse 1979, and Fiorina 1981, it is reasonable to conclude that the current body of research on local politics has not even begun to approach a state of the art comparable to that at the national level.

political context matters—that there are predicable sets of circumstances where partisanship and political ideology largely influence individual-level voting behavior and others where these factors exert much less influence. At the center of this theory is the proposition that heightened perceptions of group conflict make alternate social identities politically salient and that, as perceptions of group conflict escalate, nonpolitical group identities play an increasingly important role in candidate evaluation and electoral choice. This perspective maintains that the assumptions that underlie the partisanship paradigm may be too restrictive for local politics. In the case of local elections, partisan identities are but one of many social identities that influence individual decision making.

Because the notion of "local politics" is unduly broad, the scope of this book is limited in several important ways. First, the subject of this research is voting behavior in mayoral elections. Within the range of local elected offices, the mayor—while not always the most powerful local official in an objective sense—is generally perceived as the titular head of the municipality. Because the mayor is generally the most visible local official, mayoral elections are typically more salient than other forms of local elections. Second, this study is limited to voting behavior in large American cities. While the variety of data necessary to conduct this research imposes this restriction to a great degree, there are nonetheless a number of important substantive reasons why big city politics are an important theoretical focus.

Large cities are politically important because they generally control vast economic and financial resources. They typically administer public funds far beyond their own taxing authority, as many state and federal programs are filtered through city budgets. The control of large amounts of public money is often placed in the hands of officials who are elected by cities. Contemporary trends away from federally administered programs suggest that cities are likely to be given even greater discretionary control over public funds. And as the federal government increasingly devolves power to city and state governments, their politics become ever more relevant.

Cities are also important in that they are excellent laboratories for the study of social processes. The social diversity of cities provides an especially fruitful environment in which to study group politics. Ethnic and racial politics, for example, happen in cities in ways that they less frequently happen at other levels of government. Most American cities remain highly segregated by race (Massey and Denton 1993; O'Connor, Tilly, and Bobo 2001). Thus the politics of place so common in the campaign strategies and rhetoric of city politicians—east side versus west side, north versus south—often have important racial overtones and meaningful racial consequences. Finally, it is worth noting that the racial and ethnic diversity of the United States is only increasing. Given the profound demographic changes expected to occur in the United States over the next fifty years, there is undoubtedly much to learn from studying the politics of American cities.

The remainder of this chapter considers important research on voting behavior and on American cities and links these somewhat heterogeneous research agendas to a larger theoretical framework. This section begins by exploring several dominant voting paradigms and assessing their applicability to local elections. Since the vast majority of voting behavior research has focused on presidential elections, applying these theories to local elections requires the revision of some central assumptions. Specifically, it appears that political party membership is not always as important to local voting as it is to presidential elections.

Theories of Voting

Within the contemporary era of voting research, our earliest understanding of political behavior was closely tied to the notion of groups and group identities. The sociological approach to voting behavior argued that political cleavages were derivative of other social groupings—that secondary group memberships, in effect, translated into partisan groups. According to Berelson, Lazarsfeld, and McPhee (1954), the three most politically relevant social cleavages were (1) occupational, income, and status cleavages; (2) religious, racial, and ethnic cleavages; and (3) regional and rural-urban cleavages. From these social distinctions, they argued, most political behavior could be predicted. This approach, however, was challenged on the grounds that it was unable to explain political differences among demographically similar communities or to explain rapid shifts in partisan allegiances in regions where social changes were comparatively glacial (Key and Munger 1959; Campbell et al. 1960). Thus in the subsequent generation of political behavior research, group identities were not removed from the theoretical equation of voting but rather relegated to the role of an antecedent factor that, among other factors, influenced the more proximate set of political attitudes that directly influence the vote.

The group-centered, sociological paradigm embodied in *The People's Choice* (Lazarsfeld, Berelson, and Gaudet 1948) and *Voting* (Berelson, Lazarsfeld, and McPhee 1954) was ostensibly replaced by a social psychological perspective that focused on how individual political attitudes translate into political choice. The partisanship paradigm, as introduced by Campbell, Converse, Miller, and Stokes, fundamentally altered the way social scientists understood political behavior. And while there have been numerous revisions and challenges to *The American Voter,* the concept that party identification is central to political decision making continues to influence many theoretical formulations of voting behavior (Campbell et al. 1960; Jackson 1975; Nie, Verba, and Petrocik 1976; Page and Jones 1979; Markus and Converse 1979; Fiorina 1981).

Of particular interest to this research are the ways in which groups, group identities, and the nature of their political influence are characterized in this work. The "group influence model," as described in *The American Voter,* suggests that individuals identify with political parties in much the same way as they identify with ethnic groups, racial groups, religious groups, and other social groups. Political identities, the authors argue, are nonetheless the most influential group membership with respect to political behavior in that they are the most proximate. Political parties and partisan identification, as such, are conceived as a special case of the group influence phenomenon.

Within the theoretical framework of *The American Voter,* "groups" are characterized in terms of psychological affiliations, and the relative importance of groups with respect to electoral behavior is conditioned by the degree of one's psychological affiliation with the group and by the relative degree of group cohesiveness. Thus individuals who strongly identify with a particular group are more likely to be influenced by political group norms than are individuals with lower levels of identification. Membership in cohesive groups—groups with regular membership activities or socially differentiated lifestyles—is in an absolute sense always more influential with respect to political attitudes than is membership in less cohesive groups.

In *The American Voter*, two further factors are considered to condition the potential influence of group membership on political behavior: proximity and salience. Proximity is "a subjective dimension, a tendency to associate group and politics at a psychological level" (311). Thus the authors claim that, as the proximity between a group and the world of politics increase, the political distinctiveness of the group will also likely increase. Furthermore, as the "perception of proximity between the group and the world of politics becomes clearer, the susceptibility of the individual member to group influence in political affairs increases" (311). In order for group membership to induce distinctive group behavior, influentials within the group must effectively transmit the political standards of the group to remaining group members. In some situations, they explain, the standards of group membership are self-evident. "This is the case when important political objects of orientation embody group cues, so that the course of behavior characteristic of a good group member cannot be held in doubt" (317). An example of such instances would be when a group member is running for office against a nongroup member or when the political issues that dominate a given campaign obviously coincide with some stated or perceived objectives of the group. Thus, as conceived within this theoretical framework, group membership—either by identity or by political objectives—must be *salient* during any given election for a group distinctive vote to occur.

The political party occupies an important location within the group influence model. Secondary groups such as class, union membership, race, religion, and ethnicity are not explicitly political groups, thus the relative proximity of these groups to political objects is generally further than the proximity of party membership to the political world. Furthermore, the authors argue that the salience of political parties in national elections is always high. In general, one candidate is always a group member, the prime group goal is political victory, and all controversial issues represent subordinate goals that the group has assumed. The legitimacy of its activity in politics goes without question for the major parties at least, and the communication of their standards is perfect. Therefore, we would expect that the political influence of psychological membership in a party would be extremely potent, relative to other secondary memberships. (327)

Finally, it is the political party with its extraordinary influence on political behavior that in one sense reinforces the distinctiveness of secondary groups and their political behavior and acts as a bridge between "other social groupings and the political world. The influence of secondary groups in politics comes to have more enduring effects, as loyalties directed toward them may be transferred to abiding political loyalties" (331). In the group influence model, the political party represents a special case of the group influence phenomena. Nonetheless, the authors do acknowledge that, if there were no political parties, the psychological economy of the individual would necessitate a substitute organizing principle and that "there might be much more straightforward dependence on other groups for guidance" (328).

The theory of group influence developed by Campbell et al. was derived from a study of political attitudes and subsequent political behavior during a series of presidential elections. This study offers a powerful set of theoretical expectations about how individual values translate into political choices. And while there have been many subsequent treatises on voting behavior, *The American Voter*'s essential contribution—the idea that the distribution of political party allegiances represents a relevant baseline against which one should analyze electoral behavior— has continued to be a pervasive influence in voting behavior research.

At the root of *The American Voter*'s argument is the notion that political party membership is the most proximate and influential group membership with respect to voting behavior because the candidates and issues that emerge in the national arena make partisanship extraordinarily salient. The most defining feature of a presidential candidate is his or her partisan affiliation, and the issue debates that dominate campaign agendas are generally organized to accentuate the differing agendas of the political parties. In evaluating local elections with the same criteria, however, it is not so clear that political parties would necessarily be the most proximate or salient group membership with respect to voting.

How Local- and National-Level Politics Differ

Nevertheless the mayor of Detroit for four terms was Albert E. Cobo, a conservative businessman who opposed public housing and favored economy and efficiency. Why did the working people who voted for Williams for governor vote for Cobo for mayor? The answer may be that Detroit is a predominantly lower middle class homeowning town. In the partisan state and national elections, a UAW member votes as a liberal because the measures he supports will not be assessed against his bungalow. In nonpartisan city elections, however, he votes as a property owner and taxpayer, and in all probability (if he is white) as one who fears that a progressive city government might make it easier for Negroes to move into his neighborhood.
—Edward C. Banfield and James Q. Wilson, *City Politics*

What Banfield and Wilson clearly suggest in this quote is that voters often make stark distinctions about the stakes in local versus national elections. Local politics—and the kinds of issues that dominate local elections—are often more proximate and more discrete than are the larger symbolic issues of national elections. Local governments, while sometimes lawmakers, are principally service providers. They make sure that garbage is collected. They provide planning and zoning for economic development. They provide infrastructure for the provision of collective goods, and they work in concert with the state and federal governments to ensure that available funds reach their constituencies. They decide where parks and libraries will be built while marketing cities to industries, to other communities, and to other countries in the hopes of bringing incremental prosperity back home. They represent a city's parochial concerns to the greater universe and push its individual agendas in front of larger, more influential public and private bodies (Peterson 1981; Judd and Swanstrom 1994; Ross and Levine 2000). To most Americans, the role of their local government is to maintain or enhance their immediate quality of life, to provide necessary services, and at times to ameliorate intracity conflict. Thus the citizen's expectations of local government are inherently more connected to daily life than are his or her expectations of other governmental bodies. And as such, how people view their local leadership and why they vote for them will likely reflect the proximity of their interests.

The majority of local political decisions are less policy driven than they are allocational in nature.[3] The essential questions that dominate many, if not most, local elections focus on the priorities and allocation of local government services: who will receive how much and at the expense of whom. The "who" and "whom" within the realm of local politics do not, of course, refer to individuals but rather to subgroups within the larger municipality that represent, at times, opposing priorities and interests. Thus, the inherent focus of local government on the distribution of benefits and the explicitly competitive nature of the allocation process tend to reinforce the importance of secondary group memberships in relation to the political world. Because many of the issues in local campaigns invoke competing interests within the electorate, these interests can become salient political cues upon which much political behavior is oriented.

The ability to identify group interests and to use these perceived interests as a basis of one's political calculus is thus greatly enhanced at the level of local politics. The issues in local politics are generally smaller in number, less complicated, and more proximate than are issues at the national level. The trade-offs between policy options are more explicit, as the political environment often emphasizes the scarcity of resources and the inherent zero-sum quality of choices that have been and will be made. The outputs of local government are the services that local residents rely upon and use every day, and, as a

---

3. In this chapter and throughout this book, the term "allocational" refers to the role that local government plays in allocating goods and services throughout the community. It is conceptually contrasted with the legislative or redistributive functions prevalent at other levels of government. The allocational function assumes a finite set of goods and services and implies a degree of institutional discretion as to the nature and degree of access to these goods that different groups within the electorate will have. For a more detailed discussion of the politics of allocation, see Peterson 1981, chapter 6.

result, the degree of motivation as well as the capacity to quantify and act upon one's group interest are at the core of much local political behavior.

It would be misleading to contend that every municipal election represents concrete choices between alternatives that represent opposing group interests. Local elections are typically among the least salient form of electoral politics, and, as such, interest and turnout in these elections are normally low relative to statewide or national elections. Nonetheless, when group conflict is present in local politics, the competing sides and their respective interests are generally clear. It is this clarity and proximity that allows individuals to assess their group interests and to act on them. This is not to say that local elections are always interest driven or always competitive, but just that local issues have a tangible quality to them and that competition over scarce resources is more commonplace at this level of government.

When the issues and candidates running for local office embody competing group interests, traditional partisan identities may become less important to voting while salient group identities and group-related attitudes become more consequential. Thus in local elections partisanship may be proximate and salient to electoral choices, but it is not necessarily so.

Candidates and Parties in Local Elections

Another important difference between national and local politics is the varied nature of candidates who run for office. Throughout this nation's history major party presidential candidates (with a few notable exceptions) have been white Protestant males. Given the racial, religious, ethnic, class, and gender homogeneity of the presidential candidates, it is reasonable to presume that the most differentiating factor among contenders for the presidency is their partisan affiliations. In contrast to the lack of candidate diversity found at the national level, however, the heterogeneity of the candidate pool for local offices is in some cases greatly enhanced. Simply, the opportunity for casting a vote for "one's own" in a municipal election is often much greater than it is in a presidential election. Applying the proximity argument made by Campbell et al. (1960) to local elections, it is then reasonable to expect that, when important group differences are manifest in local candidacies, these respective group memberships may become salient to the vote.

Another distinctive feature of local candidates is that, in many instances, they do not explicitly represent a political party. Among the nation's one hundred largest cities, only 20 percent hold partisan local elections.[4] Thus for the vast majority of political contenders for local office, partisan affiliations will not appear on the ballot and party organizations will not meaningfully control individual agendas or campaigns. This is not to suggest that the partisanship of individual candidates in nonpartisan elections will be unknown to the mass electorate, but rather it emphasizes the fact that political parties are more tangential to many local electoral processes. As Peterson (1981) notes,

> Because cities have so few policy options open to them, partisan political life becomes one dimensional, a pale reflection of national political debates, a thin veneer that has none of the solidity of partisanship as it is usually understood. (112)

While national party organizations often exert little influence in city politics, the kinds of organizations that typically do mobilize voters in local elections tend to reinforce the relative importance of group memberships and their respective interests. Racial, ethnic, and religious groups, not to mention unions, are often the mainstays of local political action. And unlike national party organizations, which by necessity try to target their mobilization efforts across a broad swath of the electorate, the mobilizing strategies of local organizations are typically narrow and fairly group specific. This is not to say that political parties don't play a role in some city elections. But even in cases where local party organizations exist and try to influence election outcomes, partisan beliefs may still have little bearing on political choices should other more proximate group memberships become salient.

---

4. Author's calculation based on data from the National League of Cities.

Partisan allegiances, so prevalent at the national level, are clearly less constant in the realm of local politics. Conversely, group interest calculations that can play a minor role in presidential politics may loom rather large when voting for mayor. Nonetheless, voting behavior in local elections should not be construed as any more "rational" than the voting calculus in national elections. From the perspective of rational choice theorists such as Anthony Downs (1957), party identification represents an efficient political guidepost for most people. The costs of obtaining detailed information for each and every election are sufficiently prohibitive that individuals use party identification as an information shortcut. Thus party voting, per se, is understood as a rational behavior. In the context of national elections, party voting is particularly appropriate, as the candidates and issues more often than not represent partisan differences.

Local voting behavior, although not as consistently reliant on partisan cues, is similarly rational. Group identities, like partisan ones, embody sets of interests relevant to different groups. In the absence of a political environment that accentuates partisan differences, individuals seek substitute political cues. In a political context where racial and ethnic groups see themselves as zero-sum competitors over scarce political and material resources, group identities function as information shortcuts in much the same way as partisan attachments do at the national level.[5]

Ethnic Politics

Scholarly interest in the politics of American cities is nothing new. Indeed, cities historically have been of interest to students of American politics and pluralist democracy because the city, with its concentrated populations and genuine diversity, provides an ideal laboratory for the study of governance in a heterogeneous society. The ethnic politics research conducted in the 1950s and 1960s represents an important foundation for the contemporary study of local politics.

---

5. Similar in spirit, Herbert Simon (1985) argues that the limited computational and informational resources of individuals constrain their ability to engage in rational behavior as conceived by economic paradigms. From the psychological viewpoint, then, individuals engage in procedural or bounded rationality.

The political relationships between European immigrant groups and "Yankee" WASPs were the focus of this ethnic politics literature. And while the study of ethnic politics was somewhat bounded by time and geography, the empirical observations that informed this work and the debates that ensued from it are still relevant to current urban research.[6]

Robert Dahl (1961) in *Who Governs* argued that, as immigrant ethnic groups assimilated into the larger society, the incidence of ethnic voting would most assuredly decline and that this decline would be especially pronounced among upwardly mobile, middle-class ethnics. Dahl's assimilation hypothesis generated considerable debate among scholars over the persistence of ethnic voting, a controversy that continued for over a decade (Wolfinger 1965; Parenti 1967; Miller 1971; Gabriel 1972; Lorinska, Hawkins, and Edwards 1969). The central focus of scholarly disagreement was over the finding that ethnic voting in city elections continued even as ethnic populations became less homogenous with respect to their class characteristics. Fundamental to Dahl's thesis was the notion that class would subsume ethnicity as a determinant of voting behavior. Subsequent empirical research, however, did not confirm Dahl's expectations (Wolfinger 1965; Miller 1971; Gabriel 1972). In spite of the upward social and economic mobility experienced by many immigrant groups, ethnicity remained a powerful influence on voting behavior.

It is likely that the persistence of ethnic voting was especially puzzling to scholars in the 1960s, as the predominant paradigm in political behavior during this era—the partisanship model—did not lend theoretical support to the notion that voting behavior was instrumentally tied to ethnic identities. As Lorinskas, Hawkins, and Edwards (1969) argued,

> Nor should social scientists overlook the possibility that party appears to be the modal electoral orientation of the American voter partly because ethnic differences among candidates for major offices have been infrequent. Findings based on such elec-

---

6. The ethnic politics debate to which this discussion refers was especially prevalent in political science during the 1960s. For a review of this literature see Miller 1971.

tions are inconclusive for lack of variation in a key variable—candidate ethnicity. (898)

From this perspective, the opportunity for "identity" politics at the national level was limited because presidential candidates did not generally represent any meaningful ethnic, racial, or religious diversity. Furthermore, they suggested that, in a context of greater candidate diversity, voters might not be as reliant on party cues.

The debate over ethnic voting became somewhat muted by the 1970s, as the changing institutional and demographic characteristics of American cities—the virtual extinction of urban machines, the large-scale immigration of Southern blacks into Northern and Midwestern cities, increasing suburbanization and "white flight" from central cities, and the shift in ethnic immigration patterns—rendered traditional concerns regarding ethnic voting somewhat obsolete. Salient urban cleavages became less centered among European ethnic groups and more focused on the division between increasingly large black urban populations and their nonblack urban cohabitants. The questions of assimilation, acculturation, social mobility, and the integration of immigrants into American life did not readily apply to black populations that were now so prevalent in many urban centers. Questions of racial prejudice, residential segregation, and barriers to political, social, and economic empowerment became the focus of urban study. Race and the questions that surrounded racial politics were seen as substantively different than the prior question of the "ethnics." In truth, however, the politics of race is not wholly unrelated to the politics of national identity. Powerful group interests—ethnic, religious, or racial—continued to play an important role in the politics of American cities.

Racial Politics and Urban Voting

In 1967 Carl Stokes was elected the mayor of Cleveland and became the first black mayor of a large American city. In the years to follow, hundreds of black mayors would be elected in cities throughout the United States, and a central focus of urban research during this time period would be to analyze the factors that had led to this phenomena. As argued by Hahn, Klingman, and Pachon in their 1976 study, "the emergence of black mayors can be attributed more to the growth of the black population in cities than to the approval or receptivity of white voters" (509). Certainly patterns of white support for early black mayoral candidates supported this view. Until Tom Bradley's election in 1973 as the mayor of Los Angeles, no black mayor had been elected in a city with a predominantly white population. Furthermore, typical support among whites for black mayoral candidates did not exceed 20 percent (Hahn, Klingman, and Pachon 1976; Pettigrew 1971).

In cities where blacks did not constitute electoral majorities, the election of black mayors was contingent on candidates' abilities to mobilize black communities while attracting sufficient numbers of white votes to build electoral majorities. Early expectations—derived no doubt from the prior era when class interests were presumed to function independently of ethnicity or race—were that poor and working-class whites might form electoral coalitions with blacks, based on their mutual economic interests. Empirical analyses of these early elections, however, found that working-class whites were among the least receptive to black candidacies. Indeed, among nonblacks, higher-income and better-educated voters, ideological liberals, and especially Jews were the most supportive of black candidates (Pettigrew 1971; Murray and Vedlitz 1978).

A fundamental difference between the racial politics literature that emerged in the 1970s and the ethnic politics debate that preceded it was the absence of a central theory of racial voting. The analytical method used in much of the early research on racial voting was to describe the nature of the vote and the de facto electoral coalitions that enabled black candidates to win office (Pettigrew 1971; Hahn and Almy 1971; Hahn, Klingman, and Pachon 1976; Halley, Acock, and Green 1976; Murray and Vedlitz 1978; Browning, Marshall, and Tabb 1984; Kleppner 1985; Munoz and Henry 1986; Pinderhughes 1987; Hero and Beatty 1989; Winn 1990; Sleeper 1990; Ransom 1987; Sonenshein 1993a, 1993b; Grimshaw 1993; Browning, Marshall, and Tabb 1997). Coalitional analyses across a broad array of cities repeatedly demonstrated patterns of support that linked black, and in some instances Latino, voters with better educated, liberal whites. While few of these studies argued for any large degree of generalizability, the cumulative findings suggested that, for white voters, class was negatively related to support for black candidates and that education coupled with liberal ideology was positively related. The fundamental limitation regarding this body of research, however, was that it offered little in explaining the resistance of lower-income whites to black candidacies and little analysis as to the contextual factors that influence the degree of racial voting.

One exception to this general criticism would be the research conducted on the Los Angeles mayoral election in 1969. Three studies conducted on black candidate Tom Bradley's loss to Sam Yorty focused on attitudinal explanations for Bradley's defeat. Studies conducted by Sears and Kinder (1971) and Jeffries and Ransford (1972) maintained that the "white backlash" against Tom Bradley stemmed from the threat to white values posed by protest and black militancy. Furthermore, Pettigrew (1971) argued that perceptions of relative deprivation—that blacks were progressing faster than similar status whites—were highly correlated to working-class white resistance to black mayoral candidates. While these studies may have represented differences in scope and research methodology, a central theme nonetheless resonated throughout this work: the notion that white opposition to black mayoral candidates was functionally related to the competitive relations between these groups and the respective values and agendas to which they subscribe.

Los Angeles in the late 1960s was undeniably a tumultuous place. During the 1969 election for mayor, the city's recent race riots coupled with the campus unrest that occurred so close to election day did indeed evoke fear and a sense of conflict for many voters. The analyses conducted on the 1969 election aptly identified the impact that this context had on electoral behavior. At the same time, however, these analyses failed to capture the transitory nature of interracial discord and its relevance to mayoral voting behavior. Four years after his 1969 defeat, Bradley ran again against incumbent mayor Sam Yorty. In 1973, however, Bradley defeated Yorty and began his twenty-year and largely popular reign as the mayor of Los Angeles. The "conservative surge" in mayoral voting that occurred in 1969 had receded somewhat by 1973 and remained relatively dormant for twenty years to follow. While the research conducted on the Los Angeles mayoral election in 1969 was able to explain voter resistance to Bradley in that election, the theoretical contribution of this work was insufficiently broad to foresee Bradley's victory four years later. This example illustrates a central difficulty with much of the research on local elections. In 1969 partisanship was only weakly related to voter choice, whereas racial attitudes were strongly connected. In 1973, in a considerably different political context, partisanship was a much stronger determinant of the vote and the influence of racial resentments had waned. What research on local politics has failed to account for are the factors that engender this ebb and flow.

The Importance of Coalitions

Research conducted on the groundbreaking black mayoralties of the late 1960s and 1970s focused considerable attention on the coalitions necessary to produce a win at the ballot box (Cole 1974; Eisinger 1976; Murray and Vedlitz 1978; Browning, Marshall, and Tabb 1984; Kleppner 1985; Pinderhughes 1987; Sonenshein 1993a; Grimshaw 1993). The major players in these early electoral successes were the elite actors—politicians and activists—who negotiated electoral arrangements based on shared interests and ideologies. Leaders from the black community could at times find ideological brethren among liberal whites and Latinos. And given their collective exclusion from the halls of power in many cities, leaders from these racially and economically disparate groups had considerable incentives to build electoral alliances. Indeed, viable coalitions and electoral victories were most likely in cities where blacks constituted majorities or near majorities (Pettigrew 1971). They were also more likely to happen in reform cities where conservative governing regimes could be outnumbered by well-mobilized, insurgent, liberal coalitions (Browning, Marshall, and Tabb 1984). Cities with machine-like governing institutions such as Chicago, Philadelphia, and Baltimore didn't elect black mayors until the 1980s and, in the case of New York, the 1990s. Machine political structures offered fewer opportunities for the politics of insurgency than did their reform counterparts, as blacks and "liberal" whites were already incorporated—albeit as junior partners—into the machine establishment. Taking on the machine was a high-risk proposition for political elites whose professional livelihoods were often tied to the largesse of the status quo leadership (Pinderhughes 1987; Grimshaw 1993; Keiser 2003; Orr 2003).

Much of the coalition research on early black empowerment tacitly assumed that voters at the mass level would follow the directives of political leaders and that elite arrangements would largely result in organized and predictable patterns in the vote. In a period of time when black empowerment was exceptional and when conservative urban regimes were the norm, it was not uncommon for minority and liberal leaders, or their constituents, to be unified in their opposition to status quo power relations. Hard fought successes at the ballot box in the 1960s and 1970s were a harbinger of the surge in minority empowerment—on city councils and in mayors' offices—that would take hold in the 1980s and continue to this day. And while the mainstays of these early coalitions were the shared goals of minorities and white liberals in ousting regimes from which they were largely excluded, cohesion among the interests of black, Latino, and liberal white voters is less certain today than it was thirty years ago.

The electoral coalitions of African-Americans, liberal whites, and, in some cases, Latinos that produced the first generation of minority mayors were strikingly similar across time and place. Political leaders within minority communities often set aside their internal ideological differences to provide unified support for liberal candidates, and minority voters were generally responsive to these elite cues. Thus the scholarly foci on coalitions and elite alliances, so prevalent during this period, made enormous sense at a time when their main assumptions—the predictable unity of elite actors and the anticipated responsiveness of mass publics—were generally true. The contemporary state of urban America—the behavior of both elites and masses—is considerably more fluid today than it was in the early years of black empowerment.

Several decades of minority empowerment has resulted in a class of political entrepreneurs who, much like non-Latino white politicians, have personal constituencies and individual agendas. Officeholders tend to see their electoral mandate in narrower terms than do insurgent activists, and the current crop of minority politicians is no exception. Recent mayoral elections in New York, Los Angeles, and Houston, for example, point to decreasing levels of solidarity within and/or between minority communities. It is ever more common to see divisions within the African-American and Latino elite communities, providing black and Latino endorsements for multiple candidates in the same race. Simply, there is greater evidence of ideological fragmentation among minority leaders today than there was thirty years ago— and there is greater independence among minority voters as well.

Were one to study the politics of American cities from this earlier coalition perspective, it would be difficult indeed to identify a coherent explanation for recent mayoral outcomes across the nation. In some instances, for example, black and Latino voters have come together in support of progressive candidates. In other cases Latinos and whites have joined in support of moderate or conservative regimes. And yet in other elections black liberals and white conservatives have built coalitions to defeat insurgent Latino candidates. There is no standing coalition that routinely elects progressive, conservative, or minority mayors in the contemporary era. Political opportunities, racial group interests, and ultimately mass voting behavior are shaped by the social, economic, and political contexts within which they take place (Keiser 1997). Political leadership and elite arrangements were critical factors in the early success of minority mayors during a period of time when opportunities for empowerment were relatively scarce. And while the nature of political leadership and elite behavior continues to influence electoral outcomes, to fully understand the contemporary voting behavior of urban electorates it seems important to pay greater attention to mass publics and the motivations that underlie their electoral choices. Group interest theory and the individual-level analyses I conduct in this work fill a notable void in how we understand and interpret local electoral politics.

Social Diversity and Electoral Support
for Black Candidates

While a good deal of academic attention has been paid to the political coalitions that result in minority mayoral success, a separate body of research focuses on how social context (i.e., the demographic composition of a community) influences the attitudes and behavior of white voters. In particular, this research looks to the relative size of black populations as an explanation for varying levels of white resistance to black candidates. The central contention in much of this work is that feelings of racial threat keep white voters from supporting black candidates. This is particularly the case when blacks represent a large or growing proportion of the local electorate (Key 1949; Pettigrew 1971; Wolfinger 1974; Giles and Evans 1986; Citrin, Green, and Sears 1990).

Studies have found that, as the percentage of the black population increases within a community, there are heightened perceptions of racial threat (Giles 1977; Fosset and Kiecolt 1989; Glaser 1994), increased resistance to racial integration (Fosset and Kiecolt 1989), more evidence of racial prejudice and negativity toward ameliorative racial policy (Quillian 1996; Taylor 1998), and higher levels of racial polarization in the vote (Wright 1977; Giles and Evans 1986; Vanderleeuw 1990; Giles and Buckner 1993; Lublin 1995). Some of this research, however, has been challenged by others who maintain that interracial contact can work to minimize negative stereotyping and polarized voting—that indeed the presence of large black populations does not necessarily alienate or threaten white voters (Amir 1969; Ellison and Powers 1994; Carsey 1995; Forbes 1997; Stein, Post, and Rinden 2000; Hajnal 2001).

A number of recent studies, in an effort to reconcile these divergent findings, question the presumed linearity of the racial composition thesis. Racially conservative attitudes and race-based voting appear more prevalent in homogenous white and bifurcated (i.e., relatively equal proportions of minorities and whites) social contexts but less likely in moderately heterogeneous environments (Hero and Tolbert 1996; Tolbert and Hero 1996; Hero 1998; Tolbert and Hero 2001). Apparently, the absence of minorities alone does little to minimize racial intolerance, as extreme residential segregation results in white voters who disproportionately rely on racial stereotypes to make race-related judgments (Kinder and Mendelberg 1995). Moderate levels of social diversity create conditions for positive contact, whereas bifurcated environments tend to exacerbate the potential for competition and perceptions of threat.

The ramification of these findings in the contemporary urban setting, where the levels of racial heterogeneity typically range from moderate to high, is that varying degrees of social diversity should correspond with different opportunity structures for the election of minority mayors. In other words, white voters in cities with moderately sized minority populations should, in an absolute sense, always be more receptive to minority candidates than should white voters from cities with large minority populations, all else being equal. To the extent that racial conflict results from perceived threat, and to the extent that threat is a function of relative proportionality within the larger community, changes in demography are expected to have destabilizing effects on social and political cooperation between and among various racial groups.

Relative levels of intergroup conflict are most certainly related to the larger social context, but not exclusively so. For example, changing demography, in particular the growth of minority populations, in concert with a growing economy, can result in less discord than when similar levels of minority growth occur during periods of economic contraction (Olzak 1992; Jennings 1994). Varying levels of social inequality—and the relative mobility that racial and ethnic groups experience within local social and economic hierarchies—also correspond with differences in perceived competition and levels of conflict (Olzak 1992; Kaufmann 2002). Racial and ethnic minorities that become relegated, by virtue of discrimination, to the lower rungs of urban hierarchies are much more likely to see race relations in a perpetually competitive framework than are members of the majority. However, members of majority groups can become remarkably cohesive in a political context where perceptions of interracial hostilities are high. In sum, the relative level of social diversity in a given city is an important backdrop against which urban political campaigns are waged. Changing demography and social diversity constitute an important part of the setting for local politics. But from the group interest perspective, the contextual factor with the most direct influence on voting behavior is the level of perceived conflict among racial groups.

Social Identities and Group Conflict

Research conducted by Blumer (1958) and Bobo (1983, 1988) on the sources of intergroup hostility and racial prejudice constitute the foundation for the group conflict thesis. From a sociological perspective, ethnocentrism and group-based discrimination result from competition over symbolic and material resources. While intergroup relations in general are susceptible to conflict, intergroup hostilities tend to escalate when subordinate groups challenge status quo power relations. Groups that make up the dominant power coalition in a given community may interpret these challenges as threatening to their lifestyles, valued resources, and accepted practices. Thus competing groups tend to coalesce around their respective interests, and the results are interest-based constituencies that use group membership as a cue for political attitudes and political behavior.

According to Bobo, the potential for group conflict is enhanced when desired resources are scarce or when rewards are perceived as zero-sum. As a result, group conflict is not a static condition that characterizes intergroup relations. Rather, friction among groups will ebb and flow in response to a variety of conditioning factors, including, but not limited to, the degree to which individuals perceive resource scarcity, the relative size of competing groups, the relative cohesiveness of competing groups, and the degree to which group interests are not confounded with other, potentially salient cross-cutting interest cleavages (Giles and Evans 1986; Tedin 1994).

Group conflict theory is in fact quite consistent with *The American Voter*'s group influence model, as they both suggest that the degree of any group's political distinctiveness is contingent upon the degree of individual identification with the group and the relative degree of group cohesiveness. Where group conflict theorists go beyond the group influence model, however, is in the proposition that these factors (group identification and group cohesiveness) are dynamic and conditioned by the extent of perceived competition between and among groups. Thus under circumstances where perceptions of intergroup competition for scarce resources are low, many groups may exhibit rather low levels of group consciousness, and thus the likelihood for a group distinctive vote is commensurately low. Under circumstances where the candidates, the campaign rhetoric, or the external political environment emphasizes competition over scarce, desirable resources, group members will likely exhibit higher levels of in-group identification and will in essence become more cohesive in the face of external competition to the values and valued resources of the group.

Bobo and Hutchings (1996) argue that the degree to which members of a group see other groups as a competitive threat is linked to feelings of racial alienation.

> We conceive of racial alienation as a falling along a continuum ranging from a profound sense of group enfranchisement and entitlement most likely to occur among dominant racial group members to, at the opposite extreme, a profound sense of group disenfranchisement and grievance most likely to be found among subordinate or racial minority group members. The more that members of a racial group feel they are alienated and oppressed, the more they are likely to regard other racial groups as competitive threats to their own group's position. (10)

This proposition that alienation is linked to threat also has potential ramifications for political behavior. On the one hand, majority or dominant groups feel the least amount of alienation, and thus there is no expectation that they will consistently cast a group-oriented vote. When the relative power and privilege of a dominant group is challenged by a minority group, however, group-centered voting is more likely. Minority groups are on balance almost always more alienated than majority groups and thus are expected to cast a group interest–driven vote more consistently and to a greater degree (Gurin et al. 1999). For this reason, racial and ethnic minorities are often more unified in their respective voting behaviors (showing strong and consistent support for in-group members when they are candidates) than are non-Latino white voters.

Extreme levels of social inequality and the rigid social and economic hierarchies that shape the nature of urban interactions further explain the political cohesiveness of many minority groups (Frederickson 1999; Sidanius and Pratto 1999; Bobo et al. 1994; O'Connor, Tilly, and Bobo 2001). In spite of the considerable economic and cultural diversity found within the black and Latino communities, in-group solidarity is quite common and particularly notable when a brethren group member is on the ballot (Dawson 1994). The strong political linkages that often define urban minority groups are as much about common experiences as they are about communal culture or even shared political ideologies. As Manning Marable (1994) so clearly argues,

> In the United States "race" for the oppressed has also come to mean an identity of survival, victimization, and opposition to those racial groups of elites that exercise power and privilege. What we are looking at here is *not* an *ethnic* identification or culture, but an awareness of shared experience, suffering, and struggle against the barriers of racial division. These collective experiences, survival tales, and grievances form the basis of a historical consciousness, a group's recognition of what it has witnessed, and what it can anticipate in the near future. (31)

Minority groups—by virtue of their higher levels of alienation and their typically lower status in the urban social hierarchy—demonstrate more racial solidarity, on average, than do non-Latino whites. What we learn, however, from the group conflict research conducted by sociologists and social psychologists is that, when whites perceive minority demands as a challenge to their own privileged status, the result is group-based resentment, enhanced opposition to progressive racial policy, and an increase in their relative political cohesion.

The academic research conducted from this group conflict perspective has been largely confined to the study of racism and racial politics. This book in particular seeks a broader application to the electoral politics of American cities. Unlike the nation as a whole, cities represent concentrated electoral units where groups that may be insignificant by national standards can be tremendously significant within their local context. For this reason, group conflict and conflict attitudes may bear more heavily on local politics, because it is at the local level where this conflict is disproportionately played out.

Chapter 2 presents a theory of local voting behavior titled the group interest theory. As is evident from this current chapter, the group interest approach is an extension of the group influence model.

Integrating *The American Voter*'s original insights with a set of contextual expectations derived from the group conflict research, this new perspective provides a dynamic theory of local voting behavior, one that not only explains a variety of local political outcomes but that can also account for intercity and intracity differences in voting behavior.

2 Group Interest Theory and Local Elections

Studies of electoral politics often seek to abstract an individual from time, place, and surroundings. The epistemological foundations of such an effort is the mythically representative citizen chosen probabilistically to represent everyperson. But such a myth ignores the reality that every citizen is located within a setting, and the characterization of the citizen apart from the setting lacks meaning.

—Robert Huckfeldt and John D. Sprague,
Citizens, Politics, and Social Communication

Politics do not occur in a vacuum, and most political scientists acknowledge that social and political contexts influence behavior (Key 1949; Berelson, Lazarsfeld, and McPhee 1954; Nie, Verba, and Petrocik 1976; Huckfeldt 1986; Iyengar 1991; Jones 1994; Huckfeldt and Sprague 1995; Kinder and Mendelberg 1995; Hero 1998; Oliver and Mendelberg 2000; Leighley 2001; Oliver 2001). The inherent difficulty with any contextual theory, however, is in identifying the variety of factors that are influential to the process under study, finding a way to measure these factors, and then designing appropriate methods to test them. This study is no exception. Group interest theory is a broad contextual theory of voting that proposes to identify (1) the macrocontextual factors under which group conflict is more likely to occur in city politics, and (2) the respective effect that different levels of group conflict have on voting behavior in local elections. A schematic model of this approach is found in figure 2.1.

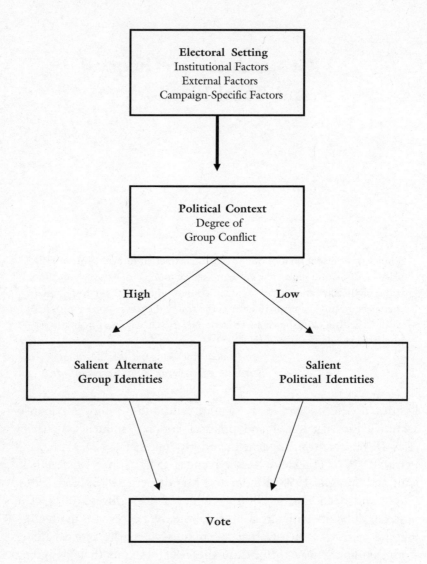

Figure 2.1.   The group interest theory of local voting behavior

Group interest theory distinguishes between the factors that make up the political setting and the political context while asserting that both are influential to electoral outcomes.[1] The important contextual factor in this theory is perceived group conflict, and the central claim is that relative levels of group conflict are predictably related to different forms of voting behavior. Conflict is defined as salient group-based resentment resulting from heightened perceptions of intergroup competition. Minority group members on average are more cognizant of interracial competition than are members of dominant groups. Sensitivities to persistent status inequalities contribute to the greater in-group solidarity and cohesiveness typical of minority groups. During periods of heightened conflict—especially when minority groups challenge status quo power relations—members of dominant groups become more attuned to group-based competition and are more likely to coalesce on this basis. For this reason, increased conflict is presumed to impact the voting behavior of dominant groups disproportionately, as their group solidarity and the salience of their respective interests become particularly evident under these conditions. (Bobo and Hutchings 1996). This was especially true when primary urban cleavages were black versus white.

In the contemporary urban setting, where members of different minority groups (particularly African-Americans and Latinos) increasingly vie among themselves for material resources and political power, heightened competition effects a similar response, with interminority solidarity giving way to group-centered voting behavior. In essence, competition incites conflict that makes group identities politically important.

From the group interest perspective, higher levels of conflict typically will result in *group distinctive voting*—electoral choices that are based on nonpolitical or alternate group identities. The rationale for this claim is that heightened levels of intergroup discord make group interests salient voting cues. In the absence of heightened tensions,

1. For a discussion of the methodological distinction between setting and context variables, see Przeworski and Teune 1970.

however, group interests are considerably more muted and less politically consequential. In their stead, traditional political cues such as partisanship should be more important to voting. Thus, context is important in this model because it influences the relative salience of different voter attitudes with regard to their political choices. As suggested in chapter 1, local voting behavior can be motivated by partisan identities, yet often it is not. The change from partisan voting to group interest voting is effected by changes in political context. In the most simplistic sense, one may contrast two possible electoral environments within which local elections take place. When perceived group conflict is relatively low, partisan loyalties will generally correspond to electoral choices, as the proximity and importance of other group memberships are commensurately low in this context. Under conflict conditions, however, alternate group memberships are likely to supplant partisan leanings with regard to the vote. Thus the observed influence of political, demographic, and attitudinal factors on voting behavior varies in response to contextual changes.

The political context is presumed to be fluid. It varies considerably between cities, and within a given city it can change significantly from one election to the next. At one level, this theory proposes an explanation for why salient voting cues change. On another level, however, this work attempts to explain changes in the political context. The degree of group conflict at any given point in time is presumably linked to a set of factors that constitute the electoral setting. And while there are an infinite number of elements that contribute to this backdrop, this analysis concentrates on three broad categories: (1) institutional factors such as local party organizations, election rules, and the local form of government; (2) external features of the electoral setting such as the demographic composition of the community, its sociopolitical history, the local economy, as well as general levels of satisfaction with local government at the time of the election; and (3) campaign-specific factors such as the candidates running for office and the important campaign issues. The following sections discuss this set of contextual factors and the expectations that I draw from the group interest perspective.

Institutional Features of the Electoral Setting:
Partisan Elections and Local Politics

One of the most notable results of the municipal reform movement that swept through many American cities in the first half of the twentieth century was the declining number of partisan elections and the waning influence of local political parties. Of the largest one hundred cities in the United States, only 20 percent currently hold partisan mayoral elections. In the Southern and Western regions of the United States, where municipal reform was particularly prevalent, the proportion of partisan local elections is even less than 20 percent.

In the wake of increasing numbers of nonpartisan elections, several studies explored the influence of nonpartisanship on local participation and behavior. Findings from this research attributed depressed local turnout (relative to the decline in national turnout), increased partisan defection, and increased racial and ethnic divisiveness to nonpartisan elections (Lee 1960; Banfield and Wilson 1963; Pomper 1966). Implicit in these findings was the contention that electoral rules somehow influence political behavior. The national decline in partisan local elections, however, occurred during a period when local party organizations were becoming weaker as well. Local organizations that recruited candidates, funded campaigns, and mobilized voters became increasingly scarce. Local elections became more candidate centered and simply did not emphasize parties or partisan loyalties to the same degree as they once had (Ehrenhalt 1991; Wattenberg 1991). Given the concurrence of these two trends (nonpartisan elections and weaker local party organizations), it is difficult to disentangle their effects. It seems logical, nonetheless, that the declining organizational strength of political parties rather than the nonpartisan character of local elections had greater influence. Party activities— membership, fund-raising, mobilization, and campaign efforts—give partisanship its vitality, not election rules. Consequently, differences in political outcomes between cities with partisan and nonpartisan elections are probably not a function of electoral design. There are many other factors that have greater weight than the form of the ballot. And while partisan identities are sometimes politically salient in local elections, holding partisan elections alone should do little to constrain group interested voting behavior.

Forms of Local Government

In addition to the partisan nature of local elections and the relative strength of local parties, the institutional arrangements in a given city also influence the political context. The prevalence of group distinctive voting behavior in local elections is motivated by individual assessments of group interests. In mayoral contests, groups compete for control over city resources. Strong-mayor systems of local government may offer greater inherent motivation for group interested voting behavior because the electoral spoils in a strong-mayor system are typically larger than they are in a weak-mayor or city manager design.

Cities with political machine traditions will also tend to encourage group-based orientations, as the political culture and the design of their political institutions often reinforce group identities and group-based claims. Old machine cities like New York and Chicago have multiple layers of government that apportion power and resources, much like their machine predecessors. Power and political patronage continue to be shared among the various groups that compose the governing coalition, and these power-sharing arrangements both acknowledge group identities and reinforce their overall importance.

Urban scholars John Mollenkopf (1999) and Michael Jones-Correa (2001a) suggest that the "vertical" institutional design of New York City enables greater minority inclusion and less political conflict than the "horizontal," fragmented governmental system of reform-cities such as Los Angeles. As Mollenkopf explains,

> New York City's political system encourages, indeed requires, groups to make deals with each other and to contain their conflicts. . . . By contrast, the depoliticized, fragmented political environment of Los Angeles County leaves few institutional channels for processing and containing intergroup conflict. (421)

From Mollenkopf's perspective, the power-sharing arrangements common to machine cities—and of New York in particular—provide a political means of conflict arbitration that mitigates the impetus for intergroup violence and organized protest. Furthermore, minority elites should have greater incentives to cooperate in New York than they have in Los Angeles.

Yet in periods of shrinking resources, or in the face of demographic changes that lead new groups to contest old arrangements, these patronage-based political systems may actually exacerbate conflict as opposed to contain it. The institutional design of New York City government, while offering more formal political apparatuses within which minority groups can negotiate, also tends to emphasize racial and ethnic group claims to a much greater degree than do political structures in Los Angeles. The inherent "group consciousness" of New York's governmental arrangements may also lead to greater persistent group consciousness among its electorate. In a political system where racial and ethnic groups are seen as the legitimate claimants of public goods, group interests, as such, are always politically in play. In reform cities, such as Los Angeles, racial groups are accorded much less formal status in the political system. Political exclusion and governmental unresponsiveness have erupted in periodic episodes of violence and rebellion in Los Angeles—more so and to a greater degree than have occurred in New York City. And during such periods of violent protest, racial group interests—especially among white voters—become a pervasive political force. Nonetheless, the everyday reform political arrangements that characterize Los Angeles politics and its institutions are considerably less tied to groups and their sense of relative entitlement than are the norms and political structures that characterize New York City. Given this contrast, the group interest perspective would expect cities with powerful mayoralties and machine traditions such as New York City to exhibit relatively higher levels of group distinctive voting on average than reform cities with weak mayors or city managers.

The External Setting: Demography, History, and the Economy

The demographic composition of cities surely influences local politics, as the number and relative size of groups competing for political power structure the options available to local politicians. In an absolute sense, group interest theory supposes that extremely diverse communities (bifurcated social contexts) are more vulnerable to intergroup competition and group distinctive voting than are less heterogeneous communities (Kinder and Mendelberg 1996; Hero 1998). Within the realm of ethnically diverse cities, those with more balanced constituent groups are more likely to exhibit group interested political behavior.

To argue that extreme social diversity increases the potential for conflict does not imply that demography, in and of itself, determines political behavior. To the contrary, the composition of the community mediates the effect of other factors that stimulate competition. Considerable research suggests that whites living in bifurcated or extremely diverse communities exhibit higher levels of racial animus and greater opposition to racially progressive public policies than do whites that reside in less diverse communities (Tolbert and Hero 1996; Hood and Morris 1997; Taylor 1998). Nonetheless, conflict is not an automatic by-product of racism or racial conservatism. As Huckfeldt and Kohfeld (1989) persuasively argue,

> Racial conflict in electoral politics is not simply a consequence of individual attitudes and predispositions. Many Americans are indeed racist and racist attitudes are central to racial conflict, but neither fact explains racial conflict. Were there significantly fewer racists in Chicago during the 1979 mayoral election than during the 1983 mayoral election? Probably not, but conditions in 1983 provoked levels of racial animosity that were unimagined four years earlier. . . . Racial conflict is fundamentally a group phenomenon, subject to environmental and structural properties that are variable through time. Thus, the pattern and consequence of racial conflict in electoral politics must be understood in terms of particular groups at particular times in particular places. (44)

Social diversity interacts with other features of the macroenvironment that directly trigger competition and conflict.

Crime, Jobs, and Social Services

By and large, the responsibility for maintaining public safety is a local mandate, as the vast majority of police officers are hired and administered by local governments. Fear of crime and perceptions of increasing crime rates are thus often particularly salient political issues in local elections. The relationship between crime rates and electoral choice is nonetheless a complicated one because crime policy is generally imbued with substantial racial overtones. This is especially true in large cities. From the perspective of many minority group members living in lower-income neighborhoods, decades of police abuse have resulted in demands for greater police reform and civilian oversight. On the other side of the crime issue, however, are calls for greater law and order and the demand for more police officers. The dividing lines in this debate, especially at the local level, are often racialized, as law and order proposals are frequently directed at minority neighborhoods. Consequently, when crime issues are particularly salient in local elections, they may provide a substantial cue for group distinctive voting.

Crime, in general, is always part of the local political agenda, and local concern over crime does not necessarily correspond with the ebb and flow in crime statistics. Individual attitudes regarding the prevalence of crime are largely shaped by the mass media. And even when crime rates decline, the local media coverage of crime may not (Entmann 1990; Alderman 1994; Gilliam et al. 1996). While crime is a persistent local concern, crime issues are particularly salient in some elections and less so in others. It seems that high-profile crimes (e.g., Polly Klass, Crown Heights, Tawana Brawley, and O. J. Simpson) may be disproportionately influential to the political context because they create interest in crime beyond what is typical. High-profile interracial and interethnic crimes, in particular, may influence the political context in that they frame the crime problem in group-related terms. Furthermore, violent protests, race riots, rebellions, and the like have an especially profound effect on political behavior, as they not only emphasize the tenuous nature of public safety but generally make racial and ethnic issues politically important as well

(Kaufmann 1996). Since crime issues are often salient in the aftermath of high-profile crimes and riots, group distinctive voting will likely be more prevalent under these circumstances.

The argument that the salience of crime increases group conflict is founded in the proposition that crime policies are often tinged with group politics. Similarly, downturns in the local economy, in particular declining local revenues to support social services, also increase the potential for intergroup competition (Gurr 1968; Horowitz 1985; Feldman and Stenner 1997; Oliver and Mendelberg 2000). Group interest theory proposes a strong relationship between the scarcity of desirable resources and group conflict. Fundamental to the group interest approach is the notion that individual perceptions of scarcity with regard to valued resources are related to the increased competition and the enhanced importance of group interest as a cue for political behavior. Downturns in the local economy, increasing unemployment rates, and declining public funds to pay for services are presumed to stimulate group interested cleavages within the community, as different subgroups begin to assess their respective access to these scarce public goods. During periods of relative economic abundance and when the municipal government is solvent, individuals are likely to perceive less intergroup rivalry than they do under more dire economic circumstances.

Retrospective Voting

On its face, the group interest theory of local voting may appear to represent a theory of retrospective voting in that, when poor local circumstances infer the failure of incumbent administrations, voters make electoral choices based on these evaluations. In the case of elections with incumbents on the ballot, group interest theory does take incumbent evaluations into account; however, the underlying motivations proposed by this approach are not the same as those in theories of retrospective voting (Downs 1957; Key 1966; Fiorina 1981). Group interest theory maintains that bad times evoke notions of scarce resources and that scarcity stimulates group-based rivalries. Voters will act to punish the incumbent only when the incumbent represents *opposing* interest constituencies. Insofar as the incumbent may still represent an individual's perceived group interests, he or she will nonetheless receive electoral support from these groups.

Consider the following example. City X is a "liberal" city where registered Democrats outnumber Republicans by more than two to one. The mayor of city X is a liberal Democrat who has always strongly defended the interests of union members. The incumbent mayor's opponent is a "free-market" Republican who proposes to privatize local service delivery in order to make public services less costly and more efficient. At election time the local economy is suffering from high unemployment, and in the prior year there were several severe strikes by city employees that brought essential city services to a halt for almost a month. A theory of retrospective voting would predict that partisan defections would likely occur on the basis that the incumbent mayor would be punished for his poor performance (Key 1966) or perhaps that voters would use the incumbent's past performance to predict the future state of the city (Downs 1957; Fiorina 1981). In contrast, group interest theory predicts that union members would more likely support the incumbent than would nonunion members and that patterns of defection would most likely result from the disparate interests of union and nonunion households. As is evidenced in this example, all of these theoretical viewpoints would expect to find substantial partisan defections under this set of circumstances—but the underlying explanations for why individuals defect are fundamentally different.

The same logic holds for racial and ethnic groups. Riots, recessions, and fiscal insolvency are generally accompanied by declining electoral support for incumbent administrations. When the incumbent mayor is a member of a racial or ethnic minority, however, brethren group members are the least likely to defect, especially when they associate the incumbent mayor with important group interests (Howell 2000). For this reason, the ability of minority mayors to sustain biracial and multiracial electoral coalitions is often damaged during recessionary periods. Ideologically based white support, in particular, can be devastated when incumbent minority mayors are seen as unable to sustain economic prosperity. This is not to suggest that minority voters never punish languishing incumbents. They most certainly do. However, the relatively high levels of in-group solidarity that typically characterize minority groups act to constrain mass group defections—especially if the incumbent is a member of their particular group.

The Sociopolitical History of Group Relations

While current events are always more proximate to the political context, the sociopolitical history of any community is nonetheless an important backdrop for local politics. Historical conflict among groups is often exacerbated in the political arena, especially when group-based tensions form the basis for candidate appeals. But historically good relationships between groups do not necessarily alleviate the potential for conflict. Group interest theory maintains that, while good historical relations between groups may create coalition opportunities, these opportunities may be sundered by the infusion of conflicting political interests.

Raphael Sonenshein, in *Politics in Black and White* (1993a), argues that the sociopolitical histories of cities influence the types of electoral coalitions that can emerge there. Specifically, he argues that certain political coalitions and political outcomes are more viable in Western cities, such as Los Angeles, than in Eastern cities, such as New York, because the historical relations among groups in these respective cities provide different opportunity structures for coalition building. The coalition among blacks, Latinos, and liberal Jews that elected Tom Bradley in 1973 was therefore possible because of the groups' shared liberal ideologies, on the one hand, and their shared outsider status, on the other. In New York, however, little incentive existed for a black-Jewish political alliance because Jews were incorporated into the political establishment long before blacks. The epilogue to this argument, however, is that the coalition between liberal Jews and blacks in Los Angeles—an alliance that Sonenshein credits for the long reign of Mayor Bradley—began to break apart toward the end of his tenure. The 1993 mayoral election further illustrated increasing strain between blacks and Jews in Los Angeles, with almost one-half of Jewish voters supporting the Republican Riordan. For as powerful as this liberal coalition was in the 1970s and 1980s, its dissolution in the 1990s seems to imply that even the strongest historical relations among groups can be undone by clashing group interests. A history of positive intergroup relations most certainly enhances the prospects for mass electoral alliances, but it does not constrain individuals from defying old patterns of support when conflicts arise.

Over the past forty years, mass electoral coalitions between minority voters and liberal whites have been most successful when they have represented challenges to existing conservative regimes. Shared outsider status is a powerful force that stimulates a sense of mutual interest beyond common policy agendas, political ideologies, and the like. As liberal whites, blacks, Latinos, and other minority groups become increasingly incorporated within local power regimes—becoming insiders themselves—strong incentives to further these coalitions may wane. When the relative size of coalition member groups changes— or when one group's political objectives fall out of line with other groups—coalitions may become unstable and eventually unravel. For minority groups in particular, the symbolic benefits of political incorporation are often equal to if not greater than the actual policy gains achieved through descriptive representation (Reed 1986; Marable 1994). To the extent that the symbolic rewards of minority empowerment are fairly group specific (Kaufmann 2003a), groups that were once contented to be minority partners in liberal coalitions may look to achieve descriptive representation of their own, even if it means abandoning previous coalition partners. In sum, coalitions founded on shared ideologies or historical bonds will ultimately be less durable than those based on the sustained mutual interests of their members (Carmichael and Hamilton 1967).

The Candidates and Their Campaigns

Even when the external setting does not precipitate intergroup rivalry, certain types of candidates and issue agendas most certainly can incite conflict. Of the potential triggers for intergroup discord, the candidates and issues in any given campaign are the most proximate and are often the most influential. In city politics, groups that are small by state or national standards can nonetheless wield great influence. Local governments represent the entry-level opportunity for many groups to seek political incorporation, and local elections represent the best chance most minority group members have for electing members of their own group. Group interest theory argues that the degree of group distinctive voting behavior is contingent upon the degree of individual identification with the group and with the cohesiveness of the group. Thus depending on the baseline strength of in-group identification and group cohesiveness, different types of groups will generally exhibit different levels of group distinctive voting.

When members of politically active racial minorities, such as African-Americans or Latinos, run for office, history suggests that black and Latino voters overwhelmingly support their own brethren candidates. Solidarity among racial minorities—especially those that suffer from discrimination and persistent economic inequalities—is high. Even if there are no compelling group-specific issues that accompany a minority candidacy, the internal cohesiveness of African-American and Latino voters (especially in contrast to non-Latino whites) would predict relatively high levels of group distinctive voting.

Simply placing a minority candidate on the ballot, however, will not necessarily stimulate heavy resistance from nongroup members. When a minority candidate is coupled with a group-specific agenda, however, there is a much greater likelihood of countermobilization from other groups that perceive their interests to be at risk. The promotion of a group interest agenda thus acts to enhance the cohesion of in-group members as well as the solidarity of opposing groups. For this reason, we should expect to see evidence of group distinctive voting when minority group members run for office and even more so when group interest agendas are pursued within a campaign. For example, when a Cuban-American runs for mayor in Miami, when Irish-Americans and Italian-Americans run in Boston, when a Mormon runs in Salt Lake City, or when gay candidates run in San Francisco, this theory presumes that ethnic, religious, and sexual orientation identities may become salient voting cues. Should these candidates embrace issue agendas that promote their group interests explicitly, however, it is likely that the enhanced cohesiveness of the candidate's in-group support will be met with greater unity from opposing groups as well.

The extent to which minority group candidates trigger a racialized or otherwise group-centered response is not entirely within their control. Even if such candidates choose to run deracialized or otherwise nongroup-specific campaigns, their opponents can make group interests salient by virtue of the kind of campaigns they choose to run. In the 1960s, 1970s, and even into the 1980s, it was quite common for white candidates to invoke racial fear tactics when trying to defeat black challengers. As described in chapter 3, Sam Yorty, in his two campaigns against Tom Bradley, made numerous references to "black block voting." Bernard Epton, Harold Washington's Republican opponent in Chicago in 1983, ran television ads that ended with the line, "Epton for Mayor . . . Before It's Too Late" (Kleppner 1985). While negative campaigning is nothing new, these kinds of explicitly racial campaign appeals were often effective in making racial considerations salient voting considerations. It is interesting to note, however, that race-based campaign tactics did not always result in mass partisan defections. The extent to which candidates were able to prime racial resentment was in part constrained by the political context—the degree of perceived racial conflict at the time of the election.

Racial appeals are still widely prevalent in the politics of American cities. Racial and ethnic minority candidates largely pursue deracialized campaign strategies aimed at minimizing the extent to which they prime white racial attitudes in the context of voting (Metz and Tate 1995). White opponents, however, can still make race salient through the use of implicit racial appeals. While it may be less publicly palatable to make references to the black bloc vote than it once was, subtle (and not so subtle) racial messages continue to pervade mayoral campaigns. Tali Mendelberg (2001) in *The Race Card* argues that explicit racial appeals are no longer particularly viable campaign strategies in that they violate widely accepted norms of equality and tend to be rebuked by voters. Conversely, implicit racial appeals—those that use code words or visual imagery to prime racial resesentment—are quite effective in generating race-based voting. In the context of local politics, where tangible group interests can loom rather large, even powerful egalitarian norms may be overshadowed, enabling candidates to engage in race-baiting strategies with little fear of white voter backlash. The level of partisan defection among whites often seen in local politics exceeds anything that is typically experienced in national-level politics. This fact alone suggests that the norm of egalitarianism may function less well at this level when salient group interests—and heightened levels of group conflict—come into play.

Issues

There are a large number of issues that arise in local elections. The most common local issues, however, tend to focus on the quantity and quality of local goods and services and access to them. As argued earlier, the primary role of local government is to allocate public goods throughout the community. Allocational politics have a distinctly competitive quality and, unto themselves, can incite intergroup friction. Furthermore, as there are multiple interest cleavages within any diverse electorate, salient issue agendas are important to local campaigns because they define the locus of competition within the community.

Contemporary urban cleavages often coincide with racial and ethnic differences. The mass in-migration of Southern blacks into large urban centers, substantial "white flight" from cities to suburbs, and the large influx of new immigrants into major cities have increased the relative presence and influence of urban minorities in a number of large cities. Furthermore, and inasmuch as the increasing relative poverty of American cities has commensurately accelerated the demand for a wide array of city services, local issues such as taxes, police, and schools often result in race- or ethnicity-based interest groups. Other local issues such as development and redevelopment policies, local service privatization, and environmental protection do not fall as easily within the interracial and interethnic fault lines. Groups that coalesce on one set of salient issues will not necessarily be linked on other issue dimensions. Thus the challenge for local candidates is to focus campaign issues in such a way as to maximize their appeal to potential winning coalitions. The role of issues in local politics is therefore central to the salient interests and electoral coalitions that emerge.

Partisan Beliefs and Political Ideology

Apart from the factors that cause the political context to change, there are also individual-level characteristics that mediate the effect of conflict on voting behavior. In particular, the strength of prior political beliefs is assumed to be such a mediating factor. As depicted in figure 2.1, salient political identities and salient group interests both potentially have direct effects on individual voting decisions. As intergroup hostilities escalate, the importance of group interest as a political cue will increase relative to the independent effects of partisanship and ideology. Conversely, when intergroup competitiveness is low, partisanship and ideology should be more strongly related to voting behavior than are alternate group identities. Thus, as was suggested earlier, partisan-driven voting behavior functions as a default setting in the overall design of this model.

The relative strength of partisan and ideological commitment also impacts the extent to which interest motivations become politically manifest at the individual level. Strong partisans are less susceptible to interest-driven motivations than are their weaker partisan counterparts. Individuals with strong ideological or partisan predispositions are the least influenced by self-interest motives (Tedin 1994). Also, voters with median levels of political interest and low levels of attitude crystallization will be the most susceptible to opinion change (Converse 1964; McGuire 1968; Zaller 1992.) In other words, strong partisanship and deeply committed ideological beliefs act to constrain individuals from attitude change. Consistent with these findings, the group interest theory expects that intergroup conflict will have the greatest impact on weak and leaning partisans and on moderate ideologues, as they will be the most affected by changes in political context.

That the political context does not equally affect all parts of the electorate should not diminish its importance. A central purpose of this research is to explain political outcomes in local elections, and most elections are in fact decided at the margins. Weak partisans and moderate ideologues often represent swing constituencies that are crucial in determining election outcomes. Insofar as one can better understand their electoral behavior, one is likely to understand a great deal about why some candidates succeed in local elections and why others do not.

The group interest perspective is a broad theory that touches on many aspects of local politics, attempting to integrate a large body of research conducted on voting and urban politics into a more comprehensive statement about the processes at work in local elections. Current theories of local voting cannot explain patterns in voting behavior that vary over time and place. Explaining such patterns demands theories that directly take changing political environments into account. The core claim from this approach is that group interests supersede partisan interests when group conflict escalates. Using election case studies and public opinion data, this research adds new evidence regarding the attitudes that motivate voter choices in local elections.

A Tale of Two Cities

The empirical focus of this work is on the nation's two largest cities: Los Angeles and New York. Admittedly, these are not typical American cities. They are larger than all other American cities and more racially and ethnically diverse than many. Nonetheless, they are particularly instructive for a variety of important reasons. In one sense, they are important because the success of two Republican mayoral candidates in these largely Democratic cities brought our scholarly limitations regarding mayoral voting behavior into sharper focus. Understanding how Rudolph Giuliani and Richard Riordan were able to attract large numbers of Democratic voters tells us a great deal about the peculiarities of city politics. Understanding the ebb and flow of racial politics—why voting is racially polarized in some elections and not in others—is a puzzle well suited to these cities and their political histories.

Another important consideration in the choice of New York and Los Angeles is that these cities provide desirable variation across a number of important factors. The imposing financial and logistical costs of multicity studies often limit the kinds of research conducted on local politics. As a result, the generalizability of local political research is a persistent concern. With this in mind, the objective of this work was to provide significant variation in political context as well as the other systemic factors that influence voting behavior directly and indirectly.

Demography

The populations of New York and Los Angeles number over 8 million and almost 4 million residents, respectively. New York City has the larger black population, approximately 24 percent compared to 11 percent in Los Angeles (see table 2.1). In contrast, Los Angeles has a much larger Latino population (47 percent) and a smaller non-Hispanic white population (30 percent) than New York. Based solely on the demographic composition of these cities over the past twenty years, one might suspect that minority voters have dominated their politics for quite some time. In practice, however, non-Latino whites made up the vast majority of voters in both cities up to and including the elections of 1993. Increasing Latino mobilization over the past five years has largely altered the electoral makeup of Los Angeles and New York, however. As of the most recent mayoral contests, black, Latino, and Asian voters constitute approximately half of the cities' electorate, with non-Hispanic whites rounding out the other half. As will be discussed in later chapters, the increasing size and electoral presence of the nonwhite populations in both of these cities, as well as the growing percentage of Latinos and the shrinking proportion of African-Americans, have had a significant effect on both the strategies of political elites within these cities as well as mass voting behavior.

Institutional Differences

There are important institutional differences between New York City and Los Angeles. New York City has partisan mayoral elections and a relatively robust local party structure. In contrast, Los Angeles is a classic Western reform city with at-large primaries, nonpartisan runoff elections, and little in the way of local party organizations. Los Angeles and New York represent the virtual ends of the partisan spectrum. Thus to the extent that partisan elections and strong local party organizations enhance partisan identification as an electoral cue, one would expect consistently greater levels of partisan voting in New York than in Los Angeles. This, however, is not typically the case.

Another potentially important point of variation is the respective structures of their local governments. New York City has a strong-mayor system of local government and is arguably one of the most powerful mayoralties in the country (Mollenkopf 2003). The mayor of New York City wields substantially more power than does the mayor of Los Angeles. In addition, the large public sector employment base in New York City and the mayor's influence over public employee unions and the city budget make the electoral spoils in New York City particularly consequential. Los Angeles, by contrast, represents a weak-mayor system with a relatively impotent chief executive. Recent charter reform in Los Angeles has marginally increased the mayor's authority over agency appointments, but these changes did not occur until 1999, and even now there is little comparison in the relative influence of these two offices. In Los Angeles, the mayor's influence is generally restricted to appointments of important city-wide agencies and commissions; the mayor has little control over the city budget and the allocation of city resources. In sum, these cases represent a wide range of institutional authority—from high in New York to quite modest in Los Angeles.

TABLE 2.1. New York and Los Angeles: Demographic Composition, 1990 and 2000

	New York City		Los Angeles	
	1990	2000	1990	2000
Total population (in thousands)	7,332	8,423	3,485	3,895
Non-Latino white	43%	35%	37%	30%
Black	29%	24%	14%	11%
Latino	24%	28%	40%	47%
Asian	7%	10%	10%	10%

Source: U.S. Census data, 1990 and 2000.

Distinctive Social and Political Histories

Other important differences between Los Angeles and New York derive from their unique social and political histories. New York City, for example, has a long history of salient ethnic and racial group cleavages, and New York voters continue to attach great importance to racial and ethnic group membership. In particular, it is the ethnic diversity of New York's white populations that sets it apart from Los Angeles.

For many decades, New York City politics were run by a coalition of white ethnics—primarily those of Irish-Catholic, Italian-Catholic, and Jewish descent. The ethnic and religious cleavages that were so prominent during the first half of the twentieth century, however, became somewhat subsumed by racial divisions in the 1960s. As Glazer and Moynihan (1970) aptly describe,

> Ethnic considerations have always been primary in New York City politics, where the top three spots of each party are regularly divided among a Jew, an Italian, and an Irishman (sometimes a white Protestant noses out one of the others, most recently the Irishman, who now represents the smallest of the three major white ethnic groups); where the Borough Presidency of Manhattan has been reserved to Negroes for some years; where the old Board of Education was regularly divided among three Jews, three Catholics, and three Protestants. . . . What is new is that these arrangements, which were adjustments to the reality of race and ethnic difference, have now taken center stage. (xxviii)

New York City politics moved from an informal accommodation of the city's major groups to a more competitive arrangement. In particular, white ethnic voters became more united in the late 1960s, especially when they perceived their interests to be at odds with the black and Latino communities that were competing against them for resources and political power. While the racial conflict described by Glazer and Moynihan was only beginning by 1970, it has continued

to be a pervasive force in the local politics of New York City (Mollenkopf 1992). What sets New York City apart from Los Angeles is
the *persistence* of racial and ethnic conflict.

Research Design

My empirical investigations cover ten mayoral elections in Los Angeles and New York. I rely on historical accounts of individual elections,
voter registration records, official election returns, interviews, and
public opinion data to explore the influence of political context on
mayoral voting behavior. In Los Angeles, there is survey data back to
1969, and the case studies include six important mayoral elections
over the past thirty-four years: 1969, 1973, 1989, 1993, 1997, and
2001. The New York City research includes analyses of the 1989,
1993, 1997, and 2001 mayoral contests.

To a large degree, the decision to focus on these cities and the
selection of the case study elections were driven by two important
considerations: the desire to analyze individual-level voter choice and
the need to control for changing political contexts within the same
electorate. The longitudinal approach I undertake in this book, looking at multiple elections over a thirty-four-year time frame, provides
excellent leverage on the question of context and how changes in
context influence adjustments in the basis for individual-level voting
behavior. Unlike much of the previous case study research, this book
offers a broad theory of urban political behavior that uses voters as the
principle unit of analysis. Because voters—and the influence that context has on the voting calculus—are central to this endeavor, this
series of mayoral elections in Los Angeles and New York (with their
available public opinion data) provides excellent opportunities for
hypothesis testing.

In Los Angeles survey data have been obtained from several
sources. The 1969 data were compiled by Tom Pettigrew as part of a
larger study on black mayoral candidates. The 1973 data uses two
sources: one from a partial replication of the 1969 study conducted
by David Sears and Donald Kinder and the other from a Los Angeles
city survey conducted by California pollster Mervin Field. Public
opinion data from 1989 through 2001 are compiled from *Los Ange-*

les Times polls. The New York City survey data were also obtained from a variety of sources, including Voter Research, CBS/*New York Times,* and ABC/*New York Daily News* polls.

An ideal data set for this research would consist of standardized public opinion results from all city elections. This type of standardized survey (much like the American National Election Survey) would allow researchers to be more confident in the reliability of their measures, to replicate their analyses over time, and to make exact comparisons among different cities and different elections. There is no such instrument available to students of urban politics, thus media polls, when available, provide the best source of data for individual-level analyses. The 1969 (Pettigrew) and 1973 (Sears and Kinder) polls were both conducted by political scientists, with exact replication of question wording in the latter survey. The samples, however, in both were restricted to white voters only. The 1973 Field Research poll was conducted prior to the mayoral runoff election in 1973 and includes 1,048 respondents. In the case of the more recent Los Angeles and New York polls (1989 to 2001), they were all obtained from large, reputable media outlets. The number of respondents was over 1,000 in each, and in some of the exit polls there were as many as 4,000 surveyed.

The first half of this chapter presented a number of expectations derived from the group interest framework. The central claim of this approach is that *changes in the political context influence the attitudinal basis for voting behavior and that, in particular, increasing levels of group conflict correspond with greater amounts of group distinctive voting.* The analyses conducted on elections in New York and Los Angeles primarily focus on exploring the validity of this claim. The survey data from each election provide a means of comparing individual-level considerations and behaviors. General support for these expectations is evident if group interests (apart from party identification) are more instrumental to voting behavior when group conflict is high than when it is low. To appropriately test this view of local politics, several things must take place. First, it is important to measure group identities, partisan identities, and alternate group interests. It is further critical that there is an appropriate method to compare their relative importance to voting behavior.

This study accomplishes this objective by using opinion data and by identifying a set of "racial interest" attitudes that are then compared with partisan beliefs, political ideologies, and other demographic factors in regard to their relative influence on the vote. Thus the analytical focus of each election study is on quantifying the extent to which partisan beliefs, ideology, and racial interests explain variance in local voting. Racial interests, as conceived in this analysis, represent attitudes regarding the equitable distribution of power and resources among competing groups in the community. Thus survey questions that focus on local government accommodation of various groups and the perceived fairness of this level of accommodation are particularly well suited for this analysis. Questions that pertain to individual feelings about intergroup relations are also used as a measure of conflict orientation because they reflect the individual's relative comfort with the state of power relations in the city at the time of the survey. Where possible, these factors are evaluated using multivariate regression techniques with mayoral voting as the dependent variable.

The central expectation in this research is that racial interests matter more when the political environment is fraught with group conflict. And while the survey data utilized in this research provide a means to measure racial attitudes and their relationship to the vote, they do not provide a similarly robust measure of the "level of conflict." Ideally, there would be survey questions that asked respondents to assess the current level of group conflict relative to prior periods and this question would be asked in each of the subject cases. With such a measure it would be very easy to compare one election to another and even to compare them between cities. While some surveys actually do ask questions similar to this, they are not available for all of the cases in this study. Identifying periods of intense group conflict is nonetheless essential to this task. In lieu of survey data, I rely on secondary sources to assess levels of conflict. For each of the subject elections, a detailed history has been compiled using newspaper accounts, magazines, academic reports, and interviews. The result of this process is a subjective assessment of overall levels of conflict ranging from low to high—or, in the case of multiple elections within the same city, from less to more.

3 From Rioting to Watergate: Los Angeles, 1969 and 1973

The 1969 and 1973 Los Angeles mayoral elections represent an ideal set of elections within which to test the group interest expectation that conflict makes racial interests salient to voting. The 1969 mayoral election in Los Angeles featured a conservative incumbent Democrat, Sam Yorty, against a more liberal black Democrat, Tom Bradley. Yorty, who had been the mayor since 1961, was the subject of much ridicule, and popular expectations in the media and the scholarly community were that Bradley would win. He did not. The political context in 1969 proved to be a deleterious backdrop against which to elect the city's first black mayor. Four years later, however, in a far different context with considerably less racial discord, Bradley won an easy victory over the incumbent Yorty.

Both of these elections featured nasty, acrimonious campaigns that played on the racial fears of white Angelenos. While Yorty was able to succeed in 1969, facilitated by the conflictual political backdrop, Bradley was able to defeat him in the more amenable political context of 1973. The initial part of this chapter recounts the history of Los Angeles mayoral politics in the late 1960s and early 1970s, beginning with the Watts Riots in 1965. In the second part of the chapter, I use public opinion data from both elections to show how changes in the political context resulted in different types of voting behavior. Negative racial sentiments were closely correlated with white voting behavior in 1969. By 1973—a different political climate to be sure—race mattered less than it had before.

The Watts Riots, 1965

For Los Angeles as well as the country, the late 1960s were turbulent times. The centerpiece of this era was the Vietnam War, and by the late 1960s the divisive and acrimonious debate over the nation's involvement in this conflict was at its apex. Accompanying the public discourse on the war were a myriad of campus protests, the emergence of a militant black power movement, the assassinations of Dr. Martin Luther King Jr. and Senator Robert Kennedy, and race riots in cities across the country. Indeed, the latter half of this decade was punctuated by social and political upheavals that were vividly broadcast every evening on the national news.

Los Angeles was the setting for one of the many urban uprisings during this period. In 1965 an altercation between a black man, Marquette Frye, and the California Highway Patrol erupted into what became known as the Watts Riots. The riots lasted for six days, resulting in thirty-four deaths, over one thousand serious injuries, nearly four thousand arrests, and approximately $40 million (1965 dollars) of destroyed property (Sears and McConahay 1973). The response by political elites to the riots and the rioters reflected the underlying ambivalence of the white electorate to the racial uprisings that occurred in many urban cores. Liberals, especially liberal Democrats, expressed sympathy to the communities affected by the riots and concern for the overall plight of the urban poor. The elite political response to the Watts Riots was not uniformly sympathetic, however. Many moderate and conservative political leaders responded to the Watts uprising with a call for greater law and order. Among those in the political leadership who saw the Watts Riots as a law and order issue were Ronald Reagan, then governor of California, and Sam Yorty, mayor of Los Angeles.

This division that was observed among political elites in their response to this social upheaval was also seen in the attitudes and political preferences of nonblack voters. Moderates and conservatives were not only unsympathetic to rioters, protesters, and the like, but they demonstrated substantial intolerance toward civil disobedience and considerable support for police and National Guard use of force (Page and Shapiro 1992). The proportion of the public who opposed public protests in general and felt that protests by students, blacks, and antiwar activists should be discontinued was above 70 percent in both 1968 and 1969. The level of anxiety over protesters began to wane with the declining salience of these movements, however, and by 1974 the proportion of the public who disapproved of protest movements had declined from 74 percent in 1968 to 52 percent (Page and Shapiro 1992, 351).

The national concern over protests and civil unrest came with a vocabulary—code words that evoked fear and uncertainty. "Leftists," "liberals," "radicals," "militants," and "communists" were some of the labels affixed to the period's protesters. And to be associated with leftists, militants, and communists during the late 1960s was a political liability, especially for candidates seeking white electoral support. In addition to the generalized fears that were so prevalent at the time, the state of California in particular was a hotbed of campus unrest. Violent protests at the University of California, Berkeley; Stanford University; and San Francisco State University had brought in the National Guard and stimulated substantial antiradical rhetoric from state legislators and especially Governor Reagan. As noted in the *Nation* in 1969:

> Against a background of campus disturbances in California, race is a pervasive political factor this year in the state. Governor Reagan, who is taking a "hard line" against student militants, was never more popular than he is today. (March 31, p. 404)

While the majority of campus militancy had been located in northern California, protests spread to UCLA and San Fernando State College less than a week before the Los Angeles mayoral runoff elections. The proximity of these protests, both geographically and temporally, to the mayoral campaign only served to exacerbate the fearful reactions of the local electorate. This environment of suspicion provided an explosive backdrop for the mayoral campaign of 1969 and on its face did not present a promising environment in which to become the first black mayor of Los Angeles. Nonetheless, Tom Bradley garnered 42 percent of the vote in the primary election and was predicted by political pundits to be the likely winner. His loss to Yorty by a 53 percent to 47 percent margin in the runoff election was considered a surprising upset. However, given the context within which this election took place, coupled with the campaign strategies employed by both candidates, hindsight suggests that this outcome was indeed not surprising.

Sam Yorty—The Maverick Incumbent Mayor

In 1969 the incumbent mayor in Los Angeles was conservative Democrat Sam Yorty. He had won the mayor's office originally in 1961, in a surprise defeat of then Republican mayor Norris Poulson. The core of his original coalition was made up of middle-class homeowners from the San Fernando Valley and blacks and Latinos from Los Angeles's less affluent neighborhoods. In his early campaigns, he ran as a populist railing against the establishment and Downtown business interests. He ran as an outsider and as a reformer, wooing Valley residents with promises of greater influence in city government and attracting the black community with promises to reform the police department and to keep Police Chief Parker under close scrutiny.

Yorty, from his earliest political days, was considered somewhat of a character. Outspoken and colorful, the mayor was a former state assemblyman and was an outsider even within his own political party. He often deviated from the California Democratic party orthodoxy, and his endorsement of Richard Nixon over John F. Kennedy in 1960 further frayed the weak ties that remained between him and state party organizations. As was noted by the *Nation* (April 21, 1969, 485), "He is a flamboyant type who began his political career as a liberal and has since moved consistently to the right." While his political roots were found in populist-style liberalism, his evolution, once mayor, was a shift from a maverick outsider to the consummate insider.

> Sam Yorty in the 1930s spoke for Los Angeles' social underdogs, the rural to urban migrant, the unionizing worker, the low-paid consumer. His electorates were composed of the little men disdained by the big forces controlling national wealth and

claiming social deference. Today, however, as his supporters have become political and social advocates of the status quo in which they are relatively well off, Yorty has moved away from fighting to get things for his clientele to fighting to keep things for it. (Maullin 1971, 41)

Yorty's original electoral coalition consisted of working-class and middle-class whites, as well as substantial numbers of black and Latino voters. His victory in 1961 is often credited to the enormous support received from the black community, and early signs from his first administration suggested that his commitment to his black constituency was sincere (Sonenshein 1993a). Yorty did increase the number of blacks appointed to city commissions and within the mayor's office (Ainsworth 1966). Equally important, however, he did not challenge Police Chief Parker with respect to the widespread misconduct reported by minority communities. As a result of his turnabout with Police Chief Parker and other factors, the mayor's support in the black community declined substantially, and by 1965 blacks overwhelmingly supported his opponent, James Roosevelt.

By 1969 Yorty's support citywide was waning. His administration had been beset by scandals. Three of his former city commissioners had been convicted of accepting bribes, and a fourth was awaiting trial on similar charges. Yorty had gone from being simply colorful to the butt of much local humor.

> His hawkish advice to Washington on how to win the war in Vietnam became standard fare for cartoonists; in fact it has been said that Los Angeles under Yorty was the only city in the nation to have its own foreign policy. (*Nation*, April 21, 1969, 485)

Yorty had rather a grandiose sense of his position, as evidenced by his frequent travels abroad. The mayor visited more than a dozen foreign countries while in his first two terms and was often criticized for his frequent trips. The mayor was not supported by the generally conservative *Los Angeles Times,* and in an editorial endorsing Bradley, the editors wrote the following regarding his tenure:

The incumbent Sam Yorty has an eight-year record of bickering and weak leadership, racial divisiveness and clowning absenteeism on world-wide junkets, collusion and bribery among his appointed commissioners, and tirades against the agencies of justice in metropolitan Los Angeles. (May 25, 1969, G6)

These critical opinions of Yorty were not far adrift of mainstream public opinion, and his unpopularity in Los Angeles was clearly evident in the primary election, when as the incumbent he received only 26 percent of the vote. If the 1969 election had been a referendum on his mayoralty, he would have lost. Nonetheless, Yorty deftly played on the fear and uncertainty that permeated the times; by asserting that Tom Bradley was a dangerous radical who associated with Black Panthers and communists, he was able to salvage victory in 1969.

Tom Bradley—The Challenger

In contrast to Mayor Yorty, Tom Bradley was a rather serene figure. While not a native Angeleno, Bradley moved to Los Angeles with his family when he was seven years old. He graduated from Los Angeles Polytechnic High School, attended UCLA, and eventually left the university to pursue a career with the Los Angeles Police Department (LAPD). He received a law degree from Southwestern Law School by completing night school while working on the police force. After twenty years on the force, he retired from his rank of police lieutenant to practice law. Bradley had come from a poor family, and his accomplishments were accordingly seen as a triumph of great individual achievement. As Raphael Sonenshein (1993a) notes in *Politics in Black and White:*

Bradley's "up from poverty story" became a staple of his political career. Its metaphors proved appealing to both blacks and whites. Bradley's isolation in a white world, his role as a pioneer entering uncharted territory, and his extraordinary academic, professional, and athletic achievements made him a suitable subject for symbolic recognition. His life became a metaphor for individual black upward mobility in the face of great odds. (60)

His political style was one of soft-spoken conviction. Unlike that of many of the trailblazing black mayors (Detroit's Coleman Young and Atlanta's Maynard Jackson, for example), who called for greater racial equality and economic justice in somewhat confrontational terms, Bradley's approach was decidedly conciliatory and understated. While his objectives to increase the economic and social well-being of poor communities of color were clearly articulated, his rhetoric steered clear of the inflammatory tones used by many of the militant black and Latino leaders during this period. Bradley was acutely aware that in order to win citywide office he could not afford to alienate large numbers of white voters. He also had great faith that his race alone would not be an obstacle to becoming mayor.

The core of Bradley's electoral coalition consisted of blacks and liberal whites—especially liberal Jews. In the 1950s and early 1960s he had become involved with several liberal political groups, most notably the Democratic Minority Conference and the California Democratic Council. It was from within these groups that he forged many close political alliances that would rally to his cause in 1969. Many high-ranking Bradley campaign operatives were Jewish, as were many of his most generous financial benefactors. The connection between the black and Jewish communities has been described as linkage of liberal ideologies and mutual interests (Sonenshein 1993a). Blacks, liberals in general, and Jews in particular had seen little political empowerment in Los Angeles. Thus their shared status as outsiders, coupled with their mutual attraction to a progressive, liberal political agenda, contributed to an alliance that would over the course of the next twenty years alter the symbols and substance of Los Angeles municipal politics.

Bradley knew that in order to win he would have to gain support from the large, yet poorly mobilized Latino community. He made direct appeals to the Latino community on the basis of their perceived interest in greater social and economic equality. The ties between the black and Latino community were somewhat tenuous, however.

Inasmuch as they may have shared similar goals for the betterment of their communities, they nonetheless were often competing against one another for political power within their respective (and shared) districts, as well as for more tangible interests such as housing and jobs. The tension between black and Latino goals and experiences was well described by Bradley pollster Richard Maullin (1971):

> Bradley's campaign, however, tended to impose the perspective of the solidarity-oriented cultural nationalists among the Mexican-American population. The black-brown coalition in effect was telling Mexican-American voters that their social and economic goals would only really be achieved when the blacks also received justice. This message negated much of the experience of thousands of Mexican-Americans, who by virtue of not being black, had greater access to non-ghetto housing, higher income and less social hostility from whites than blacks experienced. (51)

The Bradley campaign believed that they were well positioned to challenge Sam Yorty in 1969. Registered Democrats outnumbered registered Republicans by almost two to one in Los Angeles. Furthermore, Bradley's candidacy was endorsed by all of the California Democratic leadership as well as by many key Republicans. His distinguished twenty-year career with the LAPD along with his dignified, soft-spoken call for racial harmony were factors that he believed would be welcome to Los Angeles voters. That Yorty was an unpopular incumbent besieged with controversy was an added bonus. The 1969 campaign for mayor was as acrimonious as any in Los Angeles's history, and at its end the incumbent Yorty scored an upset defeat. These were not normal times in Los Angeles, however. And this conflictual political context, coupled with a campaign strategy targeted to incite the latent fears of white voters, was sufficient to defeat Bradley.

The 1969 Campaign

In a calmer time, Los Angeles might have done so (elect a black man), but against the ominous background of a poisonous war, black revolt and campus riots, Yorty stirred old passions and new anxieties. (*Nation,* June 16, 1969, 750)

Tom Bradley's bid for mayor began as a grass roots campaign utilizing the membership and resources of the California Democratic Council (CDC). Bradley had been politically active within the black community and the Democratic party, and his years of political activity were repaid by thousands of local activists politicking for him and helping to mobilize sympathetic voters. His grass roots efforts were rewarded on April 1, 1969, when Bradley, at that time a city councilman, received 42 percent of the citywide vote and was advanced to the runoff election. Bradley had received over 100,000 more votes than the incumbent Yorty and was only a mere 8 percentage points away from having taken the election outright. Furthermore, Bradley's "get out the vote" campaign appeared to have been fruitful, as the 65 percent turnout rate in this primary election was substantially higher than the 59 percent rate in 1965.

The unanticipated primary results took the somewhat complacent mayor by surprise. Yorty had little inclination to lose his office without a fight, and his response to the Bradley challenge came in the form of a racially charged campaign intended to paint his opponent and his cohorts as dangerous radicals intent on turning Los Angeles into a "black city." Yorty claimed that "to elect Tom Bradley would be an invitation to violence in this city" (*Time,* June 6, 1969, 28). He ran advertisements with Bradley's picture and a caption that read, "Will your family be safe?" He charged Bradley with being antipolice and argued that, if Bradley were elected, thousands of police officers would walk off their jobs. Almost nightly television broadcasts of campus violence at Berkeley, Stanford, and San Francisco State helped fan Yorty's brush fire of fear. "The anarchy that began on our campuses now threatens to make inroads into our city," one of his flyers shrilled. He argued, "No mayor can administer a city by accommodating militants" (*Newsweek,* June 9, 1969, 31). Equally damaging to the Bradley campaign was the revelation, made public by Yorty, that one of Bradley's top campaign officials, Don Rothenberg, had been a member of the Communist party as recently as 1956. Bradley's response to this charge was not to fire Rothenberg but to argue that his membership and interest in the party had long since lapsed and thus was not pertinent to him or his campaign. His loyalty to Rothenberg, however, only added further fuel to Yorty's leftist, radical, communist, black power tirades.

Yorty's explicit attempt to use the backdrop of social unrest to his electoral advantage was accompanied by a fervent call for law and order. Ironically, it was Bradley, not Yorty, who had served for twenty years on the police force. Yet in spite of Bradley's distinguished service, the police issue went to Yorty. As Maullin (1971) noted, "Bradley never ducked the issue of campus unrest and militancy, but his quiet tone and preference for a 'reasonable' answer were pale next to Yorty's demagoguery" (47). Internal polls by both campaigns showed that concern over campus unrest and potential violence was utmost in voters' minds. Yorty capitalized on this issue agenda, while Bradley and his advisors, squeamish at jumping on the law and order bandwagon, were ineffectual in countering his attacks. As Sonenshein (1993a) explains,

> In those days, the law and order issue was fairly new, and among many liberals, it was seen as nothing more than a code word for racism. White liberals and Blacks had great difficulty developing a popular position on crime that would not seem to embrace anti-Black views. Yet crime was a central issue to voters. (92)

Given the divisive rhetoric and widespread interest in the mayoral contest, large voter turnout was expected. The actual turnout at 76 percent was well above anyone's expectations. Black turnout was especially high. The average turnout in Los Angeles's three predominantly black council districts was 6 percentage points higher than the average for the nonblack districts in the city (Gilliam and Kaufmann 1998). Nonetheless, Yorty won the runoff by a 53 percent to 47 percent margin, and Bradley lost his electoral bid. While Bradley won nearly unanimous support from black voters, Yorty succeeded in damaging Bradley's support among white and Latino voters. Among white Protestants and Catholics, Bradley received 32 percent of the vote, and among Jews he only received 52 percent of the vote (Maullin 1971). Although Bradley picked up over 96,000 votes in the runoff campaign, the mayor gained over 260,000 votes, suggesting that his campaign strategy was highly successful.

The Aftermath: Critical Analyses of Voting Behavior in 1969

The Bradley candidacy and the mayoral contest generated substantial interest from the news media, not only in Los Angeles but nationwide. While Bradley would not have been the first black mayor to be elected in a large city, he would have been the first to be elected in a large city with a relatively small black population. Carl Stokes in Cleveland, Richard Hatcher in Gary, and Kenneth Gibson in Newark were all black men who had won the mayor's office in large American cities. Cleveland, Gary, and Newark, however, all had black populations in excess of 35 percent, and the white support these candidates received in their respective elections did not exceed 20 percent (Pettigrew 1971). In contrast, the black population in Los Angeles made up only 18 percent of the city total; thus for Bradley to win, he needed to gain much greater levels of support from the white community than did his black predecessors. While Bradley's white support far exceeded that of other black mayors, he nonetheless fell short of victory.

Bradley's enormous electoral success in the primary coupled with his unexpected defeat in the runoff election stimulated some attention from the scholarly community as well. Two studies in particular used public opinion data to investigate the underlying attitudes of white voters and their correlates to voting behavior in this election. Using different data sets and somewhat distinct theoretical approaches, both of these studies nonetheless identified fear and concern over challenges to the status quo as highly related to political behavior in this election. Jeffries and Ransford (1972) conducted a study of white voters in the San Fernando Valley subsequent to the 1969 mayoral election. Their hypothesis proposed that "protest and dissent in our society is producing an angry backlash ideology in the white majority based on law and order, patriotism, and left wing threat" (371). To test this hypothesis they developed an ideological measure that they labeled "Troubled American Beliefs" (TAB) and set out to demonstrate that attitudes concerned with law and order, fear of communism, and a desire for greater patriotism were highly correlated to the mayoral vote decision. They argued that the common element among these three attitudinal variables was a perception of threat from internal or external forces and a need to reaffirm social stability. Jeffries and Ransford's findings did indeed support their argument that the vote was correlated with these attitudinal variables, and they further suggested that these attitudes were not unique to the working class but rather crosscut socioeconomic cleavages. "In terms of normative behavior like voting, those who are highly 'troubled' vote their fears, be they white-collar professionals or blue-collar men" (371).

Similar in spirit to Jeffries and Ransford, David Sears and Donald Kinder (1971) argued that political ideology coupled with symbolic racial attitudes were highly related to the 1969 vote. Furthermore, they acknowledged that the circumstances surrounding this election—its somewhat unique political context—evoked these underlying attitudes as voting cues:

> Thus, the conservative surge in voting is best explained by the voter's long standing political conservatism and traditionalism. . . . Evidently this conservatism has been strongly evoked by the social changes in the media—especially the very disrespectful campus radicals and the scary black militants—and has started to override the powerful restraining force of Democratic Party identification. (84)

Both of these studies suggest that the "white backlash" in 1969 was related to the perceptions of threat posed by radical war protesters and militant black activists and to the fact that Yorty played on these fears as a principle part of his runoff campaign strategy. Both studies also suggest, however, that TAB or symbolic racism was likely to become a more prevalent part of electoral politics given the changes taking place in race relations. Neither was able to foreshadow the fact that Bradley would come back to beat Yorty in four short years and that he would maintain his electoral coalition for the next twenty.

The 1973 Rematch

It was a political grudge fight—a replay of the bitter 1969 campaign. . . . Yorty, 63, overtook Bradley in a runoff last time around, mainly by placing him somewhere between Eldridge Cleaver and H. Rap Brown in the American political spectrum, and Bradley, 55, has been spoiling to settle accounts ever since. (*Newsweek,* April 19, 1973, 32)

In so many ways the 1973 mayoral election mirrored the prior election between Yorty and Bradley. The candidates were the same, as were most of the issues. The fundamental difference between 1969 and 1973 was the electoral climate, and it was this change in political context that enhanced Bradley's electoral prospects and eventually contributed to his election. Eight years had passed since the Watts uprising. Public opinion, which had been so divided over the Vietnam War, had shifted toward greater consensus regarding the need to end the war. Campus unrest had subsided, and the focus of the national media turned from civil rights to Watergate.[1] The shift in focus from riots to Watergate was not inconsequential to the 1973 mayor's race in Los Angeles. On the contrary, heightened public concerns over government corruption made issues of mayoral accountability, financial trustworthiness, and dirty campaign tricks salient and important. Yorty's 1969 campaign strategy played on the heightened fears of white voters in the context of the riots and campus protests that defined the late 1960s. In 1973, however, public attention had largely shifted away from social unrest. Yet Yorty did not change his campaign tactics in 1973, and this coupled with his own financial scandals left him vulnerable.

Similar to 1969, Bradley emerged as the front-runner after the

---

1. While arguments in chapters 1 and 2 suggest that local politics are generally focused on local sets of political issues, Watergate is an example of a national issue that had fallout even at the local level. The extraordinary events surrounding the Watergate hearings and Nixon's eventual resignation were especially powerful in the context of the Los Angeles mayoralty because of Yorty's vulnerability on the corruption issue. By 1973 four of his appointed commissioners had been convicted of accepting bribes. Many stories accusing Yorty of unscrupulous, politically corrupt behavior were published during this period as well.

April 1973 primary with 35 percent of the vote. Yorty was second with 29 percent. While the mayor did not substantially change his campaign tactics from 1969, Bradley realized that he had been too passive the last time in response to Yorty's blistering attacks. As a result, Bradley hired New York media consultant David Garth to design his radio and television campaign. Bradley had been labeled a radical and had been accused of being antipolice. He spent over $500,000 in a media campaign to dispel these public images.

> Bradley's campaign strategy was to reassure whites. He constantly referred to his 21 years' service on the LAPD. . . . he let nobody forget that he stood for law and order. He carefully disassociated himself from the Black Panthers, antagonizing the more militant blacks. In his low-keyed TV commercials, he was mainly seen with whites, who praised him for his police work or his efforts to save parks and beaches from developers. (*Time,* June 11, 1973)

In early May (election day was May 29), California pollster Mervin Field reported that Bradley had a healthy lead over Yorty, 43 percent to 29 percent with 20 percent undecided. By the middle of May, however, Bradley's lead appeared to be deteriorating and Yorty jumped on this opportunity. Approximately one week before election day Yorty sent a campaign telegram to several thousand households in predominantly white neighborhoods. "The April 3rd primary saw extremely low turnout," the mailer said. "In comparison, Watts had a phenomenally high turnout. Black bloc vote went massively for Bradley. Radical elements could control our police department and city services, as in Berkeley. . . . If we are to win, maximum turnout (in the runoff election) is vital" (*New Republic,* June 9, 1973, 8). In addition to this mailer, he placed a full-page advertisement in the *Herald Examiner* on election eve asserting Bradley's ties to the Black Panthers. Yorty did his best to reignite the fears that had saved his third term. His efforts, however, went unrewarded in 1973. "In 1969 the issue of racism was strong enough to offset antipathy toward Yorty," observed Field. "This year whites were less fearful, and Bradley was not viewed as that much of a threat" (*Newsweek,* June 11,

1973, 29). On May 29, 1973, Tom Bradley became the first black mayor of Los Angeles by a margin of 56 percent to 44 percent.

The 1973 mayoral election of Bradley has been interpreted as a watershed event in urban history. Bradley was the first black man to be elected mayor of a large city where the black population was relatively small and where his margin of victory included almost half of the white voters in the city. Perhaps as momentous as his initial victory was the relative ease with which Bradley held together his electoral coalition for the next twenty years. So widespread was Bradley's multiracial and multiethnic support throughout the city that few challengers emerged during his twenty-year reign, and none of the competition was substantial enough to even force a runoff.

Explaining the Outcome in 1973

While Bradley's 1969 defeat generated several scholarly studies, Bradley's victory in 1973 did not stimulate as much academic interest. There was, however, one study conducted by Hahn, Klingman, and Pachon (1976) that examined the cleavages and coalitions in 1969 versus 1973. Their analysis suggested that Bradley was successful in attracting higher percentages of Latinos and whites in 1973 and that improvement within these groups led to his victory. They argued that the difference between the 1969 and 1973 campaigns was Yorty's decision to make Bradley's race less of an issue in the latter. They concluded their paper with the observation that black candidates are inherently vulnerable to the possible injection of race as a campaign issue and that, when the race card is dealt, the potential for victory is devastated.

Mayor Yorty, however, did not forget to inject racial issues into the 1973 campaign. As evidenced from his campaign materials, he most explicitly attempted to generate race-based fears. He called Bradley a "radical left-winger" and a "sort of black nationalist" (*Los Angeles Times,* May 24, 1973, A1). He suggested that the police department and other civil services would be taken over by dangerous radicals. He attempted the same tactics that had brought him victory four years prior. The difference, however, was in the receptivity of the public to his campaign. In the political context of 1973, racial fears were less salient than other factors, and as a result his message fell on deaf ears. More than any other factor, the declining levels of racial anxiety among white voters in 1973 made racial cues less salient and enabled Bradley's momentous victory.

Comparing White Voting Behavior in 1969 and 1973

From a group interest perspective, the political context helps shape the issues and subsequent group identities that become salient voting cues in any given election. Individual voter attention—from traditional political alliances (such as party affiliation) to other salient group memberships (such as racial identities)—changes with increasing levels of group conflict. Since interracial tensions were very high in 1969, group interest theory would expect racial attitudes to have greater predictive power than more general political attitudes with regard to the vote in this election. By contrast, racial discord was much less pronounced by 1973.[2] In the context of the Watergate hearings, the political issues concerning the mass public had shifted from protest and civil unrest to matters of political accountability and integrity. And since public attention in 1973 had moved to issues with less racial content, political beliefs should be more influential in this election than they were four years prior.

It is important to note that shifting public attentiveness works at the margins and that it would be unrealistic to expect wholesale shifts in mass behavior from one election to the next. As was discussed in chapter 2, contextual factors have differential impact depending on the strength of the ideological and partisan commitment of any given individual. Strong partisans and strong ideologues are less susceptible

---

2. The analyses I conduct in this chapter pertain to white voters exclusively. The claim that interracial discord had subsided in 1973 also refers particularly to white perceptions. As discussed in chapter 1, racial and ethnic minorities—especially those who suffer from persistent discrimination—are more alienated generally and more cognizant of interracial competition than are members of dominant racial groups. In both elections, blacks overwhelmingly supported Bradley's candidacy. The swing voters who made the difference between the outcome in 1969 and 1973 were predominantly liberal and moderate whites. It was thus the decline in perceived conflict within these groups that effected lower levels of partisan defection in the 1973 election.

to contextual influences than are weak partisans and ideological moderates. Thus from one election to another it is reasonable to expect marginal differences in voter choice that, in many cases, result in different electoral outcomes. For this reason, the voting analyses explore the electorate in the aggregate as well as important subgroups where group interest motives are most likely to be evident. The following discussion presents findings from a series of bivariate and multivariate analyses designed to test the group interest expectations regarding salient voting cues in 1969 and 1973. The first set of analyses uses public opinion survey data from 1969[3] and explores the extent to which racial attitudes were important to voting behavior in this election. Because the sample from the 1969 survey was restricted to white voters, the following discussion pertains only to whites.

I explore several possible explanations for the Yorty vote. From the group interest perspective, racial attitudes are expected to be particularly important to white voting behavior. The racial attitude measure used in this analysis is a scale composed of two survey questions. The first question relates to local government responsiveness to black citizens: "In general, do you think Los Angeles city officials pay more, less, or the same attention to a request or complaint from a Negro person as from a white person?" This question taps into levels of racial resentment and is particularly relevant as it relates feelings about blacks to city government. The second question is more general and identifies attitudes regarding poor blacks and their reliance on social programs: "Do you think that most Negroes who receive money from welfare programs could get along without it if they tried, or do they really need this help?" Responses from these two questions are combined into a composite measure. From the group interest perspective, individuals who feel that city hall pays too much attention to Negroes and individuals who think blacks are too reliant on social

---

3. The 1969 data were collected as part of a larger study on black mayoral candidates under the direction of Thomas Pettigrew. They comprise personal interviews with white Los Angeles residents randomly sampled from two predominantly white council districts. The data were collected during the 1969 mayoral election campaign. Other studies using this data include Pettigrew 1971, Sears and Kinder 1971, and Kinder and Sears 1981. I am very grateful for Tom Pettigrew's permission to use the 1969 data and also grateful to David Sears and Donald Kinder for their assistance in locating this survey.

programs should be much more likely to vote for Yorty than should more racially liberal whites.

Aside from racial explanations, it is certainly possible that Yorty voting was tied to retrospective evaluations of his mayoralty. Yorty had been mayor of Los Angeles since 1961, and it is reasonable to expect that this election may have been a referendum on his job performance. This possibility is explored with a measure called "Satisfaction with Local Government Services" that combines responses to four survey questions that ask the respondent to rate his or her satisfaction with public schools, parks and playgrounds, garbage collection, and the police. Responses from these four questions are combined and scaled from low to high.[4] If mayoral voting was in fact motivated out of satisfaction with Yorty's job performance, individuals with high levels of approval should display a much higher Yorty vote than those with low evaluations, all else being equal. I also include measures of party identification, political ideology, and income.

Regarding the 1969 election, I expect individual racial attitudes to be stronger determinants of the vote than more traditional political orientations, such as partisanship and ideology. The conflictual political context in 1969 is presumed to make group interests salient and to de-emphasize other sets of political attitudes with regard to voting. To explore these expectations, I conduct logistic regression analyses for three groups of voters: the aggregate white electorate, white ideological liberals, and white Democrats. Since the logistic regression coefficients (see table A3.1 in the appendix) have no ready interpretation, I report a series of estimated probabilities of the Yorty vote.[5] These probabilities, found in table 3.1, represent the difference in the Yorty vote moving from a given independent variable's lowest to

---

4. Given the context of this election, it is certainly plausible that retrospective evaluations regarding the police and their ability to protect the community would be a more important factor than the other three retrospective evaluations. I tested for this possibility and found the cumulative retrospective evaluation scale to be the more robust predictor of the vote.

5. The estimated probabilities reported in table 3.1 are comparable to what Rosenstone and Hansen (1993) refer to as the "effect" of the independent variable. These estimates based on the logistic regression coefficients are found in table A3.1 in the appendix and are generated using the statistical programs STATA and CLARIFY.

highest values, letting all the other independent variables take their natural values.[6] Large differences indicate that the variable in question has a potent influence on voting behavior, whereas smaller differences imply a more modest impact.

TABLE 3.1.   Estimated Probability of a Yorty Vote, 1969

	All Whites	White Democrats	White Liberals
Ideology			
Liberal	.37	.32	—
Conservative	.54	.48	—
Difference	*.17**	*.16*	—
Income			
Low	.44	.29	.34
High	.49	.64	.44
Difference	*.05*	*.35**	*.10*
Satisfaction with local govt. services			
Approve strongly	.57	.54	.59
Disapprove strongly	.29	.21	.10
Difference	*.28**	*.33**	*.49**
Party identification			
Democrat	.40	—	.33
Republican	.55	—	.44
Difference	*.15**	—	*.11*
Attitudes regarding blacks			
Favorable/govt. pays too little attention	.14	.11	.06
Unfavorable/govt. pays too much attention	.79	.74	.77
Difference	*.65**	*.63**	*.71**
Number of cases	229	126	104

Source: Los Angeles Pre-election Poll, 1969—Tom Pettigrew, principal investigator.
Note: Cell entries equal the estimated probability of a Yorty vote. The author's calculations are based on multivariate logistic regression results found in table A3.1 in the appendix.
*$p < .10$

6. I only report the reduced fit models. Other demographic variables such as gender, age, occupation, and education failed to attract significant coefficients. I also tested a range of interaction effects, especially between ideology, partisanship, and racial attitudes. Interaction effects are excluded from the final model, as they did not yield significant coefficients or substantively enhance the results.

White Voting Behavior in 1969

Clearly the results of this analysis show that negative racial attitudes were paramount considerations for Yorty voters. Among all white voters, racial attitudes are by far the most robust predictor of voting behavior. Among racially liberal white voters, the estimated Yorty vote was only 14 percent, while it was 79 percent among voters with racially conservative views. While party identification, ideology, and retrospective evaluations were also significant factors in regard to vote choice, racial attitudes were nonetheless the single largest determinant of a Yorty vote. And the extent to which racial attitudes supersede traditional political factors in explaining the vote further implies that partisan and ideological preferences may be crosscut on the issue of race. Patterns in these data provide support for the group interest thesis. The group interest perspective, however, also presumes that Democratic and liberal decisions to support conservative candidates should be particularly founded in racially motivated behavior, as these groups, in particular, defect more from their partisan and ideological predispositions. The second and third columns of table 3.1 show parallel analyses for both Democratic and liberal subgroups, further confirming the group interest hypothesis.

Similar to the findings for the white electorate as a whole, racial attitudes contribute significantly to Democratic and liberal Yorty support. For Democrats, racial attitudes, class interests, and job satisfaction attitudes influence Yorty voting. Only 11 percent of white Democrats with liberal racial attitudes voted for Yorty in 1969, compared to 74 percent of white Democrats with racially conservative views. For white liberals, racial attitudes and positive retrospective evaluations of local government both influence voter choices. Party identification and class distinctions do not, however, significantly predict Yorty voting. The cumulative results from these analyses overwhelmingly support group interest expectations. In the case of both Democrats and liberals, racial conservatism was highly related to Yorty voting where partisan and ideological differences were statistically insignificant.

In the context of the social upheaval in the late 1960s, racial attitudes clearly mattered to the electoral outcome in this election. Furthermore, individual racial attitudes were more influential to the vote than were party, ideology, or retrospective evaluations of the Yorty mayoralty. Consistent with the expectations of group interest theory, the high degree of racial conflict surrounding this election appeared to alter the electoral calculus for many voters. The salience of race and racial group interests in this election weakened the normally powerful effects of party and ideology on the vote and, to a great degree, effected a conservative outcome.

There were several important factors that made racial attitudes salient in this election, and Tom Bradley's race was certainly among them. Group interest theory, however, presumes that the mere presence of a black candidate is insufficient, in and of itself, to make racial identities extraordinarily salient for white voters and to necessarily induce large numbers of partisan and ideological defections. For racial identities and attitudes to be salient among white voters, the political context should be fraught with some level of racial discord. For many cities, interracial conflict is a chronic condition of urban political life. And when this is the case, it does not take much to make racial interests salient to voters. Los Angeles, prior to the 1965 Watts Riots, did not have a history of chronic interracial friction. Extreme racial economic inequalities were certainly evident in Los Angeles throughout this period, and it would be unrealistic to presume that racial minorities living in Los Angeles, especially those at the bottom of the social/economic hierarchy, did not sense substantial competition between their groups and dominant whites. For white voters, however, issues of racial competition had been relatively muted. Had there been less pervasive social and racial unrest at the time of this election, Bradley most likely would have won. The racially charged context in 1969—coupled with a black mayoral candidate—made racial interests extraordinarily important, as is evidenced thus far.

The 1973 mayoral rematch was nearly identical to the race in 1969, except that the underlying social and political context had changed dramatically. The race rioting that had been so prevalent in the late 1960s had abated, as had the widespread campus protests over the Vietnam War. Watergate was now front-page news in Los Angeles and around the nation. Simply, racial issues had slipped into the background of public concern while politics—issues of integrity and political accountability—were now front and center. Given the change in political context, and as a result of less discord, one would expect that voting in 1973 would be less tied to racial attitudes and more related to general partisan and ideological dispositions. However, given Bradley's presence as a black candidate and the continued racial nature of the campaign discourse, it would be quite unreasonable to expect racial considerations to disappear entirely.

Bradley Voters in 1973

Tom Bradley was more successful in 1973 than he had been four years previously, defeating Sam Yorty by a margin of 56 percent to 44 percent. As shown in table 3.2, Bradley's margin among voters increased and his expanding support was especially pronounced among whites and Latinos, where his margins improved by 9 percentage points and 8 percentage points, respectively. Furthermore, his successes were evident citywide. From 1969 to 1973, Bradley's share of the vote increased 12 percent in the San Fernando Valley, 10 percent on the Westside, and 8 percent in the predominantly black council districts located in South Central Los Angeles.

Part of the increase in proportional support for Bradley can possibly be explained by the decline in voter turnout between 1969 and 1973. Overall turnout (as a percentage of registered voters) was a record 76 percent in 1969. By 1973 the overall rate had declined to 64 percent. And while voting in the black council districts remained the highest in the city at an average of 74 percent (down from an average of 81 percent in 1969), turnout declined in the largely white

TABLE 3.2. Bradley's Percentage of the Mayoral Vote by Ethnic and Racial Groups, 1969 and 1973

	1969	1973
Black	89	91
Latino	43	51
White	37	46

Source: Hahn, Klingman, and Pachon 1976, 514.

San Fernando Valley and Westside by 14 percent and 11 percent, respectively. It would be misleading, however, to suggest that Bradley's victory can be explained entirely by this fact. Even if all of the voters from 1969 had voted in 1973, and even if 100 percent of the incremental voters had cast their vote for Yorty (an improbable assumption to be sure), Bradley would still have won in 1973 by more than ten thousand votes. Furthermore, there is no reason to believe that this group of 1973 nonvoters had substantially different candidate preferences than was demonstrated by the electorate as a whole (Cavanagh 1993). Thus to explain the shift in voter preference from 1969 to 1973, one must look beyond turnout differences.

Racial Attitudes, Partisanship, and Voting Behavior, 1969 versus 1973

The most direct test of the group interest hypothesis would be to model the Yorty vote in 1973 with the identical variables used in the 1969 analysis. And while Sears and Kinder conducted an election poll in 1973 that included many of the same measures used by Pettigrew in 1969, the 1973 data could not be located. Fortunately, Kinder and Sears (1981) report several useful bivariate comparisons of data from these years in their analysis. The following discussion uses their findings as well as a 1973 Field poll to explore the differences in voting behavior between 1969 and 1973.

Table 3.3 reports correlations between candidate preference and series of racial and political attitudes. The top half of the table presents correlations between three racial attitude questions and the vote. The interrelationships between each of the three racial attitude measures and the vote were quite high in 1969, ranging from gamma coefficients of .49 to .69. In 1973, these relationships continue to be statistically significant; however, they decline in magnitude substantially (by an average of 33 percent). Simply, racial attitudes continued to be important in 1973 but were less important to the vote than they had been in 1969.

Conversely, partisan considerations were very weakly associated with the vote in 1969, with a Pearson's *R* coefficient of .29. By 1973, however, party identification was more strongly associated with candidate preference; the correlation between party identification and the vote had increased to .44. As anticipated, in 1969 racial attitudes were strongly correlated with the vote, whereas political attitudes were less so. By 1973, the importance of racial attitudes in regard to electoral choice had declined, while partisan and ideological beliefs were much more strongly associated. Given that the principle difference between these two elections was one of context, these data imply that the political context was important to the respective salience of group memberships with regard to the vote.

Conclusion

Group interest theory proposes that social identities and group interests can bear heavily on local electoral choice. Individuals possess

TABLE 3.3.   Racial Attitudes, Political Attitudes, and the Vote: Los Angeles, 1969 and 1973

	Correlation with Candidate Preference	
	1969	1973
Racial attitudes		
Do you think that most Negroes who receive money from welfare programs could get along without it if they really tried, or do they really need the help?	.69**	.56**
Do you think Los Angeles city officials pay more, less, or the same attention to a request from a black person as from a white person?	.55**	.30**
In Los Angeles, would you say many, some, or only a few blacks miss out on jobs or promotions because of racial discrimination?	.49**	.32*
Political attitudes		
Party identification	.29**	.44**
Ideology	.42**	.50**

Note: Racial attitude entries are gamma coefficients from Kinder and Sears 1981, table 1. Political attitude entries are Pearson's R coefficients. 1969 data is from the Pettigrew survey; 1973 data is from the Field poll.

   $*p < .05$ $**p < .01$

multiple group identities, and the nature of the political context powerfully influences the extent to which various group interests become salient in regard to political choices. When the political context is characterized by heightened intergroup tensions, electoral cleavages are likely to form around these rivalries. In the absence of such discord, traditional partisan and ideological identities are likely to be important and highly related to local vote choice.

Voting analyses from Los Angeles in 1969 and 1973 provide preliminary support for these claims. Whereas black council member Tom Bradley lost the mayor's race in 1969 to the unpopular white incumbent, analysis of 1969 public opinion data suggests that conflicted racial attitudes were largely responsible for Bradley's loss. Yorty's racially inflammatory campaign coupled with a volatile political context rendered racial identities highly salient to the vote. Four years later, however, partisan identities were considerably more important and influential to voting than were racial identities. Extreme levels of intergroup conflict, so prevalent in 1969, had largely subsided by 1973 and had been supplanted by a different set of concerns over political integrity and accountability. This change in political context appears to have influenced the basis upon which individuals made their respective electoral choices.

The profoundly racialized nature of the vote in 1969 was unusual for Los Angeles, as heightened conflict among racial and ethnic minorities in Los Angeles had never been a central feature as it had in many other large U.S. cities. Bradley's twenty-year reign as mayor provides further testament to this fact. After his competitive mayoral contest in 1973, Bradley went on to win each of the next four mayoral elections in the primary. Had there been a period of heightened interracial tension during this time, it is likely that Bradley would have been more seriously challenged. The remainder of the 1970s and the decade of the 1980s were, in relative terms, calm waters for the city of Los Angeles. Racial tensions began to mount, however, in the early 1990s. And in 1992, when four Los Angeles police officers were acquitted of beating a black motorist named Rodney King, Los Angeles once again erupted in riots. The Bradley years had been the calm before the storm, and the political context surrounding the riots once again shifted the public attention to issues of race and racial interests.

The mayoral election in 1993 was the first in twenty-four years where there was no black candidate on the ballot. The political context was nonetheless imbued with substantial racial overtones. Chapter 4 examines the 1993 mayoral election and explores the extent to which racial attitudes were implicated in its outcome, much as they had been in 1969.

4 "Tough Enough to Turn L.A. Around": Los Angeles, 1973 to 1993

Tom Bradley's election in 1973 was considered historic, as he was the first black mayor in a large American city to be elected by a predominantly white electorate. As impressive as his 1973 victory was at the time, his twenty-year mayoralty was further evidence of his appeal to voters of all racial and ethnic groups. Unlike voters in other large cities (e.g., Philadelphia, Cleveland, Baltimore, and Chicago), the largely white Los Angeles electorate embraced their African-American mayor in each of his subsequent four electoral bids. So dominant was Bradley at the polls that he won each of his reelection bids with a majority of the nonpartisan primary vote.

By 1993 much of Bradley's popularity had waned. His fifth term had been wracked by financial scandals, and the 1992 riots further dampened his public support.

Embraced by the world of the white and powerful, Bradley had returned the affection. His quiet style and patrician manner put the city at ease and allowed the better-off to indulge in the fantasy that there were no serious ethnic or racial problems—among whites, blacks, Asians and the fast-growing Hispanic population—in their sunny paradise. But the people who had once found comfort in Bradley's quiescence would be looking for a more dynamic leader in 1993, and Bradley sensed that. (*New York Times Magazine,* April 18, 1993, 21)

Bradley's decision to retire at the end of his fifth term in 1993 generated substantial interest in the mayoralty among the Los Angeles political elite. In all, fifty-two contenders entered the primary candidate pool. Of these fifty-two, Michael Woo, a Democratic city council member, and Richard Riordan, a Republican businessman, emerged as the runoff contenders. No Republican had been mayor in Los Angeles since Norris Poulson's defeat to Sam Yorty in 1961. As such, Riordan was considered an underdog in the 1993 campaign. As was suggested numerous times during and after the mayoral campaign, this was Woo's race to lose (*New Republic,* May 5, 1993).

The expectation that Woo would beat Riordan handily was most certainly founded on the assumption that partisanship would play an important role in the election. For the past several decades, a majority of the Los Angeles electorate had supported Democratic candidates, and in 1993 there were twice as many registered Democrats as Republicans in the city. Thus from a partisan viewpoint, the Democrat should have been the easy victor in 1993. Yet not only did Woo not win the election, but he lost by an eight-point margin—46 percent to 54 percent. Contrary to most conventional wisdom about Los Angeles politics, two-thirds of white Los Angeles voters cast their ballot for the Republican candidate.

Clearly a partisan theory of voting behavior can not adequately explain this election outcome, as it would offer no rationale for why nearly 40 percent of the city's Democratic voters supported Riordan and why the electoral choices in the city were so racially polarized. From a group interest perspective, it seems clear that the conflictual political context in 1993 made racial and ethnic group identities and interests politically salient in this election. The central argument in this chapter is that the Los Angeles uprising in April 1992 resulted in heightened perceptions of group-based conflict—especially among white voters. As a result, racial identities and racial group interests were particularly consequential to the 1993 election. And as contextual cues are argued to be especially influential to weak partisans and moderate ideologues, racial motivations should be particularly pronounced among these groups.

In addition to the changes in political context brought about by the uprising in 1992, the local economy in Los Angeles had also faltered during this period. The depressed local economy coupled with the large-scale violence of the riots contributed to an exceptionally turbulent political environment. As a reaction to this conflict, alternate group identities were more salient to the vote than were traditional political memberships and attitudes. In the case of white voters, who made up over 70 percent of the electorate, racial attitudes are presumed to be strong determinants of the vote.

The degree of racial polarization in the 1993 election was especially profound, given the absence of a black candidate in this election. It is quite common for racial identities to become salient when a member of a racial minority is running for office. This is especially true for African-American candidates competing against whites (Murray and Vedlitz 1978; Lieske and Hillard 1984; Reeves 1997). As argued in chapter 2, the mere presence of a minority group member may be sufficient to stimulate group interested voting behavior within the represented group; however, group solidarity should vary depending on the baseline strength of in-group identification. Furthermore, a group interest–oriented political agenda coupled with such a candidacy will likely increase the relative salience of group identities and may stimulate competition and enhanced cohesiveness from competing groups. Michael Woo, the Democratic candidate in 1993, is a native-born American of Chinese descent. While this nationality group certainly represents an ethnic minority in Los Angeles, there was (and is) no general perception that Chinese-Americans support a distinctive political agenda or that they are natural allies of other more politically active minority groups such as blacks and Latinos. In this case, Woo *consciously* sought support from disadvantaged racial and ethnic minority groups and promoted himself as a candidate particularly sensitive to minority concerns. In other words, by virtue of his campaign strategy, Woo designated himself a minority candidate. And as will be evident from the analyses later in this chapter, this minority-oriented political strategy was indeed sufficient to stimulate substantial resistance from the white electorate.

The first part of this chapter discusses the Bradley era from 1973 to 1989, with a particular focus on two areas. First, this section describes the political history of this period, highlighting its electoral politics as well as Bradley's sustained mayoral popularity. Second, this section gives an account of the social and economic context during the Bradley years, noting the economic expansion that characterized this period as well as the relative absence of high-profile interracial violence from 1973 to 1992. This section is important to the remainder of this chapter, as it is the basis of comparison from which I make the claim that the political context in 1993 was a sharp departure from the one that preceded it. The second part of this chapter focuses on the political context in 1993 and the mayoral campaign. Using public opinion data, I explore voting behavior in the 1993 mayoral election.

The Bradley Years

Tom Bradley was the mayor of Los Angeles for twenty years, and his political longevity must be credited in part to his soft-spoken political style and his ability to sustain his popularity among diverse constituents. His commitment to the black community came in various forms, most notably in greater access to public jobs (Sonenshein 1993a), but Bradley was also a strong ally to the business community. The mayor was decidedly in favor of pro-growth policies that were attractive to both the business sector and disadvantaged minority communities. By empowering moneyed business interests within the local government, he was able not only to maintain their financial support but also to discourage any serious potential challengers for four consecutive terms.

Table 4.1 shows Los Angeles mayoral election returns from 1969 to 1989. Aside from Bradley's contests with Sam Yorty in 1969 and 1973, he won each of the remaining four elections in the primary. Furthermore, and equally impressive, his reelection margin increased in four consecutive elections—from 56 percent in 1973 to 68 percent in 1985. Even in 1989, when the mayor's competition included a black Democratic council member, Bradley's citywide support was strong enough to avert challenges from both a conservative white and a liberal African-American candidate at the same time. Part of the reason why Bradley was so successful in his tenure as mayor was that he was able to discourage serious competition by his own fund-raising prowess. His ties to wealthy Downtown and Westside business interests provided a reliable base of financial support at election time. Apart from his financial strength, however, the mayor also maintained an enormously high approval rating for sixteen of his twenty years in office.

Table 4.2 indicates levels of public approval for Bradley from 1979 through 1993. For black, white, and Latino voters, his approval ratings remained high through his reelection in 1989. Often, the longer a politician stays in office, the more enemies he will make. This did not appear to be true for Bradley. While African-American and Latino voters consistently showed higher rates of approval than whites, white approval for the mayor did not drop below 70 percent for his first

TABLE 4.1. Los Angeles Mayoral Election Returns, 1969–89

Year	Election Type	Total Votes	Turnout (%)	Bradley Vote (%)	Major Opponents	Opponent Vote (%)
1969	Primary	731,423	66	42	Yorty	26
					Ward	17
					Bell	14
1969	Runoff	856,474	76	47	Yorty	53
1973	Primary	674,555	57	35	Yorty	29
					Unruh	17
1973	Runoff	780,845	64	56	Yorty	44
1977	Primary	498,315	42	60	Robbins	28
					Jarvis	10
1981	Primary	472,989	37	64	Yorty	32
1985	Primary	463,435	34	68	Ferraro	31
1989	Primary	334,764	24	52	Holden	28
					Ward	15

Source: City of Los Angeles, Office of the City Clerk—Elections Division; Los Angeles County Registrar of Voters.

TABLE 4.2. Bradley Approval Ratings by Race, 1979–93 (in percentages)

	1979	1981	1985	1989	1993
White	72	71	73	70	29
Blacks	81	89	84	77	58
Latinos	74	82	79	78	44

Source: Los Angeles Times Polls, selected years.

four terms in office. Thus Bradley's sustained job approval strongly implies multiracial support for his mayoralty. Unlike the racially motivated opposition to his candidacy in 1969, voting behavior in the following five elections does not reflect anywhere near this level of racial content. Even when he ran against antibusing candidate Allan Robbins in 1977, he was largely able to sustain his white electoral base.

Shortly after the mayoral primary in 1989, Bradley was charged with financial improprieties that negatively impacted his public approval. In the wake of these financial scandals, his approval ratings among whites dropped to 46 percent and among blacks dropped to 60 percent (*Los Angeles Times* Poll, May 1989). The mayor was resilient, however, and by March 1991 his approval rating among whites and blacks had rebounded to 56 percent and 66 percent, respectively. The Los Angeles riots in 1992, however, substantially damaged his public standing. Most strikingly, white approval for Bradley dropped to 27 percent in May 1992 and remained at these low levels throughout the remainder of his fifth term (*Los Angeles Times* Poll, May 1992). In September 1992 Bradley announced his intention to retire.

While Bradley's electoral success was in part contingent on his ability to discourage strong competitors and his substantial popularity, several factors helped the mayor retain his impressive support. In particular, the period of the late 1970s and early 1980s was a time of enormous economic growth for the city. Concurrent with the expanding population, over 570,000 jobs were created in Los Angeles from 1980 to 1990 at an average annual growth rate of 3.5 percent (U.S. Bureau of the Census). Household income and property values also escalated during this period, and the city unemployment rate fell from a high of 9.7 in 1983 to a low of 4.6 in 1989 (U.S. Bureau of Labor Statistics). Simply, times were good for a large portion of the Los Angeles electorate, and there were no compelling economic issues to weaken the mayor's approval.[1]

---

1. This is not to suggest that the national recession in 1982 and 1983 was not felt in the Los Angeles economy as well. Unemployment in Los Angeles increased in these two years to 9.3 percent and 9.7 percent, respectively. As good fortune would have it, for both Ronald Reagan and Tom Bradley, the peak of the economic recession did not fall during election years. By 1985, the year of Bradley's third reelection campaign, unemployment had declined to 7 percent and he was elected by his largest margin ever.

In addition to the robust economy that accompanied most of Bradley's tenure, there were no race riots or high-profile racial incidents with the police during his mayoralty. This relative tranquility further contributed to the absence of racial hostility in local politics. The decade of the 1980s was, however, a period of rapid ethnic transformation for the city of Los Angeles. In 1980 non-Latino whites made up almost half of the city population (48 percent), with African-Americans representing approximately 17 percent and Latinos representing 28 percent. By 1990 the city had grown by over 500,000, and all of this growth was attributable to the increasing Latino and Asian communities (see table 4.3). By 1990 there were over 547,000 new Latino residents in the city (a 70 percent increase), while the non-Latino white and black populations declined by 8 percent and 2 percent, respectively (U.S. Bureau of the Census). This amount of rapid demographic growth spurred by immigration might normally have led to increasing levels of interracial conflict; however, the widespread availability of jobs and sense of economic well-being, among white city residents particularly, appears to have mitigated against this. Yet predictably, when the California economy in the early 1990s fell into a recession, anti-immigrant rhetoric became heated and immigration-related issues came to the fore. It was not until after the riots and the worsening economy that immigration became a hot political topic in Los Angeles. Given the dramatic demographic

TABLE 4.3. Changing Racial and Ethnic Composition in Los Angeles, 1980–90

	1980	1990	Difference
Whites	1,419,413	1,299,604	(119,809)
	48%	37%	−8%
Blacks	495,723	487,674	(8,049)
	17%	14%	−2%
Latinos	816,076	1,390,673	574,597
	28%	40%	+70%
Other	235,638	307,447	71,809
	8%	9%	+30%
Total Population	2,966,850	3,485,398	518,548

Source: U.S. Census, 1980 and 1990.

Note: Percentages in column 3 equal the percentage change in total population by subgroup.

changes happening in Los Angeles during the 1980s, most of which was arguably immigration related, it is all the more telling that immigration and immigration "policies" per se did not become politically important until after the economic downturn. As argued at the outset of this book, group conflict is exacerbated during periods of scarcity, and it wasn't until there were pending budget shortfalls and climbing unemployment rates in Los Angeles that immigrants and immigration became politically contentious.

In large part, Tom Bradley benefited from good economic times during his tenure as mayor. From his election in 1973 through most of his fifth term, which ended in 1993, there was little of the overt racial rancor so prevalent in the late 1960s. Bradley received broad electoral support among all racial and ethnic groups. Racial identities and racial interests were not particularly salient at the polls, and as a result Bradley achieved easy victories in all of his reelection bids. On March 3, 1991, however, an amateur cameraman captured Los Angeles police officers beating a black motorist named Rodney King. On April 29, 1992, a largely white jury would exonerate these four LAPD officers on assault charges. The Bradley era, and all the peaceful interracial accommodation that characterized this period, was officially over.

The Political Fallout from the Los Angeles Riots

Almost as quickly as the verdicts were rendered, crowds began to gather in black neighborhoods throughout South Central Los Angeles. The riots,[2] as they were, began with isolated attacks on white and Latino motorists in South Central Los Angeles. By 6:00 P.M. looting began, and within hours buildings were set aflame (Tierney 1994). The civil unrest lasted six days and resulted in over 16,000 arrests, 52 fatalities, and nearly $1 billion in property damage (Sears et al. 1994).

---

2. Terms such as "riot," "rebellion," "racial unrest," and "civil insurrection" are used interchangeably in this text to describe the events in 1992. Some scholars have noted that the different labels affixed to incidents of civil unrest carry substantively different connotations regarding their substance and purpose (Masotti and Bowen 1968). No such distinction, however, is made here.

The public response to the rebellion was very mixed and often divided along racial lines. There was considerable consensus across racial and ethnic groups that the King verdict was a sham. "Fully 96% of blacks disagreed with the verdict as compared to roughly three-quarters of Asian and Latino respondents and just under two-thirds of white respondents" (Bobo et al. 1994). When asked to label the riots as "mainly a protest" or "mainly a way to engage in looting and street crime," 68 percent of black respondents saw these events as a protest compared to only 37 percent among whites, 39 percent among Latinos, and 43 percent among Asians.[3] Indeed, there was enormous public antagonism toward the LAPD in the wake of the King beating, so much so that the public overwhelmingly supported a myriad of reform measures targeted to increase civilian oversight of the police department. In spite of this, the rebellion had a polarizing effect on the city—especially between blacks and whites. The verdicts, while criticized by most, were still not seen (among nonblacks) as sufficient justification for the criminal recklessness of the riots.[4]

By 1993 the uprising had passed, yet there remained a sense among many of the city's residents that peace within the city was fragile and that the police force was too small or otherwise unprepared to safeguard the security of its residents from future outbreaks of urban violence. To compound this situation, the city was deep in an economic recession. Los Angeles was losing jobs, the unemployment rate was nearly 10 percent, and the city's bleak economy put additional strain on its social services, which were generally regarded to be at the breaking point. The issue of spending on social services focused the community on its ever-growing immigrant population, and there was a groundswell of opinion that the large immigrant population in Los Angeles was at least partially to blame for the financial squeeze the city was facing. In early 1993 the governor of California, Pete Wilson,

---

3. These data are taken from the 1992 Los Angeles County Social Survey.

4. It is interesting to note that while Latinos were active contributors to the civil unrest (they represented the highest number of arrestees) they were not part of the political fallout. Unlike many in the black community who felt that the riots were predominantly a protest, Latinos generally did not embrace this view (Bobo et al. 1994). Perhaps for this reason the political conflict that resulted from the riots centered on differences between blacks and whites.

announced his intention to ask the federal government for immigrant-related cost reimbursements, which stimulated substantial public debate over the financial burden of illegal immigration. As explained in the *Los Angeles Times,*

> A recent survey of Los Angeles city residents by The Times Poll indicated that the public generally is unhappy about the immigrant situation. Six in 10 said: 'There are too many foreign immigrants in Los Angeles.' This was true of six in 10 Latinos, as well as African-Americans and Anglos. (February 15, 1993)

Concern over crime, residual anxiety from the riots, and the increasingly salient immigration issue pitted ethnic and racial groups against one another. *Newsweek* reported that "All the important indicators are heading down, and the city's self-confidence is in tatters. The Bradley legacy, an era of good feelings at little or no political cost, seems like ancient history now" (April 19, 1993, 28). This was the backdrop for the 1993 mayoral election in Los Angeles.

The 1993 Primary

While the Los Angeles riots in April 1992 were at the core of the growing interethnic conflict in Los Angeles, Bradley's decision to retire in a sense exacerbated tensions in the community. A void in political leadership throughout the city was strongly felt. The multiracial, multiethnic governing coalition that had dominated so much of the Bradley era had broken apart into a wide array of angry constituencies looking for their voices to be heard above the rest. This would be the first time in more than five decades that an incumbent would not be seeking reelection in Los Angeles, and the opportunity for previously excluded groups to gain power in the city was not lost on them.

The unique circumstances surrounding this election—Bradley's intention to retire, the recent violence, and the serious economic recession facing the city—brought forth a myriad of primary contenders. In all, fifty-two candidates participated in the nonpartisan primary. The most serious of these candidates included three city council members—Mike Woo, Joel Wachs, and Nate Holden—attorney Stan Sanders, Deputy Mayor Linda Griego, State Assemblyman Richard Katz, and businessman/attorney Richard Riordan. Like the city itself, these candidates represented a rainbow of ethnicities, races, interests, and ideologies. The struggle ahead for each of them was to distinguish themselves from this large field of contenders.

Mike Woo was from the beginning the perceived front-runner. A Chinese-American, Woo had represented Hollywood's thirteenth council district since 1985. Shortly after the riots, he had been the first city official to call for Police Chief Daryl Gates's resignation. His public opposition to Chief Gates was appreciated in the black community, and his reward came in the form of strong endorsements from many politically influential black leaders. Woo was a liberal, and his record at city hall was replete with support for many liberal causes.

> On the city council he made his reputation as a champion of street vendors, political refugees, and gay activists. Although he made crime fighting a centerpiece of his mayoral campaign, he came late to the cause having built his base in South Central Los Angeles on the strength of his opposition to former Police Chief Daryl Gates. (*Los Angeles Times,* June 6, 1993)

Woo had strong financial backing for his campaign and had cultivated necessary political ties within the black, Latino, and Asian communities. He announced his candidacy early and was considered by most political insiders to be Bradley's probable successor.

In addition to Woo, Councilman Joel Wachs and State Assemblyman Richard Katz—both of whom are Jewish and from the San Fernando Valley—were also considered strong candidates. The San Fernando Valley, located in the northern region of the city, makes up more than one-third of the city's voters, and Valley residents from as far back as the 1920s have long considered themselves underrepresented in Los Angeles municipal government.[5] The San Fernando

---

5. Periodically Valley residents have considered the possibility of secession from the city of Los Angeles. As noted in the *Los Angeles Times* (June 6, 1993, B3), the first threat of secession from Valley residents came in the 1920s: "The complaint then was much the same as it is today: that the valley pays a disproportionate share of taxes and does not get back a fair share of city services." Most recently, voters in Los Angeles defeated a Valley secession measure in 2002.

Valley in 1993 was largely white, more Republican than the rest of the city, and typically supported more conservative political candidates. Had Wachs or Katz been able to reach the runoff, they would likely have been serious competitors for the mayoralty. Valley voters represented 43 percent of the electorate in the runoff and would probably have thrown much of their collective support to a "native son." In spite of this, Wachs and Katz had little name recognition outside of the Jewish community and the San Fernando Valley. Both of them were less well known than Michael Woo. Furthermore, the fact that two notable Valley politicians were running against one another diluted the potential strength of the Valley vote.

Linda Griego, the most notable Latina in this race, was able to raise campaign money from both Latino and women's groups. A businesswoman-turned-deputy mayor, Griego had a brief political record that offered her little leverage in this overcrowded primary field. Attorney Stan Sanders and Councilman Nate Holden constituted Woo's competition for the black vote. Holden had a long political history in Los Angeles, but his campaign for mayor was hindered by ongoing accusations of sexual harassment. Sanders, by contrast, was a new face and most likely would have met with greater success had he started his campaign earlier. By the time Sanders threw his hat into the ring, most of the influentials in the black community were solidly behind Woo.

The most obvious wild card in the primary race was the millionaire attorney/businessman Richard Riordan. Although Riordan was well known in and around city hall, he was a virtual stranger to the Los Angeles electorate. Within political circles he was known for his generous contributions to a wide array of political campaigns. Among the Los Angeles business community he was also quite prominent. A venture capitalist specializing in leveraged buy-outs of failing companies, he had made millions in partnership with junk bond king Michael Milken. Riordan had enormous personal wealth and financed his own campaign. And while it was true that he could afford to buy the name recognition that he initially lacked, a white, Republican millionaire who had amassed his fortune through junk bond deals with Michael Milken seemed an unlikely successor to the black Democratic mayor of Los Angeles. Riordan, however, easily distinguished himself from the remainder of the primary field. He publicly refused to take out-side campaign funds and positioned himself as a political outsider with no personal stake in this race aside from his desire to help the cit-izenry of Los Angeles. Furthermore, his campaign slogan—"Tough Enough to Turn L.A. Around"—stood apart from the conciliatory rhetoric of other candidates and implicitly suggested that his oppo-nents were "soft."

> Riordan strategy No. 1 is to campaign as the Perot-like outsider. Problem is, as the single largest donor in L.A. politics over the past decade (to candidates of both parties often seeking the same office), Riordan personifies the permanent government—the more so since his law firm got million dollar contracts from the government bodies he contributed to. . . . An improbable outsider, singularly unable to tap into public indignation at gov-ernment's follies, Riordan will likely demonstrate that the oxy-moron "billionaire populist" is inimitably and exclusively Perot's. (*New Republic,* May 3, 1993)

In spite of the opinion held by many in the media that he could not successfully play the role of the outsider, Riordan's campaign was nonetheless effective. By the date of the primary election in April, he had succeeded where most of the other primary candidates had failed and had created a distinctive and clear image for himself among the electorate. While his large war chest was certainly responsible for part of this success, his message of "tough love" for the city of Los Ange-les struck a cord for many of this city's voters and was especially appealing to higher-income whites in the San Fernando Valley and the Westside.

The Runoff

After the primary votes had been counted in April, Richard Riordan and Mike Woo had received 32 percent and 25 percent of the vote, respectively. And even though Woo did not win the primary, it was still the expectation that a majority of the support for the losing pri-mary candidates would shift to him. Conventional wisdom dictated that this was Mike Woo's race to lose. And he did. The differences between Woo and Riordan were enormous, and the campaign style of each reflected these differences. Woo, the only son of a Chinese immigrant, was born and raised in California. He completed his undergraduate education at the University of California, Santa Cruz, and received his master's degree in urban planning from the University of California, Berkeley. Woo applied for conscientious objector status during the Vietnam War, but the war ended before he was called for service. Woo, forty-one years old, was a young, ideological politician who showed great concern for the plight of the urban poor. Clintonesque in many ways, he proposed to institute an urban Peace Corps that would put young people to work in the inner city.

Woo saw his primary advantage in the campaign as a potential mediator among the fractious ethnic and racial groups in the city. As *Time* magazine reported, "By campaigning as a conciliator, Woo seeks to inherit the coalition of minorities and liberals that supported Bradley. Says he: 'I want to be the mayor who unites the city,' the one 'closing the gap between the haves and have-nots'" (April 19, 1993). Like Riordan, he supported enlarging the number of police officers in the city. His critics, however, portrayed him as being soft on crime. He was also maligned as an unsavory insider, using his political clout to his personal advantage. Early in the campaign he was accused of enlarging his hillside home while pushing council legislation that would prohibit these types of projects. There were also questions regarding his handling of campaign funds.

More devastating than these early charges of impropriety, Woo was criticized harshly for his lack of vigilance in his own Hollywood council district. In a four-page color flyer sent to homes across the city by the Riordan campaign, the council member was accused of having failed his constituency with regard to the economy, neighborhood redevelopment, and violent crime. Citing stories and quotes from a number of Woo's constituents, Riordan sent voters messages such as the following:

> I remember that Mike Woo promised to put more police on our streets. But there are less police now than just three years ago. I'm afraid of what will happen to our city if he becomes Mayor.

I don't want any other families to have to go through what's happened to us.

I voted for Mike Woo in 1985 and 1989, but I'll never vote for him again. He's abandoned our neighborhoods, our children, and left us to fend for ourselves.

If Mike Woo becomes Mayor, I'm considering selling my business and leaving Los Angeles. I can't afford to run a business with a Mayor who cares more about politics than he does about his own community.

In spite of Riordan's well-funded attacks on Woo's record and his character, the councilman received endorsements from the *Los Angeles Times,* County Supervisor Gloria Molina (the most powerful Latina in the city), the Reverend Jesse Jackson, and President Bill Clinton. Riordan, by contrast, was publicly endorsed by the *Daily News of San Fernando Valley* (a local Valley newspaper) and a former Los Angeles police chief, Tom Reddin. Privately, however, he was supported by many of the city's more affluent business leaders, as he had been a popular member of the Los Angeles business elite for many years.

Richard Riordan, at sixty-three, was a full generation older than Mike Woo. Born and raised in New York, Riordan graduated from Princeton in 1952 and received his law degree from the University of Michigan in 1956. Riordan had fought in the Korean War and moved to California after his graduation from law school. Though he began his career as an attorney, he was also a successful businessman, investing in many high-tech firms in the late 1960s and 1970s. He was an active member of the Catholic Church and a confidant of Archbishop Mahoney. His desire to be mayor was clearly not for financial gain, as his power and influence over local government were likely greater as a private citizen. Riordan's mission, as he articulated in his blueprint for Los Angeles, was to bring peace and prosperity back to the city:

As mayor I will get tough on crime, drug dealing, gangs and violence. I will replace rhetoric with substance, fear with security, fiscal incompetence with managerial accountability, polarization with cooperation, and alienation with pride.

Unlike the conciliator Woo, Riordan emphasized his tough pragmatism in his campaign, the centerpiece of which was an assault on crime that would begin with three thousand new police officers. He described Los Angeles as a "war zone" that would not regain its economic vitality until the streets were safe again. As a Republican in a largely Democratic city, he ran a nonpartisan campaign devoid of ideological rhetoric. In all he spent $6 million of his own personal wealth to become the mayor of Los Angeles.

The heart of Woo's campaign was to paint his opponent as a ruthless, corporate-raiding Republican who threw "thousands of Californians" out of work while lining his own pockets. Woo did not have nearly the financial resources of his wealthy competitor, however, and turned to the Democratic National Committee (DNC) to partially finance his media campaign. Mailers and television ads highlighted Riordan's alliance with junk bond king Michael Milken. The DNC assailed him on his pro-life stance and sent mailers with pictures of Robert Bork, Pat Roberston, and Ronald Reagan, calling them "Dick Riordan's anti-choice alliances." Finally, in the week before the election, public disclosures revealed that Riordan had been arrested for drunk driving twice—once in the 1960s and once in the 1970s. This was the scandal that Woo hoped would undo his opponent. At the same time these public disclosures were made, however, Riordan's mother passed away, and the candidate left town to attend her funeral. Instead of showing Riordan fending off questions by the relentless press, local news coverage featured pictures of Riordan walking beside his mother's casket at her funeral in New York. On Tuesday, June 8, Riordan beat Woo by a margin of 54 percent to 46 percent.

Understanding the Vote

How could a liberal Democrat like Mike Woo lose in a city where almost two out of every three registered voters are Democrats and where two out of every three residents are members of a racial or ethnic minority? Clearly the answer to this question lies in the fact that many of the groups that were expected to vote for Woo did not. He did poorly within his own party, he did poorly among ideological moderates and conservatives, and he did poorly among white voters (see table 4.4)

As clearly evidenced in table 4.4, the Los Angeles electorate is not nearly as diverse as its underlying population. Estimates from the 1990 census report that, of the total population in Los Angeles, 37 percent were white, 14 percent were black, and 9 percent were Asian, with a plurality of the population, 40 percent, being Latino. Strikingly, the Los Angeles electorate in 1993 did not reflect this level of social diversity. Of the *registered* electorate, white voters represented 65 percent; blacks, 15 percent; and Latinos, only 11 percent (Sonenshein 1993b, 9). In the 1993 runoff election, 72 percent of voters were non-Latino whites, compared to 12 percent black and 10 percent Latino (*Los Angeles Times* Exit Poll, June 1993). These figures suggest that white voters were slightly overrepresented in this election, just as nonwhite voters were slightly underrepresented. Regardless of these small mobilization differences, however, white voters had *always* represented large majorities in Los Angeles electoral politics.

Tom Bradley, in his multiple bids for mayor of Los Angeles, understood the importance of the white vote. While the mayor was sensitive to racial and ethnic concerns, his political agenda was nonetheless oriented more toward business development than toward social services and as such attracted many white voters. By contrast, Mike Woo did not tailor his political messages to the largely white electorate. He did not overtly ignore the white vote, but it appears that he may have miscalculated their interests in the postriot environment of Los Angeles. He promoted himself as the "multicultural" candidate who would bring groups together and mend the interethnic fissures that had been widened by the riots. A liberal Asian-American with reasonably strong backing from the African-American and Latino communities, Woo argued that he was uniquely positioned to secure future peace in Los Angeles, as it was he who could bring these communities together. The majority of white voters, however, did not vote for the multicultural candidate who had great insight into working with Los Angeles's minority communities. They instead voted for a white man who had great insight into the needs of the white communities—specifically the San Fernando Valley and the Westside.

TABLE 4.4. **Description of the 1993 Los Angeles Mayoral Vote (in percentages)**

% of voters who are		% who voted for	
		Riordan	Woo
	Race/Ethnicity		
72	White	67	33
12	Black	14	86
10	Latino	43	57
4	Asian	31	69
	Ideology		
30	Liberal	27	73
43	Moderate	63	37
27	Conservative	79	21
22	White liberal	31	69
31	White moderate	75	25
20	White conservative	92	8
	Party		
63	Democrat	39	61
6	Independent	70	30
30	Republican	91	9
	Income		
14	Under $20K	42	58
25	$20K to 39,999	52	48
22	$40K to 59,999	60	40
39	$60K and up	62	38
	Religion		
39	Protestant	63	37
24	Roman Catholic	63	37
19	Jewish	49	51
	Region		
18	Westside	55	45
44	San Fernando Valley	71	29
21	Central L.A.	40	60
17	South L.A.	27	73

Source: Los Angeles Times Exit Poll, June 1993.
Note: Number of respondents equals 3,402.

Woo ran his campaign with a message of multiethnic unity and performed well among his targeted ethnic and racial constituencies, winning 86 percent of the black vote, 69 percent of the Asian vote, and 57 percent of the Latino vote. Yet he won only 33 percent of the white vote. He received 72 percent of the nonwhite vote in a city were nonwhite people represent almost two-thirds of the population, and he lost the election handily. In 1993 it would have been virtually impossible to win a citywide election in Los Angeles without appealing to white voters, as this group represented over 60 percent of the registered electorate. Woo's campaign strategy, however, appeared to be more focused on minority concerns within the city than on the needs of its large, middle-class, white constituency. His strategy succeeded in garnering widespread support from minority communities, but his success within these communities came at the expense of the white vote and ultimately at the expense of victory.

Ideological Response to the Campaign

Mike Woo, by reputation and deed, was a liberal candidate. The majority of Los Angeles voters are not liberals, however, and he suffered great losses among the ideological middle and right. Looking at Los Angeles voters in terms of their ideological alignments, it is apparent that moderates represent the largest segment of the electorate (43 percent) and that liberals (30 percent) slightly outnumber conservatives (27 percent). Woo garnered a substantial portion of the liberal vote but performed poorly among moderates and conservatives. Seventy-three percent of liberals voted for him, whereas he was only able to capture 37 percent of the moderate and 21 percent of the conservative vote. Furthermore, his unattractiveness to moderates and conservatives was only exacerbated among whites. Sixty-nine percent of white liberals voted for him, but among white moderates and white conservatives, who represented over half of the voting electorate, Woo only received 18 percent of the vote (see table 4.4).

The most significant of these findings is that Woo performed so poorly among moderates, especially white moderates. One would expect the Democrat to perform well among liberals, and it was somewhat preordained that he would not appeal to conservatives. However, in this election, as in most, the decisive swing vote came from the ideological center. At minimum, Woo needed to split the middle with Riordan if he wanted to have a chance at victory. Understanding his poor showing among moderate voters, especially among moderate white voters, appears to be key in understanding the dynamics of this election.

Woo's campaign strategy was to paint Riordan as a conservative Reagan Republican. Given the lack of support that Los Angeles voters have given to Republicans in the past, this appeared to be a reasonable strategy. In 1992 Los Angeles had cast 63 percent of their presidential vote for Democrat Bill Clinton, 63 percent of their senate vote for Democrat Dianne Feinstein, and 68 percent of their other senate vote for liberal Democrat Barbara Boxer. Woo had reason to believe that Los Angeles would not elect Riordan if they believed him to be a conservative Republican á la Ronald Reagan. Riordan, himself, however, fought to shake this association. He mailed out flyers with an endorsement from African-American attorney and primary opponent Stan Sanders that said, "I've known Dick Riordan for twenty-five years, and he's no Reagan Republican." He ran a campaign virtually cleansed of all ideological rhetoric and in the end was able to prevail over Woo in spite of his partisanship or his ideology. Clearly, in this election, partisanship was not a major factor in determining the vote. If it had been, Mike Woo would have won.

In the previous twenty years, Tom Bradley had sustained a diverse coalition made up of blacks, Westside liberals, and Westside and Downtown business interests. By the end of Bradley's tenure, however, this coalition had virtually broken apart. Woo counted on his ability to successfully recreate a Bradley-like coalition to draw his minority constituencies into an electoral coalition with liberal and moderate white Democrats. Yet the political setting in 1993 was not conducive to this rebuilding effort. The perceived conflation of interests among disparate groups that had characterized most of the Bradley era had been replaced by a zero-sum environment where past allies had now become competitors for scarce city hall resources. Peace and prosperity in the eternal boomtown had been replaced with widespread economic uncertainty, fear, and general distrust among the various groups making demands on the city. Voters from the Westside and San Fernando Valley were no longer satisfied to receive less than their proportionate share of city services. Economically blighted minority communities were no longer willing to tie their fates to business interests that had failed them in the past. It was in this spirit and under these conflictual conditions that white Democrats defected in record numbers and elected the first Republican mayor of Los Angeles in over thirty years.

Analysis and Findings

The central argument in this chapter is that the political environment in 1993—its proximity to the riots and the dire local economy—both was a significant departure from the Bradley era and contributed to an abnormally turbulent political context. From the group interest perspective, this extraordinary level of conflict is expected to correspond with high levels of group distinctive voting behavior. In other words, the intense interracial competition that characterized this period made racial identities and racial group interests particularly important to the vote. There was substantial racial polarization in electoral choice. Among blacks, 86 percent supported the Democrat Woo, and 67 percent of the white electorate chose the Republican Riordan. The Latino vote fell in between the racial divide, with 43 percent of Latinos preferring Riordan and 57 percent choosing Woo. On their face, these findings strongly imply a group distinctive response, especially for black and white voters. A more sophisticated understanding of these patterns requires individual-level analyses. Thus the following discussion explores voting behavior in this election using public opinion data.

The survey I use in this analysis was conducted by the *Los Angeles Times* approximately one month prior to election day and is employed to test several competing explanations for the vote.[6]

---

6. The *Los Angeles Times* Poll is a random-digit dialed telephone survey conducted May 8–10, 1993. The sample includes 1,503 respondents, all adult residents in the city of Los Angeles. Multivariate logistic regression analysis was used to estimate the relative probabilities reported in tables 4.5 and 4.6. The reported probabilities reflect the difference in estimated probabilities from the predictor's highest and lowest values, letting the other independent variables take their "natural" values. The regression coefficients and their respective significance are located in tables A4.1 and A4.2 in the appendix.

Among the more traditional political accounts for voting behavior are partisanship and ideology. The large number of Democratic defections in this election certainly implies that party affiliation was not a particularly important factor; nonetheless, measures of partisan identification and political ideology are included in this analysis. A second plausible explanation for this electoral outcome is that voters were motivated to vote for Riordan out of a desire for change in the city's leadership. Obviously, since Bradley was retiring, change was inevitable. Mike Woo, while not the same as Tom Bradley, was nonetheless a Democrat and a city councilman who represented many of the constituencies associated with the Bradley regime. In contrast to Woo, Riordan represented a stark departure from the political orientation and style of Bradley. Thus if indeed the Riordan vote was motivated out of dissatisfaction with the status quo ruling coalition, this would be evidenced by a significant relationship between individual retrospective evaluations of Bradley and the vote.

The group interest perspective suggests that racial interests should be particularly powerful explanations for the vote, given the intensely combative political environment surrounding this election. The racial interest measure assesses individual degrees of racial resentment pertaining to minority accommodation in the city. This scale includes two questions: (1) "Do you think city government has paid too much attention to blacks, Latinos and other minority groups, about the right amount, or do you think city government hasn't paid enough attention to minority groups?" and (2) "Do you think the problems facing minority groups in the inner city are problems of personal responsibility or are they more problems of racism and economic injustice?" Both questions tap into the worthiness and equity of government attention to minority groups and their respective demands, such that a positive relationship between this measure and the vote indicates that voters who feel that minority groups receive sufficient or excessive attention from government are most likely to vote for Riordan.

In addition, this analysis includes a measure referred to as "attitudes regarding illegal immigrants," which probes individuals on the degree to which they believe that city agencies, such as the police, should aid the Immigration and Naturalization Service in its efforts to identify and deport illegal immigrants. (City policy at the time opposed using local police in this capacity.)[7] Given that the population in Los Angeles represents enormous ethnic and racial diversity, individual attitudes regarding illegal immigrants (especially regarding local government's desired role in deporting them) are presumed to reflect the public's sentiments toward the ever-increasing racial and ethnic diversity in the city. Furthermore, given the large Latino presence in the 1992 uprising, it is possible that immigrant-related issues may represent another dimension of group conflict. From this perspective, a positive correspondence between this measure and the vote indicates that increasing concern over illegal immigration is related to higher levels of Riordan support.

An income variable is also included in this analysis to control for any effect that class differences may have on voting behavior. Measures of class are generally not regarded as good predictors of the vote once party identification is held constant. Furthermore, several studies conducted on municipal elections conclude that class is not generally a strong determinant of voting preferences in local elections (Salisbury and Black 1963; Halley, Acock, and Greene 1976; Lieske and Hillard 1984; Kemp 1986). Nonetheless, class-based voting represents a form of "interest" politics. And to the degree that group interests are expected to outweigh more typical political considerations in this election, it is certainly plausible that higher status Los Angelenos preferred Riordan given his own status in the community and that lower status voters preferred Woo based on his concern for disadvantaged groups. Because there was no class variable per se in this survey, income is used to identify status differences within the electorate.

The first set of analyses displayed in table 4.5 examines the attitudinal determinants of voting behavior for white, black, and Latino voters. In the most general sense, the expectation is that these separate analyses will yield different results. Group interest theory argues

---

7. It is important to note that the 1993 mayoral election took place over a year prior to Proposition 187 (which legally denies public services, including education, to illegal immigrants and their children). At the time this mayoral election took place, the public debate over illegal immigration was in its incipient stages and there were very few elite cues regarding partisan and/or ideological positions on illegal immigrant policy.

TABLE 4.5. Estimated Probability of a Riordan Vote by Race, 1993

Variable	Whites	Blacks	Latinos
Ideology			
Very liberal	.12	.14.	.47
Very conservative	.94	.64	.74
Difference	*.82**	*.50**	*.27*
Income			
Low (< $20K)	.39	.22	.34
High (> $60K)	.64	.46	.79
Difference	*.24**	*.23*	*.45**
Bradley job approval			
Approve strongly	.50	.08	.44
Disapprove strongly	.54	.53	.68
Difference	*.04*	*.45**	*.26*
Party identification			
Democrat	.49	.32	.54
Republican	.62	.42	.71
Difference	*.13**	*.10*	*.16*
Attitudes regarding minorities			
Government doesn't pay enough attention	.46	.28	.63
Government pays too much attention	.67	.51	.50
Difference	*.21**	*.23*	*.13*
Attitudes regarding illegal immigrants			
Police should not help INS	.48	.34	.25
Police should help INS	.54	.35	.72
Difference	*.06*	*.01*	*.46**
Number of cases	377	126	72

Source: Los Angeles Times Pre-election Poll, May 1993.

Note: Cell entries equal the estimated probability of a Riordan vote. Author's calculations are based on the multivariate logistic regression results found in table A4.1 in the appendix.

*$p < .01$

that conflict makes group identities increasingly salient. Therefore, the voting behavior within each of these three groups—whites, blacks, and Latinos—should reflect interest-driven considerations that are unique to each group. Were these results to appear substantively similar, this would largely disconfirm the group interest expectations. Table 4.5 presents the estimated probability of voting for Riordan within each of the variable categories. These probabilities are derived from a set of logistic regression analyses that can be found in table A4.1 in the appendix using the same methodology as the analysis in chapter 3. As these findings demonstrate, there are substantial differences among these groups regarding the factors that influence voting behavior. A more detailed discussion of these findings and their implications follows.

The White Vote

The single largest determinant of the white vote was ideology. As shown in table 4.5, an estimated 94 percent of very conservative whites voted for Riordan, compared with only 12 percent of those who were very liberal. This 82 percentage point difference between the very conservative and the very liberal is almost four times as large as any other variable difference among whites, suggesting quite strongly that Riordan's overwhelming support among white voters was strongly related to his general conservatism relative to Woo. While less influential than ideology, status differences and racial attitudes were also significant determinants of the vote. Among low-income voters (making less than $20,000 annually in 1993 dollars), the Riordan vote was only 39 percent, compared to 64 percent among the most affluent group (earning $60,000 and above). Similarly, only 46 percent of white voters with liberal minority attitudes voted for Riordan, whereas among those with racially conservative opinions, his vote was a much higher 67 percent. These findings seem to imply that white voting behavior was motivated by both ideological considerations and group interest motives.

Promises to create more jobs and to provide more police officers for Los Angeles were central to both the Woo and Riordan campaigns. Riordan, however, campaigned heavily in the largely white

San Fernando Valley, where his promises were amended with the
message that not only would he work for more jobs and more police
officers but he would allocate resources fairly throughout the city.
The implications of this campaign message were that Woo was likely
to work for jobs and police in the inner city at the expense of Valley
whites. To many white voters, Woo's agenda appeared to be tilted in
favor of minority communities over middle-class white communities.
Voters who felt that minorities already had sufficient or too much
attention from city hall were much more likely to vote for Riordan
than for Woo.

Partisanship also influenced the white vote, although to a lesser
degree than the previously discussed factors. It had been many years
since there had been a viable Republican candidate on the mayoral
ballot, and this unique opportunity was not lost on the city's relatively small Republican constituency. Over one-third of the city's
white Democrats joined local Republicans in voting for Riordan, and
it is this large defection among white Democrats that mitigates the
relative impact that partisanship had on this electoral outcome. The
Riordan vote among white Republicans was 62 percent, compared to
an unexpectedly high 49 percent among white Democrats.

In contrast to the factors previously discussed, retrospective evaluations of Bradley and attitudes toward immigrants were not
significant contributing factors to the vote. Bradley was largely
unpopular among white voters by June 1993; nonetheless, the variance in attitudes regarding Bradley's job performance does not
appear to explain the variance in the white vote. The potential explanation that the Riordan vote was primarily driven by a backlash
against the Bradley regime is not supported by this analysis. Furthermore, the highly charged immigration issue was apparently not as relevant to the white vote as were other factors.

The Black Vote

African-American voters in Los Angeles, much like black voters
nationwide, are largely Democratic and represent a more cohesive
voting bloc than any other racial or ethnic group. This election was
no exception, as only 14 percent of blacks voted for Riordan. Results

from this analysis suggest that ideology and discontent with Bradley's job as mayor were the principal factors motivating a black Riordan vote. Very conservative African-Americans were 50 percentage points more likely to vote for Riordan than very liberal blacks. Similarly, black voters who strongly disapproved of Bradley's job as mayor were 45 percentage points more likely to vote for Riordan than were strong Bradley supporters.

These findings seem especially plausible given the tales of increasing alienation within the black community by the end of Bradley's tenure (Sonenshein 1993a; Gilliam 1996; Gilliam and Kaufmann 1998). As the story goes, Bradley's initial justification for Downtown redevelopment, the centerpiece of his mayoral agenda, was to revitalize the economy in and around the central city and to direct city resources into the neighborhoods that needed the most revitalization. The results of this costly redevelopment program, however, were that real estate developers got fat while minority communities in and around Downtown continued to languish. Little of the money made on Downtown redevelopment was ever invested in these neighborhoods, a fact that was not lost on minority leaders throughout the city. Thus it makes a great deal of sense that dissatisfaction with Bradley's record would motivate some within the black community to punish the status quo leadership and to vote for a change in direction. Blacks legitimately believed that they would be natural beneficiaries from African-American leadership in city hall. These findings suggest that those who felt the most betrayed by this promise voted for Riordan.

The Latino Vote

In 1993 Latinos made up approximately 40 percent of Los Angeles residents. Were their political participation to reflect their actual numbers and were this constituency to represent a unified set of political interests, they would have undeniably dominated the political agenda. However, Latinos in Los Angeles have historically not been well mobilized politically, and as a consequence they represented only 10 percent of all mayoral voters in 1993. Furthermore, the Latino community in Los Angeles is made up of many nationality groups that do not necessarily share a sense of common identity (Bobo and Johnson 2000; Valle and Torres 2000). In general, Latinos exhibit relatively weak levels of pan-ethnic identity, which result in lower levels of minority group solidarity—especially in contrast to African-Americans (Lopez and Espiritu 1990; DeSipio 1996; Jones-Correa and Leal 1996; Kaufmann 2003b). For this reason, Latino voters in Los Angeles have rarely voted as a cohesive bloc.

Middle-class Latinos are more likely to be native-born Americans than are less affluent Latinos. This higher-status Latino subgroup, subject to longer periods of cultural socialization than their lower-status counterparts, typically represents a different set of political beliefs and interests than working-class or poor Latinos (Sears et al. 1999). Latinos with higher status and longer tenure in the United States are more likely to identify with similar status whites in society. Thus the political attitudes of this group more closely approximate white attitudes, presumably because they share similar group interests.[8] The voting behavior among lower-status Latinos can be expected to be more liberal than that of their higher-status counterparts. The internal divisions within the Latino community are well illustrated in this analysis.

The findings in table 4.5 suggest that variance in the Latino vote is largely explained by class or status differences. Higher-income Latinos, similar to their white counterparts, were 45 percentage points more likely to vote for Riordan than were poorer Latinos. The relative effects of partisanship and ideology on the Latino vote appear to have been overshadowed by status-driven voting cues. In addition, these findings indicate that attitudes regarding illegal immigrants were also a significant correlate of the Latino vote. Latinos who desire enhanced efforts in deporting illegal immigrants were 46 percentage

---

8. A recent study of intergroup attitudes in Los Angeles has suggested that attitudes toward Latinos in general are more positive among non-Latinos than are attitudes toward blacks among nonblacks (Bobo et al. 1994). Latinos, in a sense, have been the beneficiaries of antiblack discrimination, as they are generally more desired as neighbors or tenants than are blacks. The negative publicity regarding illegal (and principally Latino) immigrants threatens the relative standing of middle-class Latinos in Los Angeles. The perceived lawlessness and poverty of illegal immigrants potentially damage the standing of all Latinos, and those middle-class Latinos with the most to lose are substantially more intolerant of illegal immigration than are their poorer counterparts.

points more likely to vote for Riordan than were Latinos who oppose such measures.

To be clear, I don't believe that these results mean that mayoral choices among Latinos were rooted in immigration policy. Rather, it is more likely that differences within the Latino population on the issue of illegal immigration indicate underlying differences in tenure and cultural socialization that correlate with different sets of political values. Assimilated, middle-class Latinos are more likely to identify with white voters, just as less assimilated, working-class, poor Latinos are more likely to identify with disadvantaged minority groups. These different political orientations then correspond to divergent political interests among Latinos. Thus when group interests become salient to electoral behavior, as they did in this election, these status and socialization differences result in distinctive patterns of electoral choice.

Group Differences

The underlying attitudinal foundations for the vote among whites, blacks, and Latinos differed greatly and largely represented the unique political motives of these constituencies. White voters were apparently influenced by ideology, class interests, and attitudes toward minority groups. African-American voters overwhelmingly supported Woo but at the margins were influenced by differences in political ideology and divergent opinions regarding Bradley's job performance as mayor. The Latino vote was polarized between different status groups, with higher-income Latinos supporting the conservative Riordan and lower-income Latinos supporting the liberal Woo. Furthermore, in all three cases, group interests were more powerful predictors of the vote than was partisanship.

Group interests were important factors in this election. For white voters, however, the inordinate influence of ideology on voter choice appears to have undercut the group interest perspective. While racial attitudes significantly correspond with the vote, the single most important factor for white voters in this election appears to have been ideology, showing that, among whites, increasing political conservatism corresponds with an increased probability of a Riordan vote.

For white voters, these results suggest that their vote was driven, to a great degree, by ideological divisions in the electorate—that voters were not motivated by racial concerns but rather by ideological ones.

Riordan performed extremely well among ideological conservatives and almost as well among ideological moderates. The strength of Riordan's showing among these groups might suggest that Woo was simply too liberal for the largely moderate and conservative white constituency. Los Angeles moderates do not always swing to the right, however. Fifty-six percent of white moderates supported Bradley in his 1989 mayoral bid, and 62 percent of white moderates supported Dianne Feinstein for governor in 1990. Woo's showing among moderates was unusually low, suggesting that the response from the ideological middle in this election may have been driven by factors that were specific to this electoral context. Because ideology was apparently so important to this electoral outcome, the following analysis focuses particularly on the voting behavior of white ideological moderates.[9]

Table 4.6 replicates the preceding analysis but restricts the sample to white, ideologically moderate voters. As before, I estimate the probability of a Riordan vote across the various explanatory factors: income, Bradley job approval, party identification, minority attitudes, and immigrant attitudes. Unlike the findings for the white population in general, these results provide strong evidence of racially motivated voting among this subset. Of the entire set of possible explanations for the vote, racial attitudes are the only significant factor. The predicted Riordan vote among white moderates who felt that city government pays too little attention to minorities was 47 percentage points lower than that for their more conservative counterparts. And as moderate voters generally represent an important swing con-

---

9. The logistic regression analyses reported in tables A4.1 and A4.2 are reduced fit models. Other demographic variables such as gender, age, occupation, and education failed to attract robust coefficients. Tests were also conducted for interaction effects, but these effects were not found to be statistically significant. There was some concern that multicollinearity between the ideology and racial attitude variables was skewing these regression results, that the large ideology coefficient for white voters might actually reflect underlying differences in racial attitudes that were highly correlated with ideology. A separate analysis of these factors did not confirm this suspicion, however. Among the three ideological cohorts, racial attitudes were significant correlates with the vote for moderates only. For liberals and conservatives, racial attitudes were not able to explain any of the residual variance in the vote.

stituency in any election (and represent over 30 percent of voters in this election), their overwhelming support of Riordan and the racially motivated nature of this support strongly implicate racial attitudes in the outcome of this contest. The racially conservative nature of the Riordan vote most certainly appears to support the group interest perspective and suggests that white animosity toward minority groups and their respective demands on city resources was crucial to Woo's loss of this pivotal constituency. Woo's campaign strategy,

TABLE 4.6. Estimated Probability of a Riordan Vote among Moderate White Voters, 1993

Variable	Moderate White Voters
Income	
Low (< $20K)	.49
High (> $60K)	.73
Difference	*.24*
Bradley job approval	
Approve strongly	.57
Disapprove strongly	.65
Difference	*.08*
Party identification	
Democrat	.61
Republican	.65
Difference	*.04*
Attitudes regarding minorities	
Government doesn't pay enough attention	.45
Government pays too much attention	.92
Difference	*.47**
Attitudes regarding illegal immigrants	
Police should not help INS	.73
Police should help INS	.57
Difference	*.17*
Number of cases	114

Source: Los Angeles Times Pre-election Poll, May 1993.

Note: Cell Entries equal the estimated probability of a Riordan vote. The author's calculations are based on multivariate logistic regression results found in table A4.2 in the appendix.

*$p < .01$

which emphasized his multiethnic ties within the city, alienated those ideological moderates who felt that the city was doing enough, or too much, to accommodate minority demands at their expense.

Conclusion

Considering the overt racial polarization in the 1993 vote, coupled with the results from the preceding analyses, the group interest perspective represents a fairly strong explanation for mayoral voting in Los Angeles. There are distinctive sets of interests and motivations underlying the political behavior of white, black, and Latino voters—differences that are not explained by partisanship.

The obvious racial polarization of the vote in this election—especially among black and white voters—implies that racial interests were front and center in the election, and the results from the statistical analyses conducted in this chapter further support this conclusion. While African-American voters overwhelmingly supported Woo, a small subset supported the Republican candidate. The locus of this support came from black voters who disapproved of the Bradley mayoralty.

Latino voters were divided in their support for the two candidates. Higher-status Latinos, much like white voters, preferred the Republican candidate. Lower-status Latinos were more attracted to Woo and his message of multiracial harmony. White voters initially appeared to be more ideological than racial in their voting behavior. Upon further study, however, there is substantial evidence of racially motivated voting behavior among whites as well. Particularly, this research finds that ideologically moderate white voters, who arguably held the balance of power in this contest, were motivated by their conflicted attitudes toward minorities to vote for Riordan. This race was a highly charged contest between a white electoral majority and its minority competition for the scarce material resources and power that city hall controls. While the rhetoric of the campaign itself did not explicitly incite interracial conflict, the political context was such that a strong connection between conflicting racial interests and the vote was almost inevitable.

5 "Vote Your Hopes, Not Your Fears": New York, 1965 to 1993

The political flavor of New York City mayoral politics is in many ways a sharp departure from that of Los Angeles. In New York, racial, ethnic, and religious identities have always played an important role in the city's governance and its electoral politics. Although the contemporary dividing lines in New York City have shifted away from the interethnic cleavages among white voters that were so prominent in the earlier half of the twentieth century to the interracial cleavages that are so prevalent today, the city's political history is nonetheless a long tale of successive battles over conflicting group interests (Reibstein 1969). Candidates continue to make strong group-based campaign appeals, and group-based voting is essentially the norm.

While the Los Angeles elections discussed in the prior two chapters illustrate the ebb and flow of political conflict and how changes in the political context effect changes in the basis for voting behavior, the New York elections represent considerably less variability. Racial group interests have been a central and salient feature of mayoral voting behavior since Liberal party candidate John Lindsay's reelection in 1969. What is so fascinating about contemporary New York City politics is that the issues and attitudes that dominate local voting behavior have changed so little since then. In contrast to the mayoral politics of Los Angeles, New York City politics are almost always played out on a conflictual canvas. Group interests and group identities consistently seem to matter.

Prior to the 1960s, religion was the predominant political cleavage in New York City. Catholics and Jews represented the two largest religious groups, and they routinely competed for power and political influence. During this era, city politics were dominated by the Irish and Italian Catholics. Changing demography, however—the growing numbers of blacks and Puerto Ricans in the city and the increasing flight of white Catholics to the suburbs—mitigated the power and presence of Catholic leadership. Historically, Jews in New York had been more politically liberal than the Catholics; as such, it was not uncommon for Jews to align with black voters in support of more liberal candidates. Increasing racial conflict in the 1960s, however, strained the political ties between African-Americans and Jews in New York, and beginning in the late 1960s Jewish voters, especially those living in the outer boroughs, began voting with their Irish and Italian counterparts.

> Obviously, in the aftermath of New York's primaries and election campaign of 1969, it hardly seems as though religion defines the present, or the future, major fissures in New York life. Race has exploded to swallow up all other distinctions, or so it would appear at the moment. (Glazer and Moynihan 1970, viii)

The voters of New York City, often hailed or excoriated for their excessive liberalism in national elections, are not nearly as liberal in their mayoral choices. The vast majority of white voters have supported conservative policies and, in a relative sense, conservative candidates since John Lindsay left the mayor's office in the early 1970s. During the 1970s and most of the 1980s, interracial battles for political power took place *within* the Democratic party, creating the facade of "ever so liberal" New York. Closer analysis, however, shows us that ethnic and racial minorities lost most of their battles for liberal representation in the Democratic primaries. Thus apparent solidarity between minority voters and their white Democratic counterparts, as evidenced by voting patterns in the general elections, may have been more illusory than real.

The breakthrough for African-American voters came in 1989,

when then Manhattan borough president David Dinkins defeated Ed Koch to become the Democratic party nominee. The presence of a black candidate in this election, however, exposed deep racial cleavages in voter preferences. Any myth of black, Latino, and white Democratic solidarity was most certainly exposed by the vast number of white Democratic defections in this race.

This chapter begins with a discussion of political culture, noting the historical and institutional legacy of New York City's political culture and contrasting it with that of Los Angeles. In particular, I argue that New York's machine-like governmental design often exacerbates the politicization of group identities and tends to promote the group-based claims of its various constituents. Why is the political context in New York more consistently conflictual than it is in Los Angeles? Part of the explanation certainly hinges on the two cities' distinctive political histories and institutional arrangements.

The second part of this chapter turns to the recent history of New York City mayoral politics, beginning with the liberal Lindsay administration in 1965. Lindsay's election was seen as a victory among liberals and reformers looking to snatch control of the city government from corrupt Democratic machine organizations. Nonetheless, during Lindsay's first administration, the city was wracked by a series of tumultuous racial conflicts, and Lindsay's liberal social policies were met with fierce resistance from white voters. Jewish voters, who had been the linchpin of the liberal reform movement, broke ranks with the city's minority voters, creating new alliances with conservative white voters in the outer boroughs. The patterns in voting behavior that emerged during this racially divisive period have been replicated time and again in almost every election since.

The remainder of the chapter focuses on the two Dinkins-Giuliani contests in 1989 and 1993. While Dinkins's narrow election victory over Giuliani in the 1989 mayoral election was hailed as a watershed liberal victory, comparable in importance to Bradley's victory in Los Angeles sixteen years earlier, Dinkins was never able to rally a sufficient base of white voter support to sustain his mayoralty. To a large degree, a favorable political context in 1989 enabled Dinkins to beat Giuliani by the slimmest of margins. A serious downturn in the local economy and charges of racial favoritism against Dinkins in his first term propelled Giuliani to victory in the rematch. What is particularly interesting about these two elections, however, is how similar—and how racially charged—voting behavior was in both.

The Political Culture of New York City

New York City and Los Angeles represent vastly different political traditions. New York City has a history of machine politics. While the days of political machines may be gone in their purest form, the political culture in New York continues to demonstrate strong machine tendencies (Mollenkopf 1994, 1999). The regular Democratic clubs in the five boroughs are enormously important with regard to political nominations, endorsements, and voter mobilization. Furthermore, New York City's strong mayoralty coupled with its vast municipal budget continues to offer what amounts to be substantial opportunities for political patronage (Newfield and Barrett 1988). Party leaders trade political endorsements for key appointments to the city's influential agencies and for access to public funds. As such, the costs of mounting a challenge to the status quo power structure are high in New York City. For most of the past century, any group that dared to contest the dominant political coalition ran the risk of losing access to substantial political patronage.

Although New York City has partisan elections, its politics, for most of the recent era, have been similar to a one-party system. Registered Democrats outnumber registered Republicans by approximately five to one, and there have been only three Republican mayors in New York City since 1945. While the ethnic and racial composition of New York City has changed rather dramatically over the course of the past century, the Democratic party has nonetheless been successful in integrating new groups into their structures, offering little opportunity for interparty competition. Historically, waves of new ethnic and racial immigration to the city—such as the Jews, Italians, blacks, and Puerto Ricans—were incorporated into the party machinery as a way of derailing reform challenges and maintaining the strength of the single-party structure. Participating in the regular Democratic party organizations guaranteed access to significant polit-

ical rewards, and thus the material interests of each group were consistently tied to the success of regular Democratic candidates. Even
David Dinkins, the city's first minority mayor, came from the ranks of
the regular Democrats.

While New York's single-party structure has provided many opportunities for minority political incorporation below the level of the
mayoralty, it has also acted as an obstacle with regard to building
independent minority and/or liberal coalitions. In many cities, the
successes of minority mayoral candidates have been credited to electoral coalitions among blacks, in some instances Latinos, and white
liberals (Browning, Marshall, and Tabb 1984). In numerous cases,
biracial and multiracial coalitions were able to oust conservative mayoral regimes (Mollenkopf 1994). In Los Angeles, for example, blacks,
Latinos, Jews, and other liberal whites made up the coalition that
elected Tom Bradley in 1973. All of these groups had seen little
empowerment in Los Angeles municipal politics, and thus it was perceived to be in their mutual interests to band together and challenge
the existing conservative power structure. By contrast, Jews, blacks,
and Latinos do not similarly share outsider status in New York City.
As parts of the larger Democratic power base, Jews, blacks, and Latinos have long been incorporated into the political structure and,
more importantly, regularly compete against one another for political
power.

The structure of New York politics places most of its constituent
groups inside the Democratic party organization. And while the
Democratic coalition is highly fractious, no group is large enough to
defect without bearing the negative consequences of its defection.

> The political sponsorship of contracts and funding to commu-
> nity-based organization has perpetuated the influence of the
> prevailing political establishment. Regular black and Latino
> leaders control some of this funding as political patronage. Even
> where the state or the Koch administration grants funding to
> community-based organizations on the merits, these groups
> need sponsorship from elected officials and know that any overt
> political challenge to the Mayor would cost them their funds. As
> a result, established white politicians can compromise a poten-

tial resource for independent minority mobilization. (Mollenkopf 1990, 83)

These incentives potentially explain why minority groups in New
York City have not posed many independent challenges to the regular Democratic party and, furthermore, why they did not fully abandon Democrats such as Ed Koch, even after he appeared to turn hostile to their communities. The only racial group in New York City
that is large enough to challenge conservative control of the city is
white voters, and they clearly have the least incentive to do so.

The size of New York's municipal budget coupled with the relative
strength of the city's mayoralty also provide a strong basis for continuing conflict in New York City politics. Aside from symbolic interests
that imbue any group candidacy, the *material* interests associated
with power in New York City are much larger than they are in most
other cities. Thus New York City's long history of machine politics,
its fractious political culture, and its large material stakes all enhance
the competitiveness of its political environment relative to many
other cities. The consequence of this persistently conflictual environment is that, even if there are no additional short-term forces exacer-
bating group conflict in New York, group identities and group interests are nonetheless always salient to electoral choices.

To understand the contemporary configuration of New York City
politics, it is important to understand the circumstances that led to a
racial political realignment in the 1960s. Liberal Republican John
Lindsay began his 1965 mayoralty as a reformer aimed at derailing the
power of the regular Democrats and the corruption of city hall. Timing, however, is everything, and the racial acrimony that erupted in the
city shortly after he took office effectively muted the liberal reform
impulses of the city's white voters. The decade of the 1960s was a
period of enormous racial turmoil, and this conflict made racial interests salient to white voters and minorities alike. In this new racially
divisive context, white voters abandoned their previous support for
liberal policies, and the electoral realignment of the 1960s—with
white ethnic outer borough voters rallying together against minority
voters and liberal Manhattanites—largely remains to this day.

The Rise and Fall of the Liberal Coalition

In 1965 John Lindsay, a liberal four-term congressman from Manhattan's Upper East Side, ran for mayor on a Republican/Liberal ticket and defeated Abe Beame, a Brooklyn regular Democrat, and William F. Buckley, the Conservative party candidate. The core of Lindsay's 1965 coalition came from Republicans, Manhattan liberal reformers, and reform-minded white voters from the outer boroughs. While Lindsay did receive some support from black and Puerto Rican neighborhoods (40 percent and 33 percent, respectively), these minority voters nonetheless supported the regular Democrat Beame in much larger numbers (*New York Times,* November 4, 1965, 50). Lindsay won the mayoralty with less than 44 percent of the total vote.[1]

Lindsay was successful, in part, because his two main competitors were not strong candidates and because the extreme racial conflict that would plague New York during much of the 1960s was still in the offing. The 1965 mayoral election preceded a series of racially polarizing events, and in this period of relative calm, racial issues and racial identities were only marginally important electoral cues. Within the first year of his term, however, Lindsay issued an executive order creating a new Civilian Complaint Review Board (CCRB) to oversee charges of police brutality and misconduct, especially in minority neighborhoods. A fierce political battle ensued. The Patrolman's Benevolent Association, in virulent response to the CCRB, placed a referendum on the city ballot in 1966 in an attempt to abolish the review board. The 1966 ballot referendum elicited record levels of voter participation, and the CCRB was defeated with 63 percent of the vote.

---

1. While over 70 percent of New York City voters are registered Democrats, there are five party lines in New York City elections: Democrat, Republican, Liberal, Conservative, and Right to Life. By and large the four smaller parties in New York City yield little influence relative to the Democrats, but from time to time their nominations have allowed candidates, such as Lindsay in 1969, opportunities to run for mayor without endorsement from either the Democrats or the Republicans. For more on New York City party organizations, see Mollenkopf 1994, chapter 4.

The magnitude of the outcome was stunning. For years, the white electorate of New York City had been dominated by a coalition of liberal forces—a coalition that had been especially willing to support the demands of black and other minority groups. In addition to giving clear and consistent support to a string of liberal candidates for state and national offices, these electoral groupings had rallied behind the symbol of liberal reform in both the 1961 and 1965 mayoral elections. Yet, in the 1966 referendum, the presumed liberalism of white voters could not be translated into support for the Review Board. For the first time in recent years, white New Yorkers turned their backs on a clearly articulated liberal cause, and civil rights forces suffered their worst defeat. (Rogowsky, Gold, and Abbott 1971, 70)

The defeat of the CCRB represented a turning point in the liberal impulse of New York voters. Prior to the CCRB referendum, much of Lindsay's support came from the reform movement that was looking to weaken the regular Democratic control over city agencies and community programs. Nonetheless, Lindsay's support of the CCRB, scatter-site housing aimed at neighborhood integration, and increased spending on social welfare was opposed by many of the conservative and moderate outer borough white Catholics and Jews who had supported his 1965 bid.

Lindsay's first administration was battered by successive racial blowups. In addition to the battle over the CCRB, the acrimonious United Federation of Teachers strike in 1968 brought racial politics to the electoral forefront. The United Federation of Teachers—composed largely of Jewish teachers—came into direct conflict with many African-American parents and community activists, and the result was a contentious and impenetrable breach between these two largely liberal communities. Racial issues had a choke hold on New York City politics, and this heightened level of racial discord had considerable fallout at the ballot box in 1969. In this election the Democrats nominated the relatively conservative Mario Procaccino, who was expected to do well among Catholics and Jews in the outer boroughs. Lindsay lost the Republican nomination to John Marchi, a conservative state senator from Staten Island. As a result, Lindsay ran for mayor in 1969 on the Liberal party line.

The incumbent mayor won the election with a scant 42 percent of the vote. Nearly 60 percent of New York City voters supported one of the two more conservative candidates. Furthermore, Lindsay's base of support in 1969 was wholly different than it had been four years earlier, signaling an important political realignment of New York City voters. The mayor's 1969 coalition was made up primarily of blacks, Puerto Ricans, and liberal Manhattan reformers. In particular, his appeal among blacks and Puerto Ricans, quite weak in the earlier contest, increased significantly to 80 percent and 63 percent, respectively, while his base of white reform-oriented support had all but vanished (*New York Times*, November 6, 1969, 37). Lindsay's 1969 administration was arguably the first biracial governing coalition in the city's history.

> While it oversimplifies matters to say that New York shifted from liberal to conservative when racial conflict sheared Jews from their alliance with minorities, and sent them into alliance with Catholics, the dictum catches an element of truth. . . . While many external forces undermined white liberalism in New York, its satisfaction with being part of the establishment and its disinclination to risk that status by joining with outsiders contribute to its weakness as a force for political change. (Mollenkopf 1990, 81)

Lindsay's narrow victory in 1969 signaled a need for the mayor to expand his political base if he were to govern or to win reelection in the future. With this in mind, Lindsay pursued a set of policies in his second term that varied significantly from those in his first. Most notably, Lindsay entered into political alliances with several of the county Democratic leaders and began to engage in the patronage politics so distant from roots as a reformer (Shefter 1985). In spite of these new alliances, however, Lindsay's electoral prospects were sufficiently bleak in 1973 that he decided not to run for reelection. In his stead, the city elected Abe Beame, a relatively conservative Democrat from Brooklyn. Beame's election represented a serious blow to the reform movement in New York City municipal politics and, to a great degree, reverted power back into the regular Democratic clubs from which he came.

During the latter half of Lindsay's administration and the beginning of Beame's tenure, the city was consistently running on a budget deficit financed by short-term borrowing, largely in the form of municipal bonds. By 1975 the city was in a fiscal crisis so severe that new state and federal oversight agencies were formed to regulate the financial practices of city government. As a result of Beame's perceived fiscal mismanagement of the city, the Democratic primary voters elected Ed Koch as their mayoral nominee in 1977. Running against Republican Roy Goodman, Conservative party candidate Barry Farber, and Liberal party candidate Mario Cuomo, Koch won the general election in November with nearly 50 percent of the vote.

The Koch Era

Below the surface, however, a racial backlash was brewing in the middle class, one that had begun with the defeat of the civilian complaint review board in a 1966 referendum, and was reinforced by the bitter 1968 school strike that pitted a Jewish union against black community activists. Procaccino's victory in the 1969 Democratic primary for mayor suggested the potential of this turn to the right, but Lindsay's triumph in the general election revealed its limits and held it in temporary abeyance. At the heart of this backlash was the fear of crime, which expanded into an antagonism against black people moving into white, middle-class communities. It was the issue that, in 1971, proved to be the turning point in Ed Koch's political career, that marked his break with 1960s liberalism and the start of his quest for one great emotional issue that would make him acceptable to the white middle class of Brooklyn and Queens. (Newfield and Barrett 1988, 116)

The often caustic and racially provocative public debates in the latter half of the 1960s—over police oversight, busing, residential integration, social spending, and crime—effected a sea change in the public policy agenda and political preferences of New York City's white residents. The fiscal crisis in 1975 further exacerbated the divide between racial/ethnic minorities and whites living in the city, with white voters becoming increasingly resentful of the poverty programs that were seen to have contributed to the city's financial decline. It is thus somewhat ironic that the standard bearer for this new conservative regime would be Edward Koch, a former New York City congressman from the liberal, reform-minded "Silk Stocking" district on the Upper East Side of Manhattan.

Koch's political roots were in a Manhattan reform Democratic club known as the Village Independent Democrats (VID), whose mission during the 1950s and 1960s was to wean control of the city away from the regular Democratic clubs. In 1962 Koch was elected to the New York City council and in 1968 to the U.S. Congress. While in Congress, Koch amassed a liberal voting record supporting school busing and amnesty for Vietnam War draft dodgers. As noted by Newfield and Barrett (1988), "There was hardly an issue, cosmic or exotic, during this period (his tenure in Congress) on which Koch deviated from the liberal orthodoxy" (115).

By 1977, however, Koch had ameliorated many of his liberal views. With David Garth running his media campaign, Koch stressed both his reform agenda and his law and order approach to crime in the city. Furthermore, a series of events in 1977 enhanced the public's concern over crime and its subsequent responsiveness to the Koch campaign. First, there were the incidents of rioting and arson during a power blackout in several black communities. In the course of one evening, thirty-eight hundred arrests were made and damage was estimated in excess of $100 million (Newfield and Barrett 1988). In addition to this civil unrest, a serial killer named "Son of Sam" had killed thirteen young people since January of that year.

In response to the increasingly salient crime issue, Koch began to campaign on his support for reinstating the death penalty (which was not legal in the state of New York at that time). The death penalty was extremely popular in the conservative outer boroughs, and while the mayor would have no statutory ability to change the law, this theme nonetheless proved powerful. His principal opponent, Mario Cuomo, was against capital punishment, and Koch was able to use this issue to his advantage in both the Democratic runoff and the general election

Koch's winning coalition in 1977 was made up of liberal Manhattan reformers, blacks, Puerto Ricans, and outer borough Jews. The only major ethnic group that did not support Koch in his initial bid was the outer borough Catholics. In an effort to solidify this important constituency, Koch developed political alliances with the regular Democratic borough leadership in four of the five boroughs and thus garnered their support and that of their constituencies in his 1981 and 1985 reelection bids.

Koch's battle for the mayoralty in 1977 would be his last serious contest until 1989. Under his predecessor, Abe Beame, the city suffered a fiscal crisis that resulted in the elimination of sixty-five thousand municipal government jobs, wage freezes for city workers, and widespread cutbacks in social service programs. The Koch era, by contrast, was a period of enormous economic expansion, and by 1985 Koch had turned the $1.8 billion deficit from 1975 into a budget surplus. Koch was so popular by 1981 that he was nominated by both the Democratic and Republican parties. Thus with little electoral competition, Koch received 75 percent of the vote in the general election. In 1985, even without the Republican nomination, he received a record 78 percent (see table 5.1).

The year 1985 represented the apex of Ed Koch's popularity as well as the beginning of his political decline. By the end of his second term, the mayor had expanded his political base to include almost all groups throughout the city. He claimed support from the business community, liberal reformers, blacks, and Puerto Ricans, as well as

TABLE 5.1.   New York Mayoral Election Returns, 1981–93

Year	Election	Total Votes	Turnout (%)	Koch/Dinkins Vote (%)	Major Opponents	Opponent Vote (%)
1981	General	1,222,644	50	75	Barbaro	13
1985	General	1,112,805	45	78	Bellamy	10
1989	General	1,819,695	59	50	Giuliani	48
1993	General	1,827,465	57	48	Giuliani	51

Source: City of New York—Board of Elections.

the conservative outer borough ethnics that largely make up the regular Democrats. With a strong economy and flexible rhetoric he was able to satisfy the political bosses while giving power and resources to the wealthy Manhattan business establishment. Shortly after his inauguration in 1985, however, scandal beset his administration. The suicide of one borough president, the indictment of two others, and numerous other indictments of Koch-appointed commissioners, judges, state legislators, city hall aids, and party leaders left the mayor's administration and its ethical image in disarray. Koch had spent his entire political career denouncing political corruption, political machines, and political patronage. Now he was at the center of an enormous scandal. While there was no evidence of his direct involvement, those implicated in these scandals were some of his closest political allies.[2] Equally damaging to Koch's public support was his increasingly racially divisive public rhetoric.

> Freed from the constraints of Manhattan liberalism, Koch has seized on issues like the restoration of the death penalty and fanned the city's ethnic and racial animosities to mobilize political support. . . . Koch discovered that his denunciations of "special treatment" for blacks played well outside Manhattan, and since then he has rarely passed up an opportunity to capitalize on the city's ethnic polarization. (Rose 1989, 20)

Since Jesse Jackson's 1988 presidential campaign in New York City, Koch had been at public odds with the black community and liberals alike. Thus it became all the more important for him to solidify his outer borough white base, as it was evident that his reform-minded, liberal, and black constituencies were waning. By June 1989, Koch's public approval ratings were at an all-time low (31 percent), and his prospects for the September Democratic primary looked unpromising. In July and August, however, opinion polls showed Koch on the rebound and gaining on the front-runner, David Dinkins.

---

2. Somewhat ironically, the district attorney responsible for investigating, uncovering, and prosecuting many of these Koch cronies was none other than Rudolph Giuliani.

Yet Koch's political momentum came to a halt when, on August 23, Yusef Hawkins, a black youth, was murdered by a gang of white youths in Bensonhurst. General public outrage over this event was not shared by the unusually subdued Koch. By comparison, Dinkins portrayed a compassionate yet reasonable leadership that the city had not seen for many years. As noted in *Newsweek* (September 25, 1989),

> In the end, a gang of white teenagers may have handed the election to Dinkins. Koch was staging a comeback from a drastic decline in popularity when black teenager Yusef Hawkins was shot to death in Bensonhurst last month. Many voters credited Dinkins with defusing the situation by urging racial harmony. Koch, by contrast, put off blacks and many liberal whites by criticizing protest rallies in Bensonhurst. "The ground moved from under him," says Democratic consultant David Sawyer. "Koch represented the kind of polarization people were tired of." (21)

The mayoral primary in 1989 represented the end of an era in New York City politics. Koch, who had served three terms as New York City's mayor, was defeated in the Democratic primary by the Manhattan borough president, David Dinkins, by a margin of 51 percent to 42 percent. Dinkins's success relied primarily on his appeal to blacks, Latinos, and liberal whites. He received 93 percent of the black vote, 54 percent of the Latino vote, yet only 28 percent of the white primary vote (see table 5.2). Among white voters, he drew most of his support from liberals (51 percent), faring poorly among white moderates (20 percent) and conservatives (11 percent). Given that so few white voters had supported Dinkins in the primary, his challenge was to attract a substantial portion of Koch's white primary voters.

The 1989 General Election—New Territory

David Dinkins had a long history in New York City politics prior to becoming mayor. Associated with the Carver Democratic Club in Harlem, Dinkins had been an assemblyman and in 1973 was named deputy mayor of the Beame administration. He was unable to serve, however, once it became known that he had not filed his income taxes in the preceding years. But he did serve as the head of the Board of Elections and as city clerk, during which time he ran two unsuccessful campaigns for Manhattan borough president in 1977 and 1981. In 1985 Dinkins was finally successful in his bid for Manhattan borough president. He was a long-time member of the New York

TABLE 5.2. New York City Democratic Primary Vote, 1989 (in percentages)

		% who voted for	
% of voters who are		Koch	Dinkins
	Total	42	50
	Race/Ethnicity		
60	White	61	29
29	Black	3	94
8	Latino	41	54
	Ideology		
35	Liberal	28	64
45	Moderate	50	39
20	Conservative	48	42
22	White liberal	39	51
28	White moderate	72	20
11	White conservative	74	11
	Income		
28	Under $25K	36	58
42	$25K to 49,999	40	53
24	$50K to 99,999	41	49
7	$100K and up	57	33
	Religion		
26	Protestant	16	81
35	Roman Catholic	52	39
28	Jewish	65	26
7	White Protestant	46	46
22	White Catholic	64	24

Source: New York Times/CBS Primary Exit Poll, 1989.

Note: Number of respondents equals 2,014. Percentages may not add to 100, as there were several other candidates in the primary.

County Democratic party establishment and in 1988 was also cochair of the New York City Jesse Jackson campaign.

By contrast, Dinkins's Republican opponent in the 1989 general election, Rudolph Giuliani, was not a seasoned politician. Giuliani was the U.S. attorney for the Southern District of New York. He began his career prosecuting corrupt police officers in the 1960s and was named assistant U.S. attorney general during the Reagan administration. His notoriety stemmed from high-profile prosecutions of Mafia chieftains and Wall Street insider traders. His lack of political experience, his Republican party affiliation, and his generally ill-at-ease campaign style made him an unlikely contender for the mayoralty. Nonetheless, his tough stance on crime and drug issues, his fiscal conservatism, and his Italian ethnic roots made him appealing to conservative outer borough whites, especially Catholics.

A Republican had not won the New York City mayor's office since John Lindsay in 1965. Registered Democrats in the city outnumbered Republicans by a margin of five to one, and conventional New York wisdom was that Democrats don't lose. New York City had never had a black mayor, but Jesse Jackson's presidential primary success in New York City was considered a strong indication that a black candidate could run well in the city (Arian et al. 1991; Mollenkopf 1994). Nonetheless, the Dinkins-Giuliani match-up was new territory for New York City mayoral politics. Given the city's long history of tenuous race relations, it was almost inevitable that racial attitudes would bear heavily on this electoral outcome.

The political environment in 1989 was, in a relative sense, favorable to Dinkins's candidacy. Koch's increasing racial acrimony had made many white liberals, blacks, and Latinos uncomfortable with the status of race relations in the city and with having a racial conservative as mayor (Mollenkopf 1994). Furthermore, several racial incidents—the 1986 attack on three black men in Howard Beach by a mob of white youths, the Tawana Brawley trial, the highly publicized black assault on a white female jogger in Central Park, and the Bensonhurst incident—put further focus on the declining state of race relations in the city. Dinkins's campaign theme was heavily focused on racial healing. Although he had well-publicized ties with Jesse Jackson, Dinkins's personal style was by contrast decidedly understated and nonconfrontational. In addition, Dinkins had generally good relations within the Jewish community and had publicly supported Jews and the cause of Israel long before his mayoral bid.

By contrast, Giuliani's strength came from his record as a tough prosecutor. Concerns over crime, corruption, and drugs were the most salient issues among white voters, and Giuliani was uniquely positioned to address these issues, given his background (Arian et al. 1991).

> He seemed to have the perfect profile for the post-Koch era— young (45), driven, idealistic, incorruptible. He fit the fusion pattern precisely, a fresh breeze like La Guardia and Lindsay, a Republican-Liberal reprieve after a generation of tired, corrupt Democrats. He was the prosecutor who busted Mafia Dons, the Wall Street greedheads, and Koch's outer-borough cronies. He promised the toughness of a conservative on crime and drugs, and the compassion of a liberal on social issues. He soared in the early polls. And stumbled out of the starting gate. (Klein 1989, 40)

Giuliani attacked Dinkins on his history of tax impropriety and his ties to corrupt Democrats. Dinkins attacked Giuliani on his lack of experience and his position on abortion. Neither of the candidates was particularly popular with the electorate, but in the end Dinkins won by a margin of 50 percent to 48 percent.

Dinkins's victory in 1989 was heralded as the beginning of a new era. At last New York had joined the ranks of many large American cities by electing a black mayor. Like Lindsay's narrow victories in the 1960s, however, Dinkins began his mayoral career with a shallow base of support. Only 28 percent of the white electorate had cast votes for Dinkins, and it would take only slight defections from his white constituency to tip the scales back again. In a rare show of solidarity, all of the Democratic leadership endorsed Dinkins in 1989. But 30 percent of the city's registered Democrats defied their party leadership and supported the Republican Giuliani. Dinkins's narrow victory alone is evidence that partisanship was not particularly important to electoral choice. Given the degree of racial polarization in the vote, it is reasonable to presume that racial identities played a much larger role in this outcome than did traditional political ones.

Using public opinion polls conducted during the mayoral elections in 1989 and 1993, I explore the voting behavior in these two elections. Given the racially divisive backdrop of this period, I expect racial and ethnic concerns to be particularly salient voting considerations. From the standpoint of the group interest theory and given the persistent salience of race in New York City politics, the main expectation is that group interests will overshadow partisanship in both of these elections.[3]

Voting for Mayor in 1989

A demographic breakdown of the 1989 mayoral vote is found in table 5.3.[4] The results from the exit poll on which the table is based highlight the enormous racial polarization in the vote. Seventy-two percent of white voters supported Giuliani, and 91 percent of black voters supported Dinkins. Among Latino voters, 65 percent supported Dinkins. In addition, these data show that even among Dinkins's most likely white base—Democrats, liberals, and Jews—he engendered little loyalty. While the Democratic party establishment all strongly endorsed Dinkins's candidacy, Dinkins received less than half of the white Democratic vote (WABCTV/*New York Daily News* Exit Poll, 1989). Among white liberals, Dinkins captured only slightly more than half of the vote, while white moderates and con-

---

3. The following analyses use public opinion surveys and exit polls conducted for each of the subject elections. All of the survey data used in this chapter come from computer-assisted random-digit dialed citywide telephone surveys. The preelection 1989 New York survey was conducted in June by CBS News and the *New York Times* and includes 1,462 respondents. The 1989 exit poll was conducted by WABC TV and the *New York Daily News* and includes 2,595 respondents. The 1993 New York City preelection poll was conducted in May by WCBS TV and the *New York Times* and includes 1,273 respondents. The 1993 New York City exit poll was conducted by Voter Research and includes 1,788 respondents.

4. It is worth noting that the demographic makeup of the mayoral electorate deviates significantly from the underlying composition of the city. While non-Latino whites make up only 43 percent of the city population, they represented 56 percent of the total 1.8 million voters in the 1989 general election. Blacks are slightly overrepresented in the electorate and Latinos are substantially underrepresented. Thus in spite of the diverse, multicultural makeup of the city population, non-Latino whites constitute an electoral majority.

TABLE 5.3.   New York City Mayoral Vote—Runoff Election, 1989 (in percentages)

% of voters who are		% who voted for	
		Giuliani	Dinkins
	Total	48.0	50.4
	Race/Ethnicity		
56	White	72	28
28	Black	7	91
13	Latino	34	65
2	Asian/other	—	—
	Ideology		
29	Liberal	29	71
39	Moderate	48	52
23	Conservative	63	35
14	White liberal	47	51
23	White moderate	78	22
15	White conservative	86	13
	Party		
57	Democrat	30	70
18	Independent	62	38
21	Republican	81	17
	Income		
9	Under $20K	38	62
57	$20K to 49,999	44	56
19	$50K to 99,999	58	42
5	$100K and up	80	20
	Religion		
27	Protestant	27	73
39	Roman Catholic	62	38
16	Jewish	65	35
8	White Protestant	70	30
24	White Catholic	82	18

*Source: New York Times/*CBS Exit Poll, 1989.

servatives overwhelmingly supported Giuliani, with 78 percent and 86 percent of the vote, respectively. And while Jews were more supportive of Dinkins than either white Protestants or white Catholics, they still favored Giuliani by 65 percent to 35 percent.

The enormous racial polarization in the 1989 electoral results strongly implies that racial attitudes were important to this electoral outcome. Table 5.4 reports a series of estimated probabilities for a Giuliani vote in the 1989 election that further support this claim.[5] The lack of variance in black electoral choice and the sample size of the 1989 survey do not allow analyses of black, Latino, or liberal white voters. Thus the following analyses focus exclusively on the voting behavior of white Democrats and white ideological moderates.

The purpose of these analyses is to explore the rationale for Giuliani's support among white voters and in particular to assess the extent to which Giuliani voting correlates with racial resentment as opposed to partisan or ideological motives. The explanatory factors include measures of partisan identification, ideology, and education, as well as two racial attitude measures. The group interest explanation for voting behavior in 1989 is represented by the racial attitude measures. The first, called "status of race relations," is a scale made up of two survey questions regarding individual satisfaction with the current status of race relations in the city and with Koch's handling of race relations. The expectation is that those satisfied with the current state of racial power relations will be more likely to support the white conservative—Giuliani.

The second racial attitude measure, "attitudes regarding a black mayor," is a scale comprised of three survey questions that gauge the extent to which individuals believe that blacks have received their fair share in the city and whether having a black mayor would improve race relations and city life generally. Unlike the prior racial attitude measure, this scale focuses more directly on individual attitudes toward blacks and the prospects of a black mayor. These questions are explicitly racial in a way that the previous questions are not and capture individual ambivalence over the lack of black empowerment in

---

5. The estimated probabilities displayed in table 5.4 are based on the logistic regression results reported in table A5.1 in the appendix. For additional discussion of this methodology, see note 5 in chapter 3.

TABLE 5.4. Estimated Probability of a Giuliani Vote, 1989

Variable	All Whites	White Democrats	White Moderates
Party identification			
Democrat	.59	—	.55
Republican	.76	—	.74
Difference	*.17**	*—*	*.19*
Ideology			
Very liberal	.59	.53	—
Very conservative	.70	.68	—
Difference	*.11*	*.15*	*—*
Attitudes regarding race relations			
Disapprove Koch handling/relations bad	.44	.42	.41
Approve Koch handling/relations good	.80	.74	.76
Difference	*.36**	*.32**	*.35**
Attitudes regarding black mayor			
Blacks in NYC get less than fair share	.45	.33	.39
Blacks in NYC get more than fair share	.88	.90	.88
Difference	*.43**	*.57**	*.49**
Education			
Less than high school	.81	.78	.80
College degree or more	.55	.49	.49
Difference	*.26**	*.29**	*.31**
Number of cases	256	130	122

Source: CBSTV/*New York Times,* New York City pre-election survey, June 1989.

Note: Cell entries equal the estimated probability of a Giuliani vote. The author's calculations are based on multivariate logistic regression results found in table A5.1 in the appendix.

*p < .05

city politics and the desirability of black leadership as a solution to the city's interracial conflict. Whereas the prior variable is focused on individual comfort with change in a generic sense, this measure offers a more direct test of the racial animus component of group conflict.[6]

---

6. All of the items in the two racial attitude measures were factor analyzed to confirm their independence. The results from the factor analysis support separating these items into separate scales. Furthermore, the correlation between the two measures is a barely significant .09.

Table 5.4 reports estimated probabilities of a Giuliani vote for all white voters, white Democrats, and white moderates.[7] The findings largely confirm the importance of racial attitudes to voting behavior in this election. Among all white voters, party identification and education were both significant predictors of the vote. Republicans were 17 percentage points more likely to vote for Giuliani than were Democrats, while voters with less than a high school education were 26 percentage points more likely to support the Republican than were college graduates. Nonetheless, racial attitudes were better predictors of the Giuliani vote than either party identification or education. Among whites who disapproved of Koch's handling of race relations and believed that race relations in general were poor, only 44 percent voted for Giuliani, compared to 80 percent of those voters who thought race relations were good. The largest predictors of the vote, however, were attitudes regarding the necessity for and potential benefit of having a black mayor. For voters who believed that blacks in New York City get less than their fair share and that a black mayor would improve race relations, only 45 percent voted for Giuliani. Among voters who felt that blacks get more than their fair share and that a black mayor would not improve things, Giuliani received 88 percent of the vote. These results clearly emphasize the salience of racial attitudes to white voters in this election.

Separate analyses conducted for white Democrats and white moderates similarly reflect the importance of racial attitudes. For both of these groups, racial conservatism, satisfaction with the state of race relations, and lower educational attainment correspond with higher levels of Giuliani voting. Also interesting is that neither political ideology nor partisanship was a significant predictor in the latter two analyses. Apparently, for swing voters—in this case moderates—racial interests overwhelmed partisan interests in their electoral importance.

The cumulative findings from these three analyses support the group interest expectation that interracial conflict and corresponding race-related attitudes were important factors with respect to the Giuliani vote. Dinkins, nonetheless, managed to secure enough of the

7. Consistent with the analyses in prior chapters, the probabilities reported reflect the difference in estimated probabilities from the predictor's highest and lowest values, letting the other independent variables take their "natural" values.

white vote to win this election, and his challenge over the next four years would be to consolidate his white and Latino base while continuing to garner enthusiasm from the black community that was so crucial to his victory. Dinkins benefited in this election from a generally good economy, from liberal concern over the declining state of race relations, and from Giuliani's lack of campaign experience. These factors would change, however, over the course of the next four years. In the context of a dire economic recession, perceptions that he had shown favoritism to blacks in several well-publicized interracial incidents, and the presence of a more experienced Giuliani, Dinkins would lose the mayoralty in 1993.

The Rematch—1993

In 1977 Koch was helped in his first bid for mayor by Son of Sam, whose murder rampage drove up support for capital punishment, Koch's big issue. Giuliani's big issues are crime and drugs. What will make these salient? I'd hate to guess. (Barnes 1989)

There was indeed a change in political context from 1989 to 1993, one that would make Giuliani's law and order campaign all the more sympathetic to many in the New York City electorate. First, the local economy in New York City had been faltering since 1989. The entire nation had been mired in recession in the early 1990s, and New York City's recovery was not sufficient to forestall criticism of Dinkins and his ability to manage the city economy. Accompanying the economic downturn was increased concern over crime and interracial violence. Survey results from 1989 indicate that many voters believed a black mayor would mitigate interracial tensions in the city (CBS News/*New York Times* Poll, June 1989). Dinkins's apparent difficulty in coping with the Korean grocery boycott and the violent demonstrations in Crown Heights, a Brooklyn neighborhood, dampened much of this hope.

The Crown Heights incident was particularly problematic for Dinkins because there were public accusations that he had shown racial favoritism to blacks. The conflict between blacks and Jews in

Brooklyn began in August 1991, after a young black boy was acci-
dentally killed by an Orthodox Jewish driver. A disturbance ensued
when black youths retaliated in the Brooklyn neighborhood, destroy-
ing property and killing a seventeen-year-old rabbinical student. So
problematic was the perceived police handling of this event that New
York governor Mario Cuomo commissioned a study, the results of
which reported accounts from several white police officers that they
had been restrained from making arrests during the disturbance. The
final report of the Cuomo investigation, released shortly before the
mayoral election in 1993, forced Dinkins to answer additional
charges regarding his conduct in the wake of this violence. Both the
event itself and the timing of the report were detrimental to Dinkins's
public approval, especially for white voters.

Even though the political context did not favor Dinkins's reelection, the swing vote from Dinkins to Giuliani constituted less than
100,000 out of 1.8 million total votes. Consistent with the group
interest hypothesis, these results suggest that these two election outcomes were largely based on a set of stable attitudes that were central
to voter choice in both elections. Racial attitudes were enormously
salient in the 1989 contest, and the changes in political environment
between 1989 and 1993 only enhanced this salience. In particular,
public opinion polls from 1989 and 1993 illustrate the increasing
concern over race relations among white voters (see table 5.5). As
indicated in table 5.5, 67 percent of white New York City residents
felt that race relations were generally bad in 1989, compared to 72
percent of blacks and 74 percent of Latinos. By 1993, however, the
percentage of whites who thought race relations were bad had

TABLE 5.5.   Public Opinion Regarding Race Relations in New York City,
1989 and 1993

	1989	1993	Difference
Percentage who think race relations are generally bad			
Whites	67	82	+15
Blacks	72	76	+4
Latinos	74	75	+1

Source: CBS News/*New York Times* Polls, June 1989 and October 1993.

increased 15 percentage points to 82 percent. By contrast, the increase among blacks and Latinos was substantially less, 4 percent and 1 percent, respectively. White residents were disproportionately dissatisfied with Dinkins's management of race relations, and these feelings likely reflect increasing resentment with the black-led mayoral regime. Given the growing disillusionment with race relations, especially among whites, group interest theory would expect to find higher levels of racially motivated voting behavior in 1993 than in 1989.

Table 5.6 compares the 1989 and 1993 mayoral votes, and this comparison certainly suggests that racial considerations were even more salient in 1993. Increased racial polarization in the vote is evident in 1993. While 72 percent of white voters supported Giuliani in 1989, this percentage increased to 78 percent in the following election. Latino voters were also more supportive of Giuliani in the latter contest, with the percentage of their support increasing from 34 percent to 39 percent. Conversely, black support for Dinkins increased from 91 percent in 1989 to 95 percent in 1993.

These data also indicate that small movements within a variety of subgroups were responsible for Giuliani's victory—that no single group defection can be held solely responsible for the change in outcome. Among white liberals, Dinkins's support remained a constant 51 percent. Among white ideological moderates and conservatives, however, he lost, 7 and 10 points, respectively. There was great concern in the Dinkins camp that the Crown Heights incident would substantially damage his support among Jewish voters. Support for Dinkins among Jews did fall, but only 3 percentage points, from 35 percent in 1989 to 32 percent in 1993. More detrimental to Dinkins than the decline in the Jewish vote, however, was the increased turnout and increased loyalty to Giuliani among white Catholics. White Catholics represented 24 percent of the electorate in 1989 and 30 percent in 1993. Much of this increase in white Catholic turnout is credited to a Staten Island secession measure that was also on the 1993 general election ballot. While the total number of votes cast in the other four boroughs remained constant or declined in 1993, total votes cast in Staten Island increased by over twenty-five thousand (New York City Board of Elections). Over half of Giuliani's margin of

TABLE 5.6. Comparison of New York City Mayoral Vote, 1989 and 1993

			1989		1993	
% of voters who are			Giuliani	Dinkins	Giuliani	Dinkins
1989	1993	Total	48	50	51	49
		Race/Ethnicity				
56	56	White	72	28	78	22
28	29	Black	7	91	5	95
13	12	Latino	34	65	39	61
2	3	Asian/other	—	—	54	46
		Ideology				
29	30	Liberal	29	71	34	66
39	43	Moderate	48	52	56	44
23	27	Conservative	63	35	65	35
14	17	White liberal	47	51	49	51
23	25	White moderate	78	22	85	15
15	12	White conservative	86	13	97	3
		Party				
57	61	Democrat	30	70	33	67
18	22	Independent	62	38	69	31
21	17	Republican	81	17	93	7
		Income				
9	14	Under $15K	38	62	34	66
57	50	$15K to 49,999	44	56	49	52
19	28	$50K to 99,999	58	42	62	38
5	8	$100K and up	80	20	65	35
		Religion				
27	24	Protestant	27	73	26	74
39	45	Roman Catholic	62	38	69	31
16	17	Jewish	65	35	68	32
8	6	White Protestant	70	30	82	18
24	30	White Catholic	82	18	88	12

Source: New York Times/CBS Exit Poll, 1989; Voter Research Exit Poll, 1993.

victory can be attributed to the increase in white Catholic turnout in Staten Island and to their expanded support for Giuliani—78 percent in 1989 versus 84 percent in 1993 (Mollenkopf 1994).

In spite of the different election outcomes in 1989 and 1993, these two elections appear more similar than different. The racial polarization so evident in 1989 is even more apparent in 1993. Group interest theory would expect that, similar to 1989, racial attitudes should be a strong determinant of the vote in 1993 as well. Table 5.7 presents a series of estimated probabilities of a Giuliani vote based on logistic regression analyses (found in table A5.2 in the appendix). These estimated probabilities were calculated using the same methodology employed in the 1989 analysis. Arguably, the 1993 analysis provides a more rigorous test of the group interest hypothesis, as it controls for a wider range of possible explanations. The 1993 preelection survey asked a greater variety of attitude measures than did the 1989 survey, thus allowing for a more fully specified model. Consistent with the prior analyses, I explore the possibility of partisan and ideological motivations as well as racial ones. In addition to these factors, however, this model also includes attitudes regarding crime and safety, opinion regarding local immigrants, and feelings about Dinkins's management of the local economy.

When white respondents were asked to name the most important problem facing the city in 1993, the vast majority cited crime first and the local economy second (WCBSTV and the *New York Times* Poll, May 1993). Race relations was a distant fourth. Nonetheless, the group interest hypothesis would expect racial attitudes to be extremely important to the vote. Thus the inclusion of attitudes on crime and the local economy represents a stronger and more conservative test of the group interest hypothesis than does the 1989 analysis. The racial attitudes measure in this analysis is made up of three questions regarding Dinkins's handling of race relations and the extent to which he showed favoritism to blacks over Jews. The expectation is that dissatisfaction with Dinkins's management of race relations or perceptions that Dinkins showed favoritism will be positively correlated with Giuliani voting.

Beyond the issue of Dinkins's racial policies, there was substantial criticism of the mayor generally during his tenure. Since Dinkins was

TABLE 5.7. Estimated Probability of a Giuliani Vote, 1993

Variable	All Whites	White Democrats	White Moderates
Party identification			
Democrat	.58	—	.56
Republican	.71	—	.59
Difference	*.13**	—	*.03*
Ideology			
Very liberal	.52	.50	—
Very conservative	.70	.65	—
Difference	*.18**	*.15*	—
Attitudes regarding race relations			
Dinkins has done a good job/fair	.36	.33	.19
Dinkins has done a bad job/biased	.87	.86	.95
Difference	*.51**	*.53**	*.76**
Attitudes regarding crime/safety			
New York safer than 4 years ago	.41	.31	.38
New York less safe than 4 years ago	.68	.68	.64
Difference	*.27**	*.37**	*.25**
Attitudes regarding immigrants			
Local govt. doesn't pay enough attention	.54	.51	.46
Local govt. pays too much attention	.68	.65	.68
Difference	*.14**	*.14*	*.22**
Dinkin's handling of the economy			
Good	.34	.32	.30
Bad	.87	.84	.86
Difference	*.54**	*.52**	*.56**
Number of cases	377	191	117

Source: WCBSTV/*New York Times,* New York City pre-election survey, May 1993.

Note: Cell entries equal the estimated probability of a Giuliani vote. The author's calculations are based on multivariate logistic regression results found in table A5.2 in the appendix.

*p < .05

the incumbent in this contest, it is certainly plausible that Giuliani support resulted from negative evaluations of the Dinkins administration apart from racial issues. For this reason, opinions regarding the general safety of the city compared to four years prior and assessments of the local economy are also included. Finally, I consider the importance of immigrant-related attitudes to the vote. The rapid escalation of foreign immigration over the past ten years that contributed to the increasingly multicultural makeup of the city may have also contributed to increased tensions among racial and ethnic groups. This measure is thus intended to capture individual resentments toward immigrants and toward government policies that cater to them. The "attitudes regarding immigrants" variable is one survey question that asks respondents to assess whether local government pays too much attention to recent immigrants and reflects a somewhat different aspect of racial resentment than the alternative racial attitude measure described previously. Consistent with the 1989 analysis, estimated probabilities were computed for all whites, white Democrats, and white moderates.

Even after including a more fully specified set of explanatory factors, the results from 1993 look strikingly similar to those from 1989. With regard to the total white electorate, retrospective evaluations of Dinkins's management of race relations and the local economy are the two most significant factors with respect to the vote. Only 36 percent of voters who felt that Dinkins had done a good job of managing race relations voted for Giuliani, compared to 87 percent who felt that he had done a bad job and had shown racial bias. Similarly, 34 percent of voters who thought Dinkins had done a good job of managing the economy supported Giuliani, versus 87 percent who thought he had managed the economy poorly. Crime and safety attitudes, immigrant attitudes, partisan identification, and political ideology are also significant, albeit they show much smaller effects. The difference between Republican voting and Democratic voting for Giuliani is only 13 percentage points, whereas attitudes regarding race relations and attitudes regarding the economy yield differences of 51 and 54 percentage points, respectively. These findings are quite compelling because they demonstrate the continuing salience of

racial concerns, even when controlling for a variety of other important political factors.

White Democrats and white moderates were important swing constituencies in this election, and the results in table 5.7 demonstrate
that, for both groups, racial attitudes were more significant than were
economic concerns, crime and safety attitudes, and attitudes toward
recent immigrants. The relative strength of racial attitudes was especially profound for white moderates. In this case, the high/low difference in Giuliani voting was three times as large as that for crime
and safety attitudes and was 20 percentage points greater than the
effect of economic evaluations. The relative strength of this factor,
controlling for other traditionally important political concerns, makes
a strong case that racial considerations were extremely consequential
to the vote, especially among swing voters like independents and
moderates.

Discussion

Contemporary New York City politics represent an extraordinary
example of how conflictual political environments result in group distinctive voting behavior and undercut the electoral importance of traditional political cues. In the context of the persistent racial tensions
that characterize much of New York City politics, 1989 represented a
unique opportunity for the election of a black mayor. The relative
strength of the local economy, coupled with a liberal backlash against
Koch's inflammatory racial rhetoric, opened the door, ever so
slightly, for Dinkins. In 1993, however, he was unable to hold on to
his narrow electoral margin, as the political context shifted to a dismal
local economy and public accusations of racial favoritism.

From the group interest perspective, the relative opportunity for
liberal biracial coalitions in New York City is always low. The extreme
social diversity of the city, the relative equality in the size of competing groups, the strained historical relations among groups in the city,
the continuing influx of nonwhite immigrants, and the enormous
centralized power of the mayor's office all contribute to the city's persistent racial and ethnic conflict.

The contemporary political alignment in New York City politics resulted in large part from the numerous racial conflicts during the 1960s. Heightened racial demands in the 1960s coupled with New York's fiscal crisis in the mid-1970s served to exacerbate the racial divisions in the city, as the public demeanor toward social welfare spending became increasingly hostile in the face of diminishing public money. Minorities and their respective demands for city services were largely blamed for the city's disastrous financial straits, and the focus of city government moved away from minority concerns.

> By the late 1970s and early 1980s, tight fiscal management and promoting private investment had displaced responding to urban social programs at the top of New York City's political agenda. Not only were a series of legal requirements and fiscal monitors put in place, but all major forces on public opinion, ranging from the *New York Times* editorial board to the leaders of municipal unions, were united in agreeing on these ends. Previous proponents of increased social spending, such as liberal Democrats and officials of the poverty program, were on the defensive, while their social base had been demobilized. The policies of the Lindsay administration, and the electoral coalition that had given it power, were in disarray. (Arian et al. 1991, 7)

The patterns of voting behavior in 1989 confirm the persistence of these trends. Previously unheard numbers of Democratic New Yorkers voted for the Republican Giuliani in the face of unanimous support for Dinkins from Democratic elites. While the Democratic leadership had enormous vested interests in supporting the Dinkins regime, elite cues were nonetheless largely ignored by their white constituents.

Conclusion

New York City has been called an anomaly and is noted as one of the last racially diverse American cities to have a black mayor (Mollenkopf 1990). And while the city of New York did not elect a black mayor until 1989, it was nonetheless one of the first American cities to elect a socially progressive, liberal government. John Lindsay's election in 1965 and the ambitious social welfare agenda he pursued can be viewed as a precursor to many liberal administrations that would replace conservative mayoralties in other cities during the 1970s and 1980s. New York City's near bankruptcy in the mid-1970s, however, created a public clamor among city residents for less liberal policies. Ed Koch was elected in 1977, in large part, because of his commitment to scale back the public payrolls, "to engage in hard bargaining with civil service workers, and his desire to crack down on welfare and those he referred to as 'poverty pimps' in the community action program" (Mollenkopf 1994, 102). Fiscal malaise and interracial conflict in New York City thus enabled Koch to defeat the liberal Mario Cuomo. Similarly, when fiscal malaise and conflict were evident in other large American cities, they too would make more conservative electoral choices. The difference was that, for many cities, the fiscal crisis and heightened conflict would come much later.

6 Racial Conflict and Retrospective Voting

Republican mayors Rudolph Giuliani and Richard Riordan took office during periods of enormous economic and racial strife, double-digit unemployment, and skyrocketing crime rates. By their reelection campaigns in 1997, however, both mayors had experienced considerable success. Reductions in crime, shrinking unemployment, and robust job growth led to easy reelection victories. Voting patterns from both elections suggest that Riordan was more successful than Giuliani in capitalizing on this success and broadening his base of electoral support. Giuliani's 1997 victory relied on large majorities of white voters, as the preponderance of Latinos and blacks supported his Democratic opponent, Ruth Messinger. Riordan's reelection coalition was substantially more diverse than Giuliani's, with the incumbent winning solid majorities of the white, Latino, and Asian vote. Notably, black leadership and black voters were at odds with the mayors in both cities.

At first blush, these two overwhelming reelection victories in 1997 may appear to represent fairly straightforward cases of popular incumbents reaping the rewards of their successes. Yet even though both incumbents won rather effortlessly, profound racial cleavages continued to characterize these two elections. Racial tensions remained quite high in both cities in 1997, which largely explains the durability of the racial divide, especially between black and white voters.

When incumbents run for reelection, traditional theories of retrospective voting expect incumbent evaluations to be disproportion-

151

ately important to electoral choices among all voters. Furthermore, such theories would predict that voters who generally approved of the incumbent's performance would support reelection whereas those who disapproved would support the challenger (Downs 1957; Key 1966; Fiorina 1981). Group interest theory, however, would still expect the nature of the political context to shape salient voting cues. In a context characterized by low levels of interracial tensions, retrospective evaluations of incumbent performance will likely be powerful predictors of the vote. In a racially charged electoral environment, however, group interests should both influence incumbent evaluations and remain salient voting cues independent of them. What this suggests is that some minority voters who feel that the economy is improving and that the incumbent has been successful in achieving greater safety on the streets will nonetheless support liberal challengers to the extent that they perceive these challengers as better serving their group interests. Similarly, white voters who disapprove of the incumbent candidates may nonetheless continue to vote for them based on a similar racial interest calculus. The main purpose of this chapter is to explore the nature of retrospective voting in a conflictual political context with the expectation that racial interests retain their electoral relevance during periods of intergroup conflict—even in the face of a popular incumbent, economic prosperity, and reduced crime.

The first part of this chapter recounts the mayoral campaigns in New York and Los Angeles in 1997, noting the continuing conflict between these two white mayors and their African-American constituents. Using public opinion data from the New York election, I explore the extent to which racial identities continue to shape voter choices, above and beyond partisanship, ideology, and retrospective evaluations of the mayor. The latter half of this chapter focuses on the growing presence and importance of Latino voters in Los Angeles and New York. The year 1997 proved to be a critical benchmark in the political development of Latinos in Los Angeles and New York. For the first time ever, the relative size of the Latino electorate equaled or surpassed the African-American vote in both of these cities. Furthermore, Latino voters were more politically independent and more receptive to their conservative mayors than were their black counterparts, foreshadowing important changes in the electoral land-scape of the nation's two largest cities.

New York City Politics in 1997: Stability and Change

In 1997 the incumbent New York City mayor, Rudy Giuliani, beat his Democratic opponent, Manhattan borough president Ruth Messinger, by a substantial 57 percent to 41 percent margin. In spite of this lopsided victory, Giuliani's electoral coalition looked much like it had four years prior. Giuliani received 76 percent of the white vote, 20 percent of the black vote (compared to only 5 percent when Dinkins was running), and 43 percent of the Latino vote, a 5 per-centage point increase over 1993 (see table 6.1). Notwithstanding the fact that his opponent was Jewish, Guiliani was even more favored by Jewish voters in 1997 than he was in his previous victory (72 per-cent versus 68 percent).

Part of Giuliani's enhanced appeal most certainly stemmed from his many successes as mayor. As already noted, crime rates and unem-ployment rates in New York City declined rather dramatically during Giuliani's tenure. Simply, the quality of life for many New Yorkers had vastly improved over the past four years, and the mayor's large margin victory must be attributable, in part, to his relatively high approval ratings (66 percent overall).

While the voting behavior of the New York City electorate was largely stable, the more significant changes in 1997 were related to turnout. The overall turnout rate in 1997 was a low 38 percent. The reduced turnout in 1997, however, was not randomly distributed throughout the city. Turnout in black neighborhoods declined the most precipitously, averaging 24 percent. Notable levels of decline in predominantly white neighborhoods were also evident, an average of 21 percent. The vote in Latino neighborhoods was the most resistant to decline and on average only decreased by 16 percent. For the first time in the history of the city, the Latino vote nearly equaled the black vote. Whereas blacks represented almost 30 percent of mayoral voters in 1993, they were only 21 percent of the total electorate in 1997. Equally telling, Latino voters, who were only 12 percent of the electorate in 1993, equaled 20 percent in 1997. While one can only speculate on the reasons for sustained Latino mobilization (in light of the many factors that discouraged turnout among blacks and whites), part of their durability may reflect increasing registration rates in these Latino neighborhoods (up 11 percent from 1993). It seems plausible that Latinos' enhanced status in the governing coalition (relative to the position of blacks) may have been another important reason.

Growing Conflict between Black and Latino Voters in New York

Giuliani's success among Latino voters in 1997 likely reflects both long-term trends and short-term strategy. Latinos in New York, as in

TABLE 6.1.   Comparison of the New York City Mayoral Vote, 1993 and 1997 (in percentages)

| % of voters who are | | | % who voted for | | | |
| | | | 1993 | | 1997 | |
1993	1997		Giuliani	Dinkins	Giuliani	Messinger
		Total	51	49	57	41
		Race/Ethnicity				
56	53	White	77	21	76	21
29	21	Black	5	95	20	79
12	20	Latino	37	60	43	57
		Ideology				
30	33	Liberal	34	65	43	55
43	43	Moderate	56	43	61	38
27	23	Conservative	67	33	72	25
		Party				
61	61	Democrat	33	67	45	54
22	20	Independent	69	31	65	32
17	19	Republican	93	7	92	6
		Religion				
24	24	Protestant	26	74	40	58
45	41	Roman Catholic	69	31	66	32
17	23	Jewish	68	32	72	27

Source: New York Times/CBS Exit Poll, 1989; Voter Research Exit Poll, 1993; Voter News Service Exit Poll, 1997; Edison Media Research Exit Poll, 2001.

many other U.S. cities, have been an important yet typically under-mobilized political constituency. For most of the contemporary period, black voters have outpaced Latinos, both in their electoral activity and in their relative numerical importance to the larger Democratic coalition. Up until 1997, African-Americans had long been considered the most influential minority group within the city, while Latinos had typically been accorded a lesser status. Furthermore, competition between Latino and black leadership throughout the city was not new. In fact, attempts at interminority vote consolidation were often dashed by interminority competition for Democratic votes.

It is quite common for Latino and black candidates to compete against one another in the Democratic primaries, effectively diluting the strength of the minority vote. One classic example of this enduring rivalry came during the 1985 Democratic primary to unseat Ed Koch. Eager to challenge the incumbent mayor and faced with few viable candidate choices, leaders within both the African-American and Latino communities had tentatively agreed to support former Bronx borough president Herman Badillo, a well-known Puerto Rican candidate who had run and lost in several mayoral primaries. Before the Badillo candidacy was announced, however, several prominent black leaders decided not to back him, placing an African-American assemblyman, Herman "Denny" Farrell, on the ballot instead. Badillo, so disillusioned by the regular Democratic establishment, eventually switched parties and became a Republican. To the extent that black leadership was unwilling to put up Latino candidates to the exclusion of their own, and vice versa, Latinos and blacks in New York City were quite accustomed to canceling out each other's minority presence in the final balloting.

David Dinkins's candidacy in 1989 was the first real test of black-Latino solidarity in a mayor's race, and while a large majority of New York City Latinos supported Dinkins (64 percent), a notable 34 percent nonetheless voted for Giuliani. A similar percentage of Latinos (39 percent) supported Giuliani in his 1993 victory. Giuliani, well aware that his future success would hinge on his ability to attract a comparable percentage of minority voters, actively catered to Latino voters while in office. To a large degree, Giuliani's enhanced support

from the Latino community resulted from his explicit efforts at court-
ing them.

The group interests of the black and Latino voters in New York
and elsewhere are somewhat distinctive. Latinos, like blacks, are typically poorer than whites, yet the demands from poor Latinos are often
more particular and less institutional than are the desires of urban
blacks. Similar to that of the white ethnic immigrants who preceded
them, the political agenda of urban Latinos focuses on greater economic and educational opportunities. Unlike blacks, however, there
is typically less concern for the redress of social injustice or for systemic overhaul. The greater ethnic and cultural diversity within the
Latino community further implies less political homogeneity. Thus
for Giuliani, the Latino community appeared to represent greater
coalition-building opportunities than did the black community. The
mayor built working relationships with Latino leaders like Herman
Badillo. And Giuliani's public opposition to state policy proposals to
deny legal immigrants social services during their first year of resi-
dence was most certainly a nod to Latino interests.

The central point of contention between blacks and the Giuliani
administration was over the issue of the police. Giuliani promoted a
larger and more vigilant police force. His crackdown on "quality of
life" offenses such as graffiti and vandalism and on the ubiquitous
"squeegee men" was praised by many New Yorkers. His new and
more aggressive "street crimes unit" was also credited for declining
crime rates; however, many black political leaders argued that reductions in crime were being achieved at the expense of the civil liberties
of poor minorities, blacks in particular. The brutal beating of Haitian
immigrant Abner Louima during Giuliani's first term and the police
shooting of African immigrant Amadou Diallo during Giuliani's second term are two highly publicized examples of the types of incidents
that fueled the continuing political battle between the black community and Giuliani's police force. Since his election in 1993, the mayor,
a former federal prosecutor, had given broad support to the police
and had consistently opposed proposals for their independent oversight. His continuing support of the police force created an impenetrable breach between his administration and leadership in the black
community. In this context, the racial polarization in his support is

quite understandable. White voters and Latinos, to a lesser degree, were willing to accept incidents of police brutality in exchange for a 40 percent decline in the city's crime rate. Black voters apparently were not.

Retrospective Voting and the Persistent Salience of Group Interests in New York

From a group interest perspective, voting in the 1997 New York City mayoral election largely reflects the continuing salience of racial identities in voting behavior. Much like the previous two elections, large numbers of white liberals (54 percent) and white Democrats (45 percent) defected from their otherwise ideological and partisan leanings to support the incumbent Republican mayor, whereas a minority of both blacks (20 percent) and Latinos (43 percent) were similarly moved to defect. To a large degree, these defections appear to coincide with rates of mayoral approval. In general, white voters exhibited the highest approval rates, blacks showed the lowest, and Latinos were somewhere in between (see table 6.2). It is clear that, in spite of the growing economy and declining rates of crime, all groups in the city were not similarly satisfied.

TABLE 6.2. Retrospective Evaluations of the Giuliani
Mayoralty, 1997 (in percentages)

	Whites	Blacks	Latinos
Condition of the City Economy			
Excellent or Good	88	44	47
Quality of Life in NYC			
Better today than four years ago	74	31	43
Safety			
Safer than four years ago	73	36	46
Public Schools			
Worse than four years ago	31	50	44
Police Brutality			
More likely if Giuliani wins	29	68	40

Source: Voter News Service Exit Poll, New York City, November 4, 1997.

Data from exit polling in 1997 clearly indicate a lack of racial and ethnic consensus regarding the success of the Giuliani years, with the largest differences between whites and blacks. The percentage of white voters who judged the local economy as "excellent" or "good" was twice that of black voters (88 percent versus 44 percent). In this case Latinos (47 percent) were more similar in their appraisal of the economy to African-Americans than to whites. Similar patterns are found with regard to assessments of public safety, with white voters being twice as likely as black voters to say the city was safer in 1997 than in 1993. None of these three groups was particularly impressed with Giuliani's record on public schools; 31 percent of white voters thought schools had actually gotten worse compared to almost 50 percent of blacks and 44 percent of Latinos. But, notably, on the question of police brutality, whites and Latinos were in greater accord and black voters were the conspicuous outliers. When asked whether police brutality would be more likely if Giuliani were to continue as mayor, 29 percent of whites and 40 percent of Latinos agreed that it would be more likely, compared to an overwhelming 68 percent of blacks.

The disparity between blacks and Latinos on the question of police brutality may represent differences in the actual levels of police brutality experienced by their respective communities or possibly may reflect the differential salience of police brutality as an important political issue, or perhaps both. Among blacks, the correlation between "quality of life" assessments and beliefs about police brutality is significant ($R = .198$, $p < .01$), whereas for Latinos this correlation is insignificant ($R = .07$), seeming to suggest that questions of racial profiling and police brutality are less important to Latino feelings about Giuliani than they are to blacks.

Group interest theory makes specific predictions about the type of retrospective voting that occurs in a conflictual political context. While traditional theories of retrospective voting suggest that voter choice, particularly partisan or ideological defection, is largely influenced by incumbent evaluations, the group interest perspective has a somewhat different set of expectations. In particular, I argue that racial and ethnic groups will largely support brethren candidates (racial, ethnic, or ideological), sometimes in spite of their incumbent evaluations. Regarding the 1997 mayoral election, this prediction means that some dissatisfied whites will vote for Giuliani anyway based on their perceptions that he will be better for whites. It also means that many blacks and Latinos who think that the city has become a better place to live will nonetheless vote against Giuliani based on their perceived group interests as well. Admittedly, racial and ethnic identities are likely to color overall satisfaction rates. Beyond this, however, I expect that—even when controlling for partisan differences, ideological differences, and approval rate differences among blacks, Latinos, and whites—racial and ethnic differences should retain their significance. To the extent that they do, this is clearly evidence of group distinctive voting.

Using exit poll data from the 1997 New York race, I conducted a logistic regresssion analysis on voter choice. After including measures for party identification, political ideology, and income, I also include four of the five retrospective evaluation measures displayed in table 6.2 (economy, safety, schools, and police brutality). Finally, I include dummy variables for Latinos and blacks, with whites being the excluded category. If racial differences in Giuliani support were simply a direct function of differences in job approval, then the dummy variables should not be significant. To the extent that group-based differences emerge, controlling for all of these factors, one can assume that group-distinctive voting was evident above and beyond normal levels of retrospective voting. (The results of this logistic regression analysis can be found in table A6.1 in the appendix).

The findings in table 6.3 represent a set of voting probabilities derived from the regression results. They strongly support the group interest perspective. First, it is worth noting that party identification and ideology, while statistically significant, are less important predictors of voting than are attitudes regarding the state of the local economy, police brutality, safety, or the black dummy variable. For example, when controlling for all other factors, voters who felt that the city economy was excellent supported Giuliani 31 percentage points more than voters who felt that the economy was poor. By comparison, Republicans were only 19 percentage points more likely to vote for Giuliani than were Democrats. Voters who felt the city was more safe than it had been four years prior were 21 percentage points more inclined to vote for Giuliani than those who found the city less safe, whereas conservatives were only 12 percentage points more favorable toward the incumbent than liberals. Clearly retrospective evaluations of the Giuliani administration were more important influences on voting behavior than were partisanship and ideology.

Second, one should note the relative size and significance of the values for the black and Latino dummy variables. Controlling for a variety of approval measures as well as partisanship, ideology, and income, blacks were still more likely to vote for Messinger by a 28 percentage point margin, as were Latinos by a 15 percentage point margin. Clearly, differences in voting behavior among the various racial and ethnic groups are not fully explained by their respective levels of mayoral approval. Race plainly matters here—above and beyond its probable indirect influence on Giuliani's approval rates.

It is also telling that attitudes regarding police brutality are second only to economic evaluations in their relative importance to voter choice. Voters who anticipated police brutality to be more likely under Giuliani were 29 percentage points less likely to support him than those who felt it would be less likely. To a great degree, this finding both confirms the proposition that racial concerns were a primary orientation for voting behavior and further illustrates the power of this issue to divide the electorate. Whites and Latinos who did not see incidents of police brutality as attributable to Giuliani were much more likely to support him, by 30 and 41 percentage points, respectively. For whites and Latinos concerned by repeated incidents of police brutality under Giuliani, they overwhelmingly supported his opponent, Ruth Messinger (analysis not shown).

Finally, these data illustrate the somewhat greater ambivalence toward Giuliani within the Latino community than among blacks. As explained previously, Giuliani was more solicitous to Latino leadership and Latino voters during his tenure than he was toward blacks. Latinos, under Giuliani, were certainly accorded a more privileged position within the governing coalition than were African-Americans. Latino inclusion under Giuliani (and under Riordan as well) largely came at the expense of previous black empowerment. Yet given the often contentious relationship between blacks and Latinos in New York, it is not surprising that nearly half of the Latino community

TABLE 6.3. Estimated Probability of a Giuliani Vote, 1997

Variable	All Voters
Party identification	
Democrat	.50
Republican	.69
Difference	*.19**
Ideology	
Liberal	.50
Conservative	.62
Difference	*.12**
City economic condition	
Poor	.37
Excellent	.68
Difference	*.31**
Safety of NYC over past four years	
Less safe	.39
More safe	.60
Difference	*.21**
New York City public schools over past four years	
Worse today	.47
Better today	.66
Difference	*.19**
Police brutality under Giuliani	
More likely	.43
Less likely	.72
Difference	*.29**
Black vs. white	
Black	.33
White	.61
Difference	*.28**
Latino vs. white	
Latino	.44
White	.59
Difference	*.15**

Source: New York City, Voter News Service Exit Poll, 1997.

Note: Cell entries represent the estimated probability of a Giuliani vote. The author's calculations are based on logistic regression results found in table A6.1 in the appendix.

*$p < .05$. An income variable was also included in this multivariate analysis. Results were statistically insignificant and are not displayed.

showed its approval of this newfound status by supporting the incumbent mayor. This too is a reflection of group interest.

Expanding the Coalition in Los Angeles: Riordan's 1997 Reelection

The circumstances surrounding Richard Riordan's election in 1997 were in many ways similar to those in New York. Much like Giuliani, Riordan had taken over the helm of city government during a period of economic retrenchment. By 1997 the city economy was on the mend, jobs were coming back to the city, and the crime rate had declined. In spite of the improving local economy, racial tensions still ran high. The O. J. Simpson criminal and civil trials continued to fan the flames of racial discord for most of Riordan's first term, and Riordan's lack of support for the black chief of police, Willie Williams, was another source of conflict.

The pattern of support for Riordan in Los Angeles is strikingly similar to Giuliani's in New York. Only in this case, Riordan was *more* successful in attracting Latino support than was Giuliani. Certainly part of Riordan's success among Latinos can be attributed to his conscious inclusion of Latinos in his administration and his personal generosity to many schools and community groups in Latino neighborhoods. As important as these factors may have been, Riordan's commitment to children and to education was additionally appealing to Latinos. Educational reforms had been a centerpiece of Riordan's mayoral agenda. While having no statutory control over the massive Los Angeles Unified School District (LAUSD), Riordan nonetheless focused much of his personal political energies on resuscitating the languishing Los Angeles schools. The LEARN program and the push for more charter schools in Los Angeles are largely attributed to Riordan's efforts. Latinos make up approximately 70 percent of the LAUSD, and education is typically a top priority among Latino voters. Thus Riordan's success in attracting Latino support can be credited to both personal and political choices that he made while mayor. Furthermore, Riordan was able to build political alliances with many prominent Latino leaders, and his 1997 endorsements from council members Richard Alatorre and Richard Alarcon most certainly gave the mayor additional credibility in Latino neighborhoods.

Riordan was much less successful in building a following in the black community. His lack of support for then police chief Willie Williams was particularly alienating to black voters. Williams had been hired in the wake of the riots and after former police chief Daryl Gates resigned. Riordan and Williams had strained relations throughout Williams's tenure, and his firing was perceived by many blacks as a power grab to replace Williams with a more accommodating chief. Support for Williams was so high in the black community that his reappointment was listed among the top three most important issues facing the city—behind crime and education but ahead of jobs (*Los Angeles Times,* March 30, 1997). In spite of this vocal opposition from the black community, Williams was fired, and Riordan was held accountable.

Mayoral Voting in Los Angeles in 1997

Riordan's opponent in 1997 was Democratic state senator Tom Hayden.[1] Hayden's record was a laundry list of liberal causes, and his political objective was to revitalize the Bradley coalition of white liberals, blacks, and Latinos. While Hayden was successful in appealing to black voters, he was not able to attract meaningful numbers of white or Latino voters and was beaten by a margin of 61 percent to 35 percent in the low turnout, at-large primary.

A comparison of the 1993 and 1997 mayoral votes is found in table 6.4. The findings from this comparison suggest that Riordan's electoral coalition had expanded considerably since his first term. Riordan's electoral support in 1993 came predominantly from white voters, while his opponent, Michael Woo, received majorities of the black, Latino, and Asian vote. In 1997 Riordan captured large majorities among whites, Latinos, and Asians, and his only electoral weakness was among black voters. Given the heightened racial ten-

---

1. Given the absence of appropriate survey data, I am not able to replicate the New York City analysis for the 1997 Los Angeles election.

TABLE 6.4. Comparison of the Los Angeles Mayoral Vote, 1993 and 1997 (in percentages)

% of voters who are			1993		1997	
			Voters for Riordan	Voters for Woo	Voters for Riordan	Voters for Hayden
1993	1997					
		Total	54	46	61	35
		Race/Ethnicity				
72	65	White	67	33	71	26
12	13	Black	14	86	19	75
10	15	Latino	43	57	60	33
4	4	Asian	31	69	62	35
		Ideology				
30	27	Liberal	27	73	33	62
43	47	Moderate	63	37	66	30
27	26	Conservative	79	21	81	16
22	—	White liberal	31	69	—	—
31	—	White moderate	75	25	—	—
20	—	White conservative	92	8	—	—
		Party				
63	60	Democrat	39	61	47	49
6	7	Independent	70	30	58	34
30	31	Republican	91	9	91	7
		Income				
14	16	Under $20K	42	58	53	42
25	24	$20K to 39,999	52	48	54	41
22	23	$40K to 59,999	60	40	62	34
39	37	$60K and up	62	38	67	30
		Religion				
39	37	Protestant	63	37	64	32
24	28	Roman Catholic	63	37	65	31
19	15	Jewish	49	51	71	26
		Region				
18	18	Westside	55	45	64	33
44	42	San Fernando Valley	71	29	74	22
21	22	Central L.A.	40	60	55	41
17	18	South L.A.	27	73	35	61

Source: Los Angeles Times Exit Poll, June 1993 and June 1997.

sions in the city and the declining relative importance of the black vote, Riordan did not risk alienating the numerically important white vote by accommodating the political demands of blacks. Furthermore, as he was able to bolster his support within the increasingly mobilized Latino community, black votes were not necessary to sustain his electoral viability.

Like the mayoral contest in New York that same year, the 1997 mayoral election in Los Angeles drew an extremely low citywide turnout, and declining turnout was especially prevalent among white and black voters. Latino participation as a percentage of the total electorate was a record 15 percent, and for the first time Latinos outnumbered black voters at the polls. The increasing importance of Latino voters in Los Angeles and New York reflects both demographic and political trends. In New York, the Latino community is close in size to the black community but has been typically accorded less political clout due to the relatively low participation rates of Latinos compared to blacks. In Los Angeles as of the 1990 census, Latinos represented 40 percent of the city population yet traditionally participated in low numbers as well. Blacks, representing only 14 percent of the city of Los Angeles, amassed disproportionately high levels of political incorporation because of the high rates of mobilization within the black community during much of the 1970s and 1980s. Turnout differences between blacks and Latinos in both cities traditionally rendered blacks a more desirable coalition partner. The confluence of increasing Latino mobilization and a decline in black turnout may have dire consequences for future black incorporation in both of these cities. At a minimum, it is safe to say that the enhanced political importance of these growing Latino communities provides a substantial source of intergroup conflict between previously empowered black voters and their newly invigorated Latino counterparts. Furthermore, and also significant, the relative political independence of Latino voters creates a broader range of coalitional prospects than has been traditionally available to black voters in these two cities.

Conclusion

Lessons learned from the 1997 elections clearly reinforce the premise that high levels of perceived racial conflict shape voter behavior. With continuing racial discord in both New York and Los Angeles, the majority of white voters (including white Democrats) stuck with their Republican mayors, while black voters overwhelmingly favored their Democratic opponents. Latinos in both cities were less solidly Democratic than they had been in prior years, and Los Angeles Latinos in particular backed their incumbent mayor in record numbers.

All four of the candidates in these 1997 races were white, and it appeared that minority leadership in both cities was in considerable disarray. As the combined size of the black and Latino electorates continued to grow in both cities, there were few indicators that these voters would come together and seriously challenge the white establishment for control of city hall. Latinos, so long dismissed as non-voters, showed up in record numbers, even in elections that by all accounts were never close. For the first time, black and Latino voters made up almost half of these cities' electorates, yet there seemed no guarantee that they would become a united political force. As the winds of change fell upon both cities, and as Latino candidates came to the forefront of mayoral politics in 2001, new alliances seemed inevitable.

7 Down but Not Out: A Liberal Revival in 2001

By 2001 the political context in New York and Los Angeles had changed considerably. Sustained economic growth in both cities resulted in new jobs, municipal solvency, and diminished public concern over crime. The palpable racial conflict of the earlier period had largely subsided, except for continuing episodes of police misconduct that largely legitimated liberal concerns over abuses targeted at minority communities. Term limits in both cities meant that new leadership at city hall was imminent and further created opportunities for a Democratic revival in these two Republican-led cities. Los Angeles voters elected James Hahn—a liberal Democrat and former city attorney—to replace the retiring Riordan. New York also appeared to be on the brink of electing a Democrat to replace the incumbent Giuliani but, in the wake of the attacks on September 11, instead chose the Republican Michael Bloomberg over the liberal Democrat Mark Green. Nonetheless, both of these elections illustrate the potent influence that diminishing levels of black-white conflict have on voting behavior—especially on that of white voters.

The Los Angeles case, in particular, stands out as an excellent example of how the mayoral choices of white voters were less shaped by racial attitudes than they had been in the prior two elections. Palpable levels of racial conflict had declined over the past four years and, in this more congenial context white voters were much more supportive of liberal and Democratic candidates. The notable friction in this election, was between black and Latino voters, who backed different candidates in the general election. A growing Latino elec-

167

torate, faced with the possibility of new Latino leadership in city hall, rallied behind a native son, the former speaker of the state assembly, Antonio Villaraigosa. African-American voters, however, largely preferred the other Democratic candidate in the runoff for mayor, city attorney James Hahn. Race still mattered in this election, just not in the same way that it had mattered in 1993.

This chapter explores the most recent 2001 mayoral elections in Los Angeles and New York with an eye to how changes in the political context—in particular, declining black-white hostilities—affected the outcomes of these mayoral contests. Clearly, Democratic dominance in the 2001 Los Angeles mayoral election rebuts the notion that urban liberalism had permanently lost its electoral cache. What enabled James Hahn and Antonio Villaraigosa to win the top two spots in the nonpartisan primary were the same factors that had derailed Mike Woo's chances in 1993, just in reverse. Political context matters, and the Los Angeles election, in particular, illustrates the extent to which declining levels of black-white conflict resulted in less racialized voting—particularly among whites.

The 2001 elections are also notable for the apparently ruptured Democratic coalitions in both cities—between blacks and Latinos in Los Angeles and between minorities and white Democrats in New York. Changing demographics in American cities, in particular growing numbers of racial and ethnic minorities, can increase the potential for intergroup conflict, and the recent clashes between blacks and Latinos for power in Los Angeles are an apt illustration. As the size of Latino populations continues to outpace the relative proportion of black populations in many American cities, and as Latino political mobilization continues to expand, the potential for conflict between these two important minority communities will certainly increase (McClain and Karnig 1990; Waldinger 1995; Bobo and Hutchings 1996; Cruz 2000; McClain and Tauber 2001; Kaufmann 2003). The conclusion of the chapter focuses on the tension between black and Latino voters, especially in Los Angeles, as blacks strive to maintain their relevance within the traditional Democratic coalitions while Latinos push for greater levels of incorporation.

Back to Future—The Elections of 2001

In many ways the 1997 mayoral elections foreshadowed new electoral cleavages that would emerge in 2001. In particular, Latino participation increased in both cities, equaling the black vote for the first time in New York City and eclipsing blacks as the largest voting minority in Los Angeles. In the 1997 election in New York, 57 percent of Latinos voted for the Democratic candidate, Messinger. But in Los Angeles, 60 percent of Latino voters embraced their Republican mayor, evidence of growing independence from their long-term but tenuous electoral coalition with black voters. In 2001, Latinos and blacks in Los Angeles continued to support different candidates for mayor, placing white voters in the important position of a swing constituency. Had black voters in 2001 supported the Latino candidate, Antonio Villaraigosa, Los Angeles would now likely have its first Latino mayor in over one hundred years. In this case it was the electoral split between blacks and Latinos that largely foiled Latino mayoral aspirations. Nonetheless, Los Angeles voters elected the other liberal Democrat in the nonpartisan runoff, James Hahn, to replace the term-limited Riordan.

The 2001 Los Angeles mayoral election was in so many ways a marked contrast to the two preceding elections. Not only were the top two vote getters in the open primary liberal Democrats, but almost 70 percent of the primary electorate supported Democrats of one stripe or another, including 53 percent of white primary voters. Steven Soboroff, Riordan's hand-picked successor, finished out of the money in third place.

In part, the notably liberal leanings of the primary electorate reflect the dramatic demographic changes that continue in Los Angeles. As of the 2000 census, Latinos constitute almost half of Los Angeles residents, while non-Hispanic whites make up only 30 percent. Equally important, the Democratic revival in Los Angeles mayoral politics represents a striking example of how important racial conflict (or the diminution thereof) and political context are to voter choices. In an ironic twist, Riordan's successes in Los Angeles—declining crime rates, rapid job growth, fiscal solvency, and declining racial friction—

created a near ideal context for a resurgence of liberalism, especially among the city's white voters.

A Democratic Revival—Los Angeles in the Spring of 2001

The mood in Los Angeles in the spring of 2001 had changed a great deal since Richard Riordan took office eight years prior. Compared with the widespread angst and dissatisfaction so prevalent in 1993, Los Angeles voters of all stripes were remarkably contented at the beginning of the 2001 mayoral campaign. (Only 36 percent of voters saw Los Angeles as being on the "wrong track" in 2001, compared to 71 percent who felt that things were going badly in the city in 1993.) The popular fear of crime and social disorder that prevailed in the wake of the 1992 riots had become a distant memory for many Angelenos, and primary candidates struggled to find a set of pressing political issues upon which to launch a campaign. For the first time in recent history, voters—to the extent that they were paying any attention to politics—appeared focused on a relatively narrow political agenda. Peace and prosperity in the eternal boomtown had returned.

Yet in spite of the city's relative complacence, term limits created new opportunities for political leadership. The nonpartisan open primary in 2001 elicited six strong contenders for the mayoralty: Joel Wachs (I), a city councilman; Steven Soboroff (R), a businessman; Kathleen Connell (D), the state controller; Antonio Villaraigosa (D), former speaker of the state assembly; Xavier Becerra (D), a congressman; and James Hahn (D), the city attorney. Early indicators suggested that Villaraigosa, Hahn, and Soboroff would vie for the top two spots. Hahn, coming from a popular and well-known political family in Los Angeles, was expected to be the front-runner. Soboroff, while relatively unknown to the mass electorate, had both considerable financial resources and Riordan's backing. Villaraigosa, who had never held citywide office in Los Angeles, was also considered a likely front-runner given the large Latino voter presence in previous elections, his endorsement from long-time county supervisor Gloria Molina, and his financial backing from a variety of high-profile labor unions. Given the wide range of Democratic choices and the presence of two Latinos in the top six, some Democrats feared that Villaraigosa and Becerra would split the Latino vote, enabling Soboroff, the lone Republican in the race, to finish in the top two. But in spite of Riordan's relatively high approval ratings, the mayor proved to have no coattails, as Soboroff did not make it out of the primaries.

Soboroff, much like Riordan eight years earlier, focused his campaign on creating jobs and combating crime. The Westside businessman whose previous political experience included heading the Department of Parks and Recreation argued that his business background would make him an advantageous leader during the economic hard times that he foresaw as coming soon. Soboroff also distanced himself from the other primary candidates by insisting that too much attention had been paid to police misconduct while not enough attention had been paid to criminal misconduct. Soboroff, like Riordan before him, campaigned on his uncompromising crime stance. But, given the political context in 2001, his urgent call for more vigilant crime prevention was not met with a similar response. Voters were not looking to overhaul Downtown practices. They were not angry and combative. So in this more conciliatory climate, Soboroff was unable to get any political traction from his firm policies on crime.

The other moderate candidates in the race—Kathleen Connell and Joel Wachs—were similarly unsuccessful in their election strategies. Connell, the fiscal watchdog, and Wachs, who railed against special interests and their disproportionate influence at city hall, both attempted to alert the voting public of impending crises. But like Soboroff, they were unable to agitate a self-satisfied electorate into a new frame of mind. As much as campaign consultants and their clients might like to manufacture electoral climates that work to their advantage, real circumstances such as low unemployment rates and low crime rates are rarely overshadowed by clever strategy. As noted by Jaime Regalado, the executive director of the Pat Brown Institute of Public Affairs at California State University, Los Angeles, "It's hard to get a real feel for the pulse of the city. We've had relatively good times. Ethnic tension is at a low. It doesn't mean things are hunky-dory, but people are fairly content" (*Los Angeles Times,* March 22, 2001).

When the votes were counted, Villaraigosa finished in first place

with 30 percent of the primary votes. Hahn finished in second place
with 25 percent of the vote. As indicated in table 7.1, Villaraigosa
built a diverse electoral coalition attracting 23 percent of the white
vote, 62 percent of the Latino vote, 23 percent of the Asian vote, and
a scant 12 percent of the African-American vote. Hahn's largest base
of support came from the black community, where he had received
numerous endorsements from African-American leaders. Hahn had
grown up in this community where his father, Kenneth Hahn, had
served for forty years as a county supervisor, retiring in 1992. African-
American allegiance to Hahn most likely reflected the respect and
devotion that many felt for Hahn's father, who had been on the front
lines of the civil rights movement in Los Angeles long before it had
become fashionable or politically wise for whites to do so. Hahn's
solid support in the black community placed him in a uniquely advantageous position in the runoff, given that his opponent was a minority candidate. Hahn was likely to garner the vast majority of the black
vote in the runoff while Villaraigosa was expected to receive an over-

TABLE 7.1.   Los Angeles Nonpartisan Open Primary Results, April 10,
2001 (in percentages)

		% who voted for					
% of voters		Villariagosa	Hahn	Soboroff	Wachs	Becerra	Connell
	Total	30	25	21	11	6	5
	Race/Ethnicity						
52	White	23	19	30	17	3	6
14	Black	12	71	5	3	2	4
20	Latino	62	7	8	3	17	2
4	Asian	23	32	25	5	5	10
	Ideology						
47	Liberal	41	24	8	12	7	6
27	Moderate	23	29	23	13	4	5
26	Conservative	17	22	43	8	5	4
	Religion						
33	Protestant	19	37	23	9	4	5
30	Catholic	40	17	21	6	12	3
16	Jewish	26	16	27	22	1	7

Source: Los Angeles Times Primary Exit Poll, April 10, 2001.

whelming majority of Latino votes. With 56 percent of the white primary voters casting their vote for one of the losing candidates, the clear issue in this election would be which of these liberal Democrats could capture the moderate and conservative white votes.

Given the political context surrounding the Los Angeles mayoral primary in 2001—widespread satisfaction with the condition of the city and relatively little racial discord—it is not surprising that two liberal Democrats, Antonio Villaraigosa and James Hahn, topped the primary field. Similar to four years earlier, Democrats continued to outnumber Republicans by a margin of two to one. Equally important, Los Angeles voters had also become substantially more liberal over the past four years. Exit poll data suggest that the proportion of self-identified liberal voters had increased from 27 percent in 1997 to 47 percent in 2001 (*Los Angeles Times* Exit Polls, April 1997 and April 2001). This increase not only is a function of the changing racial and ethic demographics of the electorate but also reflects a rather profound increase in the liberal leanings of white voters, as 49 percent of whites identified themselves as liberal in 2001 compared to 29 percent in 1993 (*Los Angeles Times* Exit Polls, June 1993 and June 2001).

Election results in the 2001 primary clearly illustrate the declining significance of racial resentment as an important voting cue, especially among whites. Both 1993 and 2001 public opinion surveys include a question regarding the relative attention paid to blacks and other minority groups by local public officials. A comparison of public opinion from these two election years is found in table 7.2. Declining white tensions over race relations are illustrated by the increasing proportion of white voters who think that racial minorities receive the right amount of attention—52 percent in 2001 compared to 34 percent in 1993. Corresponding with this increased satisfaction with racial accommodation, liberal sentiments that racial minorities receive too little attention and conservative opinion that minorities receive too much attention both decreased by 10 percentage points. Equally telling, the correlation between this racial attitude measure and the white vote declined by more than half from .33 ($p < .01$) in 1993 to .15 ($p < .01$) in 2001. In all, the increasing comfort among whites with levels of public accommodation of racial and ethnic minorities,

TABLE 7.2.   Comparing Public Opinion in Los Angeles, May 1993 versus May 2001 (in percentages)

Does City Government Pay Too Much Attention to Minorities?

	1993			2001		
	Too Much	Right Amount	Not Enough	Too Much	Right Amount	Not Enough
Whites (*N* = 663/587)	23	34	44	13	52	34
Blacks (*N* = 192/277)	3	16	81	4	26	70
Latinos (*N* = 218/515)	11	25	65	5	34	61

Source: Los Angeles Times Pre-mayoral Election Polls, May 8–10, 1993, and May 22–27, 2001.

Note: Cells do not add to 100% because "not sure" response is not shown.

coupled with the declining political importance of these attitudes, aptly supports the group conflict theory and the importance it places on political context and voter choice. As much as any other example, the 2001 mayoral primary in Los Angeles illustrates the fluidity of voting behavior as conditioned by changes in the larger political and social context.[1]

Blacks and Latinos in Los Angeles Politics

According to the 2000 census, Latinos represent more than 46 percent of Los Angeles residents, while the proportion of whites and blacks has declined precipitously (from 1990) to 30 percent and 11 percent, respectively. And while blacks and whites continue to participate politically at levels that exceed their numerical presence, Latinos most certainly will become an ever more important political force in Los Angeles politics.

Los Angeles folklore credits Tom Bradley's 1973 election and his long reign as mayor to a coalition of blacks, Westside liberals, and Latinos that constituted his core supporters. Factually correct, this

---

1. Ideally, I would have liked to replicate the multivariate analyses from the previous chapters using survey data from the 2001 election. Given the timing of the Los Angeles Times Survey, the number of participants in the primary elections, and the selection of available questions, it simply was not possible.

happy tale of liberal alliance tends to overstate the political commit-ment of the Bradley regime to Los Angeles Latinos and vice versa. For most of the Bradley era, Latinos represented a small and poorly mobilized political community that constituted less than 10 percent of actual voters and Latino political leaders were largely excluded from positions of real political power. In fact, it took legal challenges from the U.S. Justice Department in the 1980s and the Mexican American Legal Defense and Educational Fund (MALDEF) in the 1990s to force redistricting that would allow for Latino representa-tion on local city and county governing bodies.

In addition, several statewide referenda during the 1990s such as Proposition 187, which favored restricting social services and educa-tion from illegal immigrants, and Proposition 227, which sought to abolish bilingual education in California public schools, are credited for increasing rates of naturalization among eligible immigrants and heightened mobilization activity within Latino neighborhoods. On balance these new Latino voters were disproportionately Democra-tic. Nonetheless, Latinos and blacks were quite divided over these politically contentious referenda, with narrow majorities of black voters supporting both. The absence of minority solidarity over the fate of illegal immigrants and support for bilingual education appears to have been a harbinger of things to come. At a minimum, minor-ity opinions on these referenda were clearly split, illustrating the somewhat divergent interests of African-Americans and Latinos in California.

As mentioned previously, Riordan was well liked within the Latino community. There were several high-profile Latinos and Latinas in his administration, such as Linda Griego and Rocky Delgadillo, and Riordan's political agenda catered to many Latino interests. Under Riordan, Latinos were placed in an advantaged position relative to the black community, and this was arguably the first time in the con-temporary era that this had been so. Riordan even went so far as to endorse Antonio Villaraigosa over his opponent, James Hahn, in the mayoral runoff. And while the mayor may have been unsuccessful in attracting incremental moderate white support for the Latino candi-date, his endorsement was nonetheless a powerful affirmation of his commitment to his Latino constituents.

Prior to Riordan's election in 1993, Latinos had been the perpetual bridesmaids of Los Angeles politics during a period of time when black power not only grew but in some cases became institutionally entrenched. Thus the political ascendancy of Latinos during the 1990s, coupled with the diminution of black power, created a potentially discordant backdrop for the political contest of 2001. Eighty percent of black voters supported city attorney James Hahn, while 82 percent of Latinos supported Villaraigosa. And while Hahn's unique background (the son of Kenneth Hahn) may explain a good portion of the polarization between blacks and Latinos in this contest, the lack of black support for Villaraigosa should not be solely attributed to the particulars of the Hahn family tree.

Blacks and Latinos were clearly competing for a dominant position in the city's governing coalition, and preelection polling data suggest that these groups were somewhat suspicious of each other's candidates and their respective commitments to minority issues (see table 7.3). Among white voters, 23 percent worried that Villaraigosa would pay too much attention to minority concerns if elected, although they were not so concerned about Hahn. Among blacks, 18 percent thought that Villaraigosa would pay too much attention to minorities, compared to only 8 percent among Latinos. On the other side of this equation, both blacks and Latinos showed concern that neither of these candidates would pay enough attention to minority issues. This

TABLE 7.3.   Public Opinion in Los Angeles, May 2001 (in percentages)

Will Villaraigosa/Hahn Pay Too Much Attention to Minorities?

	Villaraigosa			Hahn		
	Too Much	Right Amount	Not Enough	Too Much	Right Amount	Not Enough
Whites (*N* = 806)	23	56	9	6	56	19
Blacks (*N* = 231)	18	51	11	3	60	23
Latinos (*N* = 417)	8	68	14	3	45	27
Asians (*N* = 105)	17	63	2	1	60	21

Source: *Los Angeles Times* Pre-mayoral Election Poll, May 22–27, 2001.
Note: Cells do not add to 100% because "not sure" response is not shown.

worry was particularly pronounced for Hahn, as 23 percent of blacks and 27 percent of Latinos indicated reservations that he may not pay sufficient attention to minority communities and their needs.

Another point of contention between the African-American and Latino communities has continued to be the issue of immigration. As described earlier, Los Angeles has experienced profound demographic changes over the past twenty years, with the growth in the Latino population seriously outpacing growth among other racial and ethnic groups. Among middle-class white voters, anxiety over immigration tends to flare during periods of economic retrenchment, as was evidenced quite clearly during the early 1990s. For African-Americans in Los Angeles, however, tensions over immigration issues are persistently salient, given the ongoing competition between immigrant Latinos and lower-income blacks for jobs and housing in the city.

As demonstrated in table 7.4, Latinos and Asians, both heavily immigrant communities, tend to see immigration and its impact on the city in a more favorable light than do either whites or African-Americans. Among these four groups, blacks have the most negative perceptions of immigration, with almost one-half saying that it is a "bad or very bad" thing for the city. In contrast, only one-third of Latinos and Asians express these negative sentiments, while 39 percent of whites see immigration as, on balance, bad for the city. African-American anxiety over immigration is yet another example of

TABLE 7.4. Public Opinion about Immigration in Los Angeles, May 2001 (in percentages)

Is Immigration a Good or a Bad Thing for Los Angeles?

	Good	No Effect	Bad
Whites ($N = 815$)	34	26	39
Blacks ($N = 231$)	28	24	48
Latinos ($N = 418$)	44	23	34
Asians ($N = 97$)	41	26	34

Source: Los Angeles Times Pre-mayoral Election Poll, May 22–27, 2001.
Note: Cells do not add to 100% due to rounding error.

the competitive pressures that exist between blacks and Latinos in the city. Many of the traditionally black neighborhoods in Los Angeles are now predominantly Latino. Even Watts, the historic site of the 1965 race riots, is transitioning to a chiefly Latino neighborhood.

> Louis Smith, 67, a black retired city worker, was 31 when the Watts riot erupted. . . . Now, he's among those watching control over Watts shifting to Latinos. "They are taking it over," he said, standing in front of the El Bethel Missionary Baptist Church, which, he noted, is one of the few African American institutions remaining in the area. "In the overall picture, Hispanics are taking over the whole of Los Angeles." (Edsall 2001)

Neighborhood transition and anxiety over immigration are clearly linked within the black community. And increasing Latino aspirations for political incorporation may serve to exacerbate the sense that "they are taking over." Leaders within the African-American community have become very accustomed to being the political voice of disenfranchised minorities in the city. But as Latinos and their leaders find their own independent voices, will they be embraced by their African-American counterparts? Or will concern over their own shrinking political influence and numerical presence create even greater barriers between these two communities? Given both the material and symbolic group interests at stake in Los Angeles, growing clashes between Latinos and African-Americans seem all too likely.

The Runoff: Hahn versus Villaraigosa, 2001

On paper, the two liberal Democrats, Villaraigosa and Hahn, showed broad agreement on a variety of political issues in the 2001 mayoral race; thus it was incumbent upon the candidates to find ways to distinguish themselves in efforts to secure votes. Sixty-five percent of liberal voters had already committed to one or the other of these candidates in the open primary, leaving Hahn and Villaraigosa to battle it out for the moderate and conservative white voters, whose candidates were no longer in the race. It was particularly important to attract voters in the more conservative and disproportionately white San Fernando Valley, which constitutes over 40 percent of the Los Angeles electorate.

Hahn's strategy was to paint Villaraigosa as soft on crime, using Villaraigosa's voting record in the California Assembly to substantiate these claims. Villaraigosa, on the other hand, pointed to Hahn's poor record as city attorney in prosecuting the police misconduct that had erupted into an enormous scandal in the years prior to this election. The Rampart Division of the LAPD, located in the San Fernando Valley, was enmeshed in a police corruption scandal of enormous proportion, with hundreds of reported cases of police officers planting evidence, harming suspects, and otherwise going outside the bounds of the law. The majority of the suspected criminals who had been mistreated by the Rampart officers were Latinos living in the Valley (as were the officers), and Villaraigosa's call for greater police accountability was expected to play well among his Latino constituency. This issue was also very important to Los Angeles's white liberal community, but it fell largely on the deaf ears of San Fernando Valley whites, who were arguably more concerned with controlling crime than with civil rights abuses within the police force. Villaraigosa had also hoped to attract African-American voters with this message, as historically they too had felt victimized by the practices of the LAPD. Perhaps because this latest round of police investigations pertained primarily to Latino suspects, or perhaps because African-American allegiance to Hahn was so intransigent, Villaraigosa's call for greater police accountability made few inroads into the black vote.

Outgoing mayor Richard Riordan endorsed Villaraigosa over Hahn, and the Villaraigosa camp hoped that his endorsement would help win votes among moderate and conservative Angelenos. But the Riordan endorsement did little to boost Villaraigosa's appeal to these groups; less than two weeks before the June election, the *Los Angeles Times* (March 29, 2001) reported that Hahn was running slightly ahead in the polls—47 percent to 40 percent with 13 percent still undecided.

The crowning blow to the Villaraigosa campaign, however, came from a television ad run by Hahn.

In a television advertisement that juxtaposes grainy images of Mr. Villaraigosa with video of a crack pipe and a razor blade cutting cocaine, Mr. Hahn's camp has questioned Mr. Villaraigosa's 1996 letter supporting clemency for a convicted drug dealer whose sentence was commuted by former President Bill Clinton in his final hours in office, and concludes by saying, "Los Angeles can't trust Antonio Villaraigosa." (Purdum 2001)

The ad, which blanketed the airwaves in the few weeks prior to the runoff, was devastating to Villaraigosa. Not only had Hahn revealed an embarrassing lack of judgment on Villaraigosa's part, but he managed to undermine the ethical, nonracial image that Villaraigosa had worked so diligently to amass.[2] Harkening back to the 1969 politics of Sam Yorty (whose ad asked, "Will Your City Be Safe With This Man?"), Hahn's ad appeared to be particularly effective among white moderates and conservatives, and he went on to a rather easy victory, beating Villaraigosa 54 percent to 46 percent (see table 7.5).

Wither the Black-Latino Alliance?

By campaign's end, 80 percent of African-Americans cast their vote for James Hahn while 82 percent of Latinos supported Villaraigosa. A large majority of white voters (59 percent) backed Hahn; nonetheless, Villaraigosa was able to garner 41 percent of the white vote—8 percentage points better than Woo in 1993 and 15 points better than Tom Hayden in 1997. Villaraigosa was able to capture narrow majorities of both the Democratic and Independent voters, but Hahn successfully attracted almost 80 percent of Los Angeles Republicans, essentially handing him the victory. Clearly, if Villaraigosa had been able to attract a larger percentage of the African-American vote he would have won the election, and in postelection commentary many

---

2. Villaraigosa was one of many high-profile Angelenos who had made appeals on behalf of Carlos Vignali, the convicted drug dealer. Vignali's other supporters included the Catholic Archbishop Roger Mahony; the Los Angeles county sheriff, Lee Baca; and Hahn's most notable Latino backer, State Senator Richard Polanco. Villaraigosa, who might have countered Hahn's negative ad with one of his own, took the high road on this one and made little effort to rebut these charges.

TABLE 7.5. Comparing the Los Angeles Mayoral Vote, 1993–2001 (in percentages)

				% who voted for					
				1993		1997		2001	
% of voters who are									
1993	1997	2001		Riordan	Woo	Riordan	Hayden	Hahn	Villaraigosa
			Total	54	46	61	35	54	46
			Race/Ethnicity						
72	65	52	White	67	33	71	26	59	41
12	13	17	Black	14	86	19	75	80	20
10	15	22	Latino	43	57	60	33	18	82
4	4	6	Asian	31	69	62	35	65	35
			Ideology						
30	27	49	Liberal	27	73	33	62	41	59
43	47	29	Moderate	63	37	66	30	62	38
27	26	22	Conservative	79	21	81	16	73	27
22	—	26	White liberal	31	69	—	—	38	62
31	—	15	White moderate	75	25	—	—	71	29
20	—	12	White conservative	92	8	—	—	88	12
			Party						
63	60	70	Democrat	39	61	47	49	48	52
6	7	8	Independent	70	30	58	34	48	52
30	31	20	Republican	91	9	91	7	79	21
			Income						
14	16	11	Under $20K	42	58	53	42	47	53
25	24	19	$20K to 39,999	52	48	54	41	54	46
22	23	18	$40K to 59,999	60	40	62	34	52	48
39	37	52	$60K and up	62	38	67	30	57	43
			Religion						
39	37	32	Protestant	63	37	64	32	69	31
24	28	28	Roman Catholic	63	37	65	31	40	60
19	15	18	Jewish	49	51	71	26	54	46
			Region						
18	18	18	Westside	55	45	64	33	48	52
44	42	42	San Fernando Valley	71	29	74	22	55	45
21	22	21	Central L.A.	40	60	55	41	42	58
17	18	19	South L.A.	27	73	35	61	67	33

Source: Los Angeles Times Exit Poll, June 1993, June 1997, June 2001.

have suggested that, apart from Hahn's somewhat idiosyncratic link to the black community, Villaraigosa would have been popular there. As noted by Harold Meyerson (2001), long-time Los Angeles political observer and former executive editor of *L.A. Weekly*,

> By any number of standards, Mr. Villaraigosa should have been the logical recipient of black support. He helped form the city's Black-Latino roundtable some 20 years ago, and as president of the city's chapter of the American Civil Liberties Union had been a champion of police reform, normally (though not this year) a defining issue in black Los Angeles. He did win the backing of the city's younger black political leaders, but the older leaders, and voters, stuck with Kenny Hahn's son. Too much can be read into this rift, though. Four years ago, black Los Angeles supported a white candidate—and four years before that, an Asian candidate—against Mayor Richard Riordan, a Republican. Had Mr. Villaraigosa been running against a Republican, he would have won South-Central going away. (A25)

Further evidence to support this premise can be found in a down-ballot race for city attorney, where a Latino, Rocky Delgadillo, defeated a white councilman, Mike Feuer, capturing 59 percent of the black vote. In this case, the African-American support for Delgadillo must certainly be interpreted as a show of minority solidarity, as Delgadillo, a deputy mayor in the Riordan administration, was the moderate in this race running against the outspokenly liberal Feuer. Had this vote hinged on shared political ideology, Feuer would likely have been more successful among blacks than he was.

Having said all of this, it is still quite likely that African-American Los Angeles and Latino Los Angeles will clash in the future. It is one thing for blacks to support Latino candidates in down-ballot races. There are numerous instances around the country where minority candidates are successful in attracting diverse coalitions for lower-level office, only to be faced with a racialized response when they attempt to run for highly salient offices such as mayor. That black Angelenos embraced Delgadillo as city attorney against his white,

Jewish opponent, Michael Feuer, in no way guarantees that African-Americans will automatically support Latinos running for mayor. Meyerson is probably correct that, had Villaraigosa run against a Republican, he would have been the first choice among African-Americans, but savvy white Democrats in Los Angeles should not write off Hahn's black support as merely epiphenomenal. Latinos were more than happy to vote for Riordan in exchange for their privileged position within the governing coalition, and Los Angeles blacks—faced with the prospect of being second in line behind Latino leadership—could use their electoral clout as a bargaining chip for their own privileged levels of incorporation. The relationship between blacks and Latinos in Los Angeles is at best fragile, and the extent to which they will coalesce in future political races is conditioned by the degree of sustained conflict between them, and the range of coalition opportunities available to them.

The New York Elections, 2001

The 2001 New York mayoral contest held in November offered a different partisan outcome than that of Los Angeles, but it also is a compelling example of how group conflict can diminish partisan loyalties. Only in this case, it was the racially divisive primary strategy of the Democrat, Mark Green, that led to widespread party defections among Latinos and blacks in favor of the liberal Republican, Michael Bloomberg.

For most of the primary season it seemed that the New York mayoralty would revert to Democratic control. Much like Los Angeles, New York City had also experienced an extraordinary economic revival, crime rates were at contemporary lows, and the city was in excellent fiscal condition. Even given the persistent racial and ethnic dissension that typifies New York, circumstances seemed ripe for the Democrats in 2001. Consistent with group interest expectations, early surveys seemed to point in this direction as well. As of August 15, a CBS News/*New York Times* survey showed Mark Green, one of two front-running Democratic candidates, beating Bloomberg by 25 percentage points.

On the day of the Republican and Democratic primaries, however, two hijacked commercial airliners crashed into the Twin Towers of the World Trade Center in downtown Manhattan, changing the political focus in New York. Prior to the tragedy on September 11 it seemed reasonable to expect a Democratic victory; however, after the terrorist attacks, the political context shifted dramatically: the local economy became an issue of enormous concern; the popularity of the incumbent mayor, Rudy Giuliani, surged; and leadership became a pressing electoral consideration. Green's acrimonious and racially divisive campaign against fellow Democrat and Bronx borough president Fernando Ferrer caused a substantial rift within a frail Democratic coalition, alienating Ferrer's Latino base of support and inciting the Reverend Al Sharpton to threaten a black boycott on election day. None of these circumstances (not to mention Giuliani's last-minute endorsement of Bloomberg or the $74 million that Bloomberg spent on this campaign) benefited the liberal Green.[3] With 60 percent of the white vote, almost half of the Latino vote, and a quarter of the city's black vote, billionaire Republican Michael Bloomberg succeeded Rudy Giuliani as the mayor of New York.

New York 2001—The Primaries

For most of the prior century, conventional wisdom dictated that the winner of the Democratic primary would be the next mayor of New York. And given the lopsided proportion of Democrats in the city and the favorable political context for Democrats generally—relatively low levels of racial discord, historically low crime rates, and reasonably low unemployment rates—the Democrats were expected to regain the mayoralty in 2001. Compared to 1997, when 38 percent of New Yorkers cited race relations as the most important problem in the city (Voter News Service Exit Poll, 1997), only 4 percent considered race relations to be the most important in 2001 (Edison Media Research Exit Poll, 2001). Rather, 43 percent of New Yorkers cited public education and 22 percent chose police brutality as the most serious challenges facing New York in the 2001 election season—issues that tend to benefit Democratic candidates. Indeed, from a

---

3. The final tally of Bloomberg's campaign spending is taken from the *Washington Post,* March 31, 2002, A2.

group interest perspective, the political context was as good as it had been in recent years for the Democrats. In particular, it seemed that white voters, who had largely abandoned Democratic candidates in the past two elections, were more likely to be attracted to the Democrats this time around. In the absence of the heightened racial conflict that had plagued New York during most of the Giuliani years, group interest theory would expect Democrats to defect in lower numbers than they had previously.

The four top candidates vying for the Democratic nomination included the liberal public advocate, Mark Green; the city comptroller, Alan Hevesi; the speaker of the city council, Peter Vallone; and the Bronx borough president, Fernando Ferrer. In the Republican primary, billionaire businessman Michael Bloomberg challenged long-time New York City politico Herman Badillo. The Republican contest turned out to be a terribly lopsided race, as Bloomberg poured $20 million into his primary bid and defeated Badillo by a 66 percent to 25 percent margin.

The Democratic primary race was considerably more competitive than the Republican contest, however, as each of these four well-known candidates attempted to garner over 40 percent of the vote (the number that would make them the party nominee). Bronx borough president Freddie Ferrer, of Puerto Rican descent, was the single ethnic minority in this race, and recognizing that blacks and Latinos made up approximately half of the city voters, he targeted his initial appeals to economically disadvantaged minority communities. His early primary theme—that as mayor he would help "the other New York"—highlighted the disparities in wealth and well-being between those middle-class and upper-middle-class communities that had prospered during the Giuliani era and those that had benefited quite little from the economic successes of the 1990s. Ferrer, along with African-American leaders such as Representative Charles Rangel and the Reverend Al Sharpton, attempted to solidify a black-Latino coalition that would power Ferrer into the mayoralty. Ferrer's first-place finish in the primary on September 25 was considered an upset by many who believed Green to be the likely front-runner. As illustrated in the exit polling (see table 7.6), Ferrer's strategy to attract and mobilize the black and Latino communities was quite successful, as he garnered over half of the black vote and nearly three-quarters of the Latino vote. Ferrer only

TABLE 7.6. New York City Democratic Primary Results,
September 25, 2001 (in percentages)

% of voters		% who voted for			
		Ferrer	Green	Vallone	Hevesi
	Total	36	31	20	12
	Race/Ethnicity				
48	White	7	40	31	20
24	Black	52	34	4	9
23	Latino	72	12	12	5
	Ideology				
39	Liberal	34	41	11	14
46	Moderate	30	29	24	14
15	Conservative	41	21	30	6
	Religion				
30	Protestant	46	31	11	12
31	Catholic	42	16	29	11
21	Jewish	7	46	23	21

Source: Edison Media Research Exit Poll, September 25, 2001.

received 7 percent of the white vote, however, which posed a considerable challenge for him in the runoff against Green.

Green's public primary strategy was to build as diverse a coalition
as possible. Green had backing from several important African-American leaders such as former mayor David Dinkins and the Reverend
Calvin Butts and received more than one-third of the black vote in
the September primary, as well as 40 percent of the white vote and 12
percent of the Latino vote. His challenge was to expand his white
voter base while maintaining his vote share in the African-American
and Latino communities.

The Runoff—October 11, 2001

Green campaigned all year by portraying himself as the candidate with the broadest most diverse coalition. But while the
runoff was dominated by issues generated by the terrorist attack
on the World Trade Center, the racial undercurrent that has
been part of so many New York elections was as strong as ever.
(Siegel 2001, 7)

The runoff election, originally scheduled for Tuesday, September 11, was held on Tuesday, September 25, due to the terrorist attacks on New York City. The attacks, however, had a greater effect on this election than merely postponing it and created considerable havoc for the Green and Ferrer campaigns. Almost overnight the incumbent mayor, Giuliani, soared in his public approval. For much of the two years prior to September 11, the mayor's approval rating had been languishing, bottoming out at a low 32 percent in April 2000 (*New York Times,* April 7, 2000). By August 2001, his approval rating had rebounded to 55 percent (*New York Times,* August 15, 2001). His leadership during the terror crisis, however, buoyed his citywide popularity, driving up his approval ratings to as high as 79 percent by October 24, 2001 (Quinnipiac University Survey, October 24, 2001).

In response to the terrorist attacks and their subsequent economic fallout, and in consideration of Giuliani's enormous popularity, both Green and Ferrer were forced to rethink their campaign messages. Green, who had clashed publicly with Giuliani for years, became largely constrained from campaigning against unpopular Giuliani policies such as racial profiling in the police force. Similarly, Ferrer, who had based his early primary campaign on increased funding for affordable housing, health care, and education, was forced to focus on the economic devastation of the financial district. After Ferrer publicly remarked that communities beyond the financial district should be targeted for revitalization as well, Green ran a vituperative ad calling Ferrer's policies "borderline irresponsible," with the tag line, "Can we afford to take a chance?" In addition to the negative television advertisements, flyers on behalf of Mark Green showed up in Jewish neighborhoods with a grotesque cartoon of Freddie Ferrer kissing the Reverend Al Sharpton's behind, while voters in white areas reported receiving phone calls saying that a vote for Ferrer was like a vote for Sharpton. While Green disavowed responsibility for the flyers and the phone calls, it was clear that a new level of racial consideration had now been injected into the Democratic race.

Latino leaders were publicly outraged over the "Can we afford to take a chance?" advertisement. As expressed in a letter written by Roger Green, chairman of the state's Black, Puerto Rican, and Hispanic Caucus, to Mark Green (as reported in Noel 2001):

"By engaging in an orchestrated attack on Mr. Ferrer's competence, your campaign stimulated fear among some white voters
who still harbor doubts about the leadership skills of African
American and Latino elected officials. . . . In addition, your con-
descending criticisms and negative advertisements about Mr.
Ferrer betrayed the aspirations and ideals of a growing African-
American and Latino electorate which has supported your
numerous elections, including to the Office of Public Advocate.
Be advised that most Latino and African-American voters
viewed these attacks as a disrespectful condemnation of our collective character." (29)

Roger Green, on behalf of his African-American, Puerto Rican,
and Hispanic constituents, demanded an apology from Mark
Green—one that was not forthcoming—while the Reverend Al
Sharpton threatened Mark Green with a possible call for a black boycott in the general election. Green beat Ferrer in the Democratic
runoff by a 52 percent to 48 percent margin (44,859 votes). Green

TABLE 7.7. New York City Democratic
Primary Runoff Results, October 11, 2001
(in percentages)

		% who voted for	
% of voters		Green	Ferrer
	Total	52	48
	Race/Ethnicity		
47	White	83	17
23	Black	29	71
24	Latino	16	84
	Ideology		
43	Liberal	55	45
45	Moderate	54	46
12	Conservative	46	54
	Religion		
12	Protestant	77	23
32	Catholic	45	55
21	Jewish	87	13

Source: Edison Media Research Exit Poll, October 11, 2001.

received 83 percent of the white vote but lost 71 percent and 84 percent of the black and Latino vote, respectively. More daunting than his poor showing within minority communities in the runoff, which had been largely expected, was the deep rift that had emerged within the Democratic coalition, one that clearly contributed to his loss in November (see table 7.7).

As the Democrats Implode, Bloomberg Becomes the Mayor of New York City

"The question now is, how can he win without us?" Sharpton said. "They did all this ugliness, and they only won by 20,000 votes. He knows my phone number." (Reverend Al Sharpton, quoted in the *New York Daily News,* October 12, 2001, 7)

While the Democrats had lost the last two mayoral elections largely because they could not attract white voters, the tragic irony for Mark Green was that this time he had a substantial share of the white vote. As shown in table 7.8, 38 percent of white voters cast their vote for Green in the general election. While by objective standards, this proportion may seem low, it was nonetheless considerably higher than the 21 percent Democrats Dinkins and Messinger had garnered in the previous two elections. Where Green failed and Bloomberg succeeded was in attracting greater numbers of minority voters. David Dinkins in his victorious campaign for mayor received 95 percent of the black vote and 60 percent of the Latino vote. Ruth Messinger, the loser in a contest four years earlier that was never even close, received 79 percent of the black vote and 57 percent of the Latino vote. Had Mark Green done as well among racial and ethnic minorities as Ruth Messinger, he would now be mayor.[4]

---

4. I draw this conclusion by estimating the African-American and Latino share of the overall electorate using the exit poll percentages (23 percent and 18 percent, respectively) and then recalculating the final vote substituting Messinger's share of the black and Latino vote. In this hypothetical scenario, Green would have received an additional 35,881 votes from these two groups—overcoming his actual 35,489 vote deficit. Of course, this hypothetical scenario assumes that Green could have maintained his white vote share by not engaging in his racially divisive primary campaign. Given the relatively low level of race salience among whites in this election, it seems a plausible assumption, but an assumption nonetheless.

Of course, everything in this election did not ride on Green and his choices. Bloomberg, a billionaire and lifelong Democrat turned Republican in the year prior to the election, contributed to his own success. On the one hand, Bloomberg's extravagant campaign spending blanketed the New York airwaves, creating a fairly positive image and nearly universal name recognition. On the other hand, in the post–September 11 environment, Bloomberg's leadership and business experience were perceived as enormous assets, given the rebuilding task at hand. According to the Edison Media Research Exit Poll, 30 percent of general election voters felt that the World Trade Center attack and its aftermath had made them more likely to vote for Bloomberg, whereas only 14 percent said that it made them more likely to vote for Green. Furthermore, exit poll results suggest that

TABLE 7.8.   Comparison of the New York City Mayoral Vote, 1993, 1997, and 2001 (in percentages)

% of voters who are				1993		1997		2001	
1993	1997	2001		Giuliani	Dinkins	Giuliani	Messinger	Bloomberg	Green
			Total	51	49	57	41	50	47
			Race/Ethnicity						
56	53	52	White	77	21	76	21	60	38
29	21	23	Black	5	95	20	79	25	75
12	20	18	Latino	37	60	43	57	47	49
			Ideology						
30	33	37	Liberal	34	65	43	55	36	60
43	43	45	Moderate	56	43	61	38	53	44
27	23	17	Conservative	67	33	72	25	64	32
			Party						
61	61	65	Democrat	33	67	45	54	34	64
22	20	16	Independent	69	31	65	32	60	33
17	19	19	Republican	93	7	92	6	88	9
			Religion						
24	24	24	Protestant	26	74	40	58	40	58
45	41	37	Roman Catholic	69	31	66	32	60	37
17	23	19	Jewish	68	32	72	27	52	46

Source: New York Times/CBS Exit Poll, 1989; Voter Research Exit Poll, 1993; Voter News Service Exit Poll, 1997; Edison Media Research Exit Poll, 2001.

Green lost support between the Democratic runoff and the general election, with 27 percent of his own primary voters choosing Bloomberg in the general election. An even greater proportion of Ferrer's runoff supporters (41 percent) switched parties to vote for Bloomberg.

According to a survey conducted by Quinnipiac University on October 24, however, Green was leading Bloomberg by 16 percentage points. As noted by Maurice Carroll, director of Quinnipiac University Polling Institute,

> When we first measured Michael Bloomberg against Mark Green in June, the Republican trailed 62–20 percent. Forty million dollars later, Bloomberg has narrowed the gap to 16 points. But Mark Green is still 16 points ahead with 13 days to go. . . . Both candidates get OK favorability ratings and Green gets only tepid support from his followers, so one major blunder could decide this race.

Indeed, one major blunder could decide the race—or perhaps an endorsement from the city's iconic and extraordinarily popular mayor. A week before the general election, Rudy Giuliani endorsed Bloomberg, who cleverly turned Giuliani's endorsement into a sixty-second advertisement that blanketed the New York airwaves through election day. By November 4 a new Quinnipiac poll showed the candidates in a dead heat, and on November 6 Bloomberg bested the Democrat Green by slightly more than thirty-five thousand votes.

In part, the 2001 New York City mayoral election represents a dramatic illustration of how changes in the political context influence the basis for voter decision making. Faced with probable budget deficits and the enormous task of rebuilding the city, many voters found Bloomberg's managerial experience appealing in a way that they had not prior to September 11. Were it not for the intense interracial and interethnic conflict within the Democratic party, however, it is still likely that Green would have eked out a victory. For white Democrats, it was rather easy to defect to Bloomberg. He had spent most of his life, after all, as a Democrat, and there was little fear that he would not serve white interests, even liberal white interests. For Latinos, especially, and to a lesser degree African-Americans, Green's criticism of Ferrer in the primary represented a betrayal of the backing that these groups had given him for so many years. Green, as public advocate, had been an outspoken defender of disadvantaged minority communities; given this, his behavior toward Ferrer was considered all the more inexcusable—especially among leaders in the Latino and African-American communities.

Bloomberg heavily courted the Latino community from the start of his campaign—attempting to learn Spanish and allocating enormous resources to Spanish media advertising. Having been a Democrat most of his adult life, he is no strict conservative, thus making it all the easier for disillusioned African-Americans and Latinos to support him. From a group interest perspective, black and Latino voters would probably not have defected in such great numbers had Bloomberg been a more conventional conservative Republican, but given his history he seemed a fairly safe choice for voters alienated by what was perceived as Green's racial divisiveness.

Conclusion

When largely Democratic cities elect Republican mayors, the story is generally the same: some faction of the Democratic electorate splits off and defects for the Republican. For the mayoral elections of the 1990s—in both Los Angeles and New York—the defectors came largely from the ranks of the white Democrats, who grated at uncomfortable challenges being made by the cities' minority populations. The elections of 2001, however, represent a starkly different set of circumstances. White Democrats, in large part, returned to the fold—especially in Los Angeles, where two liberal Democrats topped the open primary field. Even in New York, where racial and ethnic conflict is at some level always entrenched in the political culture, 38 percent of white New Yorkers supported a very liberal Democratic candidate—Mark Green.

The story that sets the 2001 elections apart from those in the prior decade is found among rival minority groups that are becoming ever more numerous in these respective cities. In Los Angeles, blacks and Latinos split ranks—both supporting Democrats, albeit different ones. The election of Rocky Delgadillo to the city attorney's office certainly suggests a level of Latino-black solidarity not evident in the mayoral voting. Yet, as the number of Latinos living in Los Angeles and the rate of Latino political mobilization continue to grow, increasing political competition between African-Americans and Latinos seems inevitable.

Conversely, the New York election represents an impressive case of African-American–Latino solidarity, especially in the Democratic party runoff. The mass unity between black and Latino voters all but vanished, however, in the general election. The solidarity behind Ferrer proved quite ephemeral, as the Democratic cohesion among minority voters effectively collapsed in the runoff. As Angelo Falcon, a senior policy executive with the Puerto Rican Legal Defense and Education Fund, poignantly expressed,

> "For too long, the Democrats have taken the Latino vote for granted. . . . They have insulted us. They have ignored us, and still we voted for them. No more." (quoted in Ojito 2001, D5)

The New York election also represents a cautionary tale to white Democrats about how carefully they must tailor their campaign messages when running against racial and ethnic minorities. Negative campaigning can have profoundly alienating effects within minority communities, discouraging turnout and prompting somewhat remarkable levels of partisan defection. Green apparently thought that he could attack Ferrer's competence (and political alliances with leaders such as Sharpton) and suffer little fallout among black and Latino voters. Not so. Latino voters in New York have become increasingly independent from the Democratic party—at least in local elections—and certainly cannot be considered a faithful bloc vote. Even one-quarter of New York's black voters, the most reliably Democratic group of all, were quite comfortable pulling the lever for a Republican. As these 2001 elections in Los Angeles and New York plainly show, the dynamics of racial and ethnic group competition in the city has most certainly extended beyond the age-old black-white paradigm. These two elections are quite stunning illustrations of the changing urban politics of a new century.

8 Changing Urban Politics in the New Millennium

If there is one thing we know for certain about the shape of urban politics in the years to come, it is that change will be its most defining feature. Large American cities have undergone profound demographic transformations over the past fifty years. Southern black migration to many urban centers, suburban white flight, large influxes of new immigrants, and a recent urban renaissance drawing middle-class and upper-middle-class whites and minorities back to the cities all speak to the dynamic nature of urban life.

For much of the twentieth century, white voters held the balance of power in many American cities. But this is changing as well. Findings from our most recent census clearly show that American cities are becoming more racially and ethnically diverse (see table 8.1). Of the twenty-five largest U.S. cities, only seven have non-Latino white majorities. Four cities—Detroit, Baltimore, Memphis, and Washington, D.C.—have black majorities (albeit in the case of Washington a shrinking one). San Antonio and El Paso, Texas, have Latino majorities, while Asians represent more than one-quarter of the residents in San Jose and San Francisco, California. Twelve of the twenty-five largest cities boast no majority racial or ethnic group at all. It would seem that the social diversity of American cities is at a contemporary high.

Social scientists tend to see rapid demographic change as a precursor to racial and ethnic hostilities. In some cases it is. Increasing numbers of racial and ethnic minorities alone, however, do not guarantee group-centered, racially volatile political environments. As the stories of both Los Angeles and New York clearly indicate, underlying demography is only one of many factors that contribute to competition and conflict in American cities.

While the majority of this book has been devoted to exploring the individual-level processes at work in urban elections, this final chapter turns to several larger questions about the macroenvironment and the factors that tend to foster urban discord. What causes racial and ethnic conflict to erupt in cities? And why are some cities inherently

TABLE 8.1. Racial Composition of the Twenty-five Largest Cities in the United States (in percentages)

	White	Black	Latino	Asian
New York	35	24	28	10
Los Angeles	30	11	46	10
Chicago	32	36	26	5
Houston	31	25	38	6
Philadelphia	42	42	9	5
Phoenix	55	5	35	2
San Diego	49	8	26	14
Dallas	34	25	36	3
San Antonio	32	7	59	2
Detroit	12	80	5	1
San Jose	36	4	31	27
San Francisco	44	8	15	31
Indianapolis	67	26	2	4
Jacksonville	62	29	4	3
Columbus	67	25	3	4
Austin	53	10	31	5
Baltimore	31	64	2	2
Memphis	33	61	3	2
Boston	49	25	15	8
Milwaukee	45	37	13	3
Seattle	67	9	6	14
Washington, DC	28	59	8	3
El Paso	18	3	77	1
Denver	51	11	32	3

Source: U.S. Census Data, 2000.

Note: Cell entries represent percentages. Cells do not necessarily add up to 100% because of excluded categories and rounding error.

more conflictual than others? In chapter 2, I posed a number of hypotheses about the factors that tend to instigate intergroup conflict and group distinctive voting. The following discussion revisits these propositions in light of the case studies from the previous chapters. True, Los Angeles and New York do not constitute the universe of important urban experiences (although if you talk to an Angeleno or a New Yorker, they will insist they do). Nonetheless, the lessons learned from these two large racially diverse cities point to some important observations regarding the factors that seem to affect levels of group-based hostility.

Social Heterogeneity and Group Conflict

While there is an impressive body of academic research that suggests that increasing numbers of minorities cause heightened racial anxiety, demography and demographic changes alone do not necessarily incite interracial and interethnic animosities. Competition—between and among groups for scarce but valued resources—causes conflict and in particular leads to the kind of group interested political behavior cataloged in this book. Extreme social heterogeneity can most certainly intensify the level of conflict between groups, but socially diverse communities don't have to live on the brink of riots. The recent history of Los Angeles is a perfect example of how racial conflict can ebb and flow even in the context of extreme racial diversity and rapid demographic change. Race sometimes matters a great deal in Los Angeles politics, and at other times it matters much less.

New York, on the other hand, is a city where race and ethnicity have always been politically important. Long before African-Americans and Latinos migrated and immigrated to New York City, previous waves of European immigrants set a group conscious standard. Irish, Italian, and Jewish immigrants constituted the majority of the city in an era when religious and ethnic identities were supremely consequential to its politics. But it would be a mistake to assume that the group consciousness of New York City politics is a function of diversity alone.

For much of the twentieth century, New York City was governed by political bosses who successfully consolidated the city's ethnic and

religious minorities into a powerful voting bloc. The structure of
New York City politics—its political machine roots, its powerful
Democratic clubs, its history of political patronage—arguably contributed as much to the importance of racial and ethnic interests as
did its demography. The social diversity of New York enabled the
kind of racial and ethnic group power-sharing arrangements that
evolved there, but in this case the institutional arrangements that
characterize New York City politics contribute disproportionately to
its long history of group consciousness.

As touched upon in chapter 5, most of the city's racial, religious,
and ethnic minorities are found within the Democratic party, and few
groups are without local bases of power and political influence. And
while the single-party structure in New York City may have facilitated
relatively high levels of minority empowerment at the neighborhood
and borough levels, it has also frustrated minority aspirations for
mayor. When race and ethnicity are continually salient—and knowing
that under even the best of circumstances racial minority candidates
are likely to receive weak support from conservative white voters
within the Democratic constituency—white Democratic leadership in
the city has been notably timid in promoting these candidacies. Furthermore, African-American and Latino candidates often run against
each other in the Democratic primaries, effectively canceling out each
other's substantial share of the votes. The Latino and African-American communities in New York City are an important part of the
Democratic coalition and are quite accustomed to using their electoral clout to bargain for government jobs, contracts, and the like.
But these intraparty arrangements, where racial and ethnic group
spoils constitute the prevailing political currency, largely perpetuate
the salience of group interests in all things political.

Racial, religious, and ethnic identities matter in New York in part
because they are institutionalized factors in the political workings of
the city. The size of the municipal bureaucracy, its patronage-like
qualities, and the city government's subregional organization all reinforce the importance of group identities and contribute to the ongoing group consciousness that typifies New York. In this case, it
seems that demographic change and social diversity only work at the
margins to exacerbate group competition, which irrespectively plays
an important role in the political and social organization of the city.

In complete contrast with the history, political culture, and institutional workings of New York City politics, Los Angeles represents another case altogether. As in many of the Sun Belt cities, the city government of Los Angeles reflects a reformer's sensibility—a weak executive versus a powerful city council, decentralized city agencies, a relatively small bureaucracy, and nonpartisan elections. There is no vast web of Democratic clubs or intricate power-sharing arrangements between and among constituent groups. There is little in the way of party organization, and there are few explicitly political mass membership groups. Until Tom Bradley's election in 1973, Los Angeles city government was like most provincial local governments—basically conservative and parochial in nature and run by local politicians at the behest of business interests.

As noted earlier, racial and ethnic minorities, Jews, and other liberals had seen little access to the halls of power in Los Angeles. Unlike the Irish, Italians, blacks, Jews, and Puerto Ricans of New York, who negotiated their spoils from within the Democratic party machine, minority voters in Los Angeles would have to topple the conservative governing regime in order to attain some level of power and privilege within the city. As outsiders, minorities in Los Angeles were less inclined to play the politics of group identity, as their political viability was largely contingent on their ability to build cross-cutting racial and religious coalitions.

From 1970 to 1990, the city of Los Angeles underwent a significant demographic transformation. Non-Latino whites, who made up 59 percent of the city population in 1970, were only 37 percent in 1990. Latinos went from 18 percent in 1970 to 40 percent in 1990, while the proportion of African-Americans declined from 18 percent to 14 percent and the percentage of Asians increased from 5 percent to 10 percent. Foreign immigration was fueling these rather momentous trends. If changing demography alone had been a sufficient impetus for ethnic and racial unrest, Los Angeles by all accounts should have been a hotbed. But it was not. This was Los Angeles during the Bradley era, when white voters and racial minorities of all stripes rallied behind the city's black mayor.

Social heterogeneity and changing demographics are not the root cause of conflict. And in Los Angeles, unlike in New York, the institutional workings of the city do little to promote group consciousness in its politics. This is not to say, however, that reform cities like Los Angeles never experience the kind of group-based contentious politics experienced in cities like New York and Chicago. They most certainly do. But episodes of heightened conflict in the reform city seem to rise and fall in response to exogenous factors such as police abuses or economic strife. In the presence of such a trigger, racial discord can erupt and become a pervasive social and political force. Without the institutional maintenance of the group-based political appeals, however, conflict is more likely to subside in the reform city than elsewhere.

Recessions

In socially diverse cities, economic downturns tend to be fertile breeding grounds for the eruption of group-based hostilities. A weak economy often leads to conflict because it exacerbates feelings of scarcity. In particular, downturns in the local economy, increasing unemployment rates, and declining public revenues stimulate competition over remaining scarce resources. Group-based tensions simply run hotter when the economy is poor, all else being equal.

The case of Los Angeles is an ideal illustration of how downturns in the local economy tend to strain group relations. One only needs to contrast the economic circumstances of the Bradley years—impressive job growth and fiscal solvency—with the early 1990s to understand why rapid demographic changes during the 1980s resulted in such little relative public angst over immigration and minority accommodation. As unemployment rates hovered near 10 percent in the early 1990s, and as local hospitals were closing their doors due to inadequate public funding, questions of immigration and immigration policy became a contentious political issue in Los Angeles as well as throughout California. Immigrant populations—made up of legal as well as illegal immigrants—had been rising in Los Angeles for years with little public outcry. But as the economy began to falter, the provision of essential city services became threatened. Immigrants and minorities bore the brunt of public scapegoating. The same immigrants who had been toiling away in factories, cutting lawns, cleaning houses, and caring for the children of the affluent now were seen as an oppressive burden on the city.

It is not surprising that, as the Los Angeles economy improved during the course of the decade, the immigration issue went largely underground. The powers that be in Los Angeles—especially the business community—have few vested interests in running immigrants out of the city, as they are an essential component of the growing service economy. With immigrants often working at below the minimum wage, many businesses in Los Angeles could not be nearly as prosperous as they are, were it not for their access to this workforce. As Paul Grogan and Tony Procio (2000) forcefully argue in *Comeback Cities,* immigrants are indeed essential to the revitalization of urban neighborhoods.

> Meanwhile, inner-city neighborhoods—especially the poorest ones—need fresh supplies of people willing to plant stakes, take entry-level jobs, start small businesses, and repair and maintain property. . . . For most of our history, in city after city, immigrants with small means and only basic skills have settled in such neighborhoods, done well there—and in a generation or so, like most Americans, moved on, replaced partly by newcomers much like themselves. Now, there surely is no more hardy perennial in our national political conversation than whether immigration is a good thing for America. . . . There is almost no question, in any case, about whether immigration is good for *cities,* or about whether many inner-city markets will reach their full potential without it. (138–39)

In spite of the important role that immigrants play in cities, calls for restrictive immigration policy tend to flourish during economic recessions. Increasing numbers of ethnic and racial minorities alone, however, don't instigate these racial hostilities. Nor does social diversity dictate a racially and ethnically polarized electorate. The strength and vitality of the local economy powerfully shape the extent to which diversity translates into hostility.

Riots and Civil Unrest

Beyond the obviously detrimental effects of fiscal malaise, civil unrest, public demonstrations, and wide-scale rioting make racial identities enormously salient in the political context. Do riots cause conflict?

Clearly not. But episodes of racial unrest nonetheless have important fallout at the ballot box and in particular bring racial issues (and racial interests) to the fore, especially among white voters.

It is no accident that the two most racially polarized elections in Los Angeles's history came on the heels of civil unrest. Sam Yorty—in his 1969 campaign against Tom Bradley—capitalized on the riot-related angst and ran a racially inflammatory campaign. White voters, motivated by racial resentments and fear, overwhelmingly supported Yorty. More than twenty years later, the 1992 rebellion had a similar effect on the electoral behavior of white voters. In this case, Riordan did not run an overtly racial campaign á la Sam Yorty and Woo, his opponent, was not black. Nonetheless, the political backdrop of the recent riots made racial attitudes and racial interests enormously important to white voters across the ideological spectrum.

When minorities challenge the policies and social values of dominant majorities, the racial interests of white voters tend to become manifest in ways that they typically are not. Protests, uprisings, demonstrations, and the like may be an important means of political speech for disadvantaged groups looking to garner public attention. Nonetheless, the somewhat ironic reality is that conservative voting and conservative governments tend to flourish in postriot environments. Protest and rebellion may have their rewards at the federal level (note the empowerment zone legislation that was spurred by the Los Angeles riots), but local governments tend to go into "lockdown" mode, while many white voters—especially moderate Democrats—become uncharacteristically group interested in their voting behavior.

Candidates and Issues

While conventional wisdom seems to suggest that minority candidacies are inherently contentious, making racial issues almost automatically salient, the findings from this research do not fully support this notion. It is true that, when a member of a minority group runs for office, those most highly identified with the group tend to back these candidates regardless of other considerations. For brethren group members with a strong sense of racial or ethnic identity, group-based interests tend to trump other potentially relevant considerations such as issue positions, party identification, or political ideology.

When blacks and Latinos were on the ballot in New York and Los Angeles, racial and ethnic group members supported their own at rates higher than any other group, typically in excess of 80 percent. For racial and ethnic minorities, then, the notion that electoral support is tied to the degree of group consciousness is difficult to illustrate because racial and ethnic identities are more often than not deeply felt. The enduring salience of racial identity pertains much more to minorities than it does to white voters, which is why competition and conflict affect whites to a greater degree than nonwhites when minority candidates run for mayor.

In addition to the notion that group members with the strongest sense of group consciousness are the most apt to support their own at the polls, group interest theory also proposes that issue agendas at play in a given campaign can also influence the relative cohesiveness of groups. In particular, when candidates promote group-specific agendas during the course of a campaign, the likelihood of a group distinctive vote and the probability of countermobilization from opposing groups increase. For example, if a black candidate runs against a white candidate for mayor, it is reasonable to presume that blacks will overwhelmingly support their candidate because group consciousness and group cohesiveness among African-Americans are typically high. The extent to which whites coalesce in opposition to the black candidate is not as automatic. Whites, in general, do not possess a particularly strong "white" group consciousness. Therefore, the motivation to countermobilize against minority groups rests to a large extent on whether the political context is fraught with racial conflict. A political issue agenda that focuses on the specific needs of black constituents and pits these needs against those of other groups in the city will exacerbate the overall level of conflict and will probably result in more unity among white voters. This is not to say that other factors, apart from candidate issue agendas, do not stimulate race-based opposition to black candidates. But from a group interest point of view, issue agendas that promote race-specific politics will incite competition above and beyond whatever else is happening in a political campaign.

It is interesting to note that most of the minority candidates I discuss in this book—David Dinkins, Tom Bradley, and Antonio Villaraigosa—were all quite careful to downplay race-specific issues. For minority candidates in cities where whites constitute electoral majorities, there is little to gain by making race-based appeals. Deracialized campaigns have become the contemporary model for minority candidates, as racialized campaign strategies are notorious losers (Metz and Tate 1995).

Mike Woo's 1993 campaign in Los Angeles is particularly instructive in this regard, as his experience illustrates how potent and potentially detrimental race-based appeals are, even when they are not made by African-American or Latino candidates. Woo's central campaign theme in the postriot environment of 1993—that he would bring minority communities together in Los Angeles and that he would be particularly sensitive to their political, economic, and social needs—was explicitly racial and overwhelmingly unsuccessful. White voters in Los Angeles rejected Woo in large numbers, with over two-thirds supporting his Republican opponent, Richard Riordan. There is no reason to believe that white opposition to Woo was in reaction to *his* Chinese ethnicity, yet Woo's strategy to self-identify with Latinos and blacks, coupled with an issue agenda largely focused on racial concerns, earned him substantial resistance from white voters. Indeed, Woo received a smaller percentage of white votes in 1993 than Bradley did in his first unsuccessful bid for mayor in 1969. These results speak to the potential dissension spurred by a race-targeted issue agenda—even when the candidate is not black or Latino.

Latino Voters and Urban Coalitions

For most of the contemporary era, Latinos were minor players in the politics of most American cities. Numerous but politically inactive, they simply did not represent a large enough bloc of votes to warrant substantial attention among city power brokers. African-Americans, by contrast, were important political players, often constituting a greater proportion of urban electorates than mere numbers would predict. The strength and reliability of the African-American vote made them desirable coalition partners for liberal whites, and the urban politics of the 1960s, 1970s, and 1980s featured large numbers of such liberal black-white coalitions.

The Latino public has become increasingly mobilized, however, and now represents a growing force in the new urban political arena. Many political activists and political scientists expected Latinos to be natural coalition partners with African-Americans. After all, both of these communities are economically disadvantaged relative to whites, both have suffered at the hands of white police forces, both experience disproportionate amounts of discrimination, and both support an expansive welfare state. It seems only rational that these two groups would band together and challenge dominant, white, and largely conservative governing regimes for control of their cities. In spite of how rational all this may seem, however, real examples of these alliances are few and far between.

In fact, patterns of social and political activity in American cities indicate that African-Americans and Latinos increasingly compete for political, residential, and economic turf. Not only have blacks and Latinos shown little electoral unity, but several recent elections—notably those in Los Angeles, Houston, and Miami—attest to the fact that the political competition between these two politically important minority groups in certain cases is intensifying. Urban discord, so long seen as the dynamic between white and minority voters, has expanded. And to the extent that Latino and African-American electorates compete against one another for political influence, white voters become an ever more important piece to the "musical chairs" of urban coalition building.

Latinos in Los Angeles and New York have shown little allegiance to local Democratic candidates in several of the most recent election cycles. Once a reliable Democratic constituency (and still fairly reliable in state-level and national elections), Latinos have increasingly thrown their hat in the ring with Republican candidates, enabling Riordan, Giuliani, and most recently Bloomberg to defeat their Democratic challengers. As Meier and Stewart (1991) note, for moderate whites, Latinos are simply more attractive coalition partners. For Latinos, these alliances have resulted in greater levels of political influence and incorporation than they might have otherwise had in black-led coalitions. Simply, the growing number of Latino voters and their political independence—relative to African-American voters—have placed them in the enviable position of being courted by both the right and the left.

The big losers in these new political arrangements between Latinos and moderate whites have been urban blacks, who become quite dispensable to these governing regimes as long as Latino voters stay on board. Inevitably, however, African-American leaders will strike back. The somewhat anomalous coalition between African-Americans and conservative whites that brought James Hahn to power in Los Angeles may be such an instance. According to Harold Meyerson (2001), long-time observer of Los Angeles politics, "Mr. Hahn's coalition is a politically incoherent, one-time curiosity that should not be mistaken for a new urban political force" (A25). Yet, to the extent that black and Latino voters do not come together under a banner of minority solidarity, making moderate and conservative white voters the permanent swing vote in Los Angeles, there may be many more of these "politically incoherent" coalitions in the city's future. Unlike the urban politics of the previous era, the question of who votes for whom will be largely decided by the future relationship between blacks and Latinos in American cities.

Conclusion

Studies of mayoral voting in Los Angeles and New York suggest that there is much evidence to recommend the group interest approach as a framework for studying city politics more generally. Group identities and group interests have always played a prominent role in the workings of the city. Historically excluded groups—racial, religious, and ethnic minorities and poor and working-class people—have made their homes in American cities. City politics matter because they are the open door to greater social, political, and economic opportunity for these and other groups.

The main conclusion from this work is that heightened levels of group-based hostility affect voting in local elections, making group interests important and relevant to politics. Some cities are inherently less harmonious than others, but the results from this study strongly suggest that conflict is not endemic to all cities all the time. It is often presumed that social diversity causes interracial dissension; however, the findings from this research do not see demography as such a powerful or deterministic factor. Social heterogeneity provides a wealth of opportunity for intergroup tensions, but at most it represents the cast of players and not the final script. Economic dislocations, social and legal injustices, political agendas, petty squabbles that turn into community-wide violence—these kinds of things create conflictual political environments. When highly charged events such as these occur against a backdrop of enormous social diversity, the opportunity for the city to come apart is intensified.

Groups can get along together for years, but when interests begin to diverge, there is no reservoir of goodwill that will sustain these relations. The politics of cities is about "who gets what," and groups will stay on the same side of the political fence as long as they share in the benefits. When one group gets ahead at the expense of another, the potential for future political coalitions becomes frayed. Furthermore, as new groups emerge and become politically relevant, new relations will evolve and new lines most assuredly will be drawn.

Urban politics in the future will become even more complex. The black-white paradigm that has dominated contemporary research on large cities is readily becoming obsolete in many parts of the country. The social composition of American cities is changing, and these changes create pressures for new political alliances. This research clearly illustrates that city politics cannot be understood through a fixed lens because the politics that occur in American cities are always moving. There are few partisan anchors left in local politics, and so the psychological economy of humans requires other informational shortcuts. Primary identities such as race, ethnicity, religion, or gender sometimes provide the heuristic cues for voting behavior. What is so interesting about city politics is that these identities do not *consistently* provide these cues. Voting behavior in American cities is largely shaped by the social, political, and economic forces at work in any given election. The group interest approach is therefore important because it provides a more nuanced understanding of contemporary urban politics and a more sophisticated analytical framework from which to pursue future research.

Appendix

Chapter 3

TABLE A3.1. Logistic Regression Results: Los Angeles Mayoral Vote, 1969

	All Whites	White Democrats	White Liberals
Ideology	.97*	.84*	—
	(.37)	(.51)	—
Income	.32	2.07*	.62
	(.71)	(1.02)	(1.18)
Satisfaction with local govt. services	1.82*	2.08*	3.53*
	(.95)	(1.22)	(1.68)
Party identification	.91*	—	.67
	(.40)	—	(.68)
Attitudes regarding blacks	3.52*	3.45*	4.27*
	(.61)	(.83)	(1.06)
Constant	–2.22*	–2.58*	–1.99*
	(.57)	(.74)	(.87)
Number of cases	229	126	104
Pseudo R^2	.30	.26	.24

Source: Los Angeles Pre-election Poll, 1969—Tom Pettigrew, principal investigator.

Note: Cell entries represent unstandardized regression coefficients; standard errors are in parentheses. All of the independent variables are uniformly scaled from zero to one, from liberal to conservative, or, with regard to income, from low to high.

*p < .10

Chapter 4

TABLE A4.1.   Logistic Regression Results by Racial/Ethnic Group for Los Angeles Mayoral Vote, 1993

	Whites	Blacks	Latinos
Ideology	5.88**	3.86**	1.71*
	(.78)	(1.23)	(.87)
Bradley approval	.33	3.77**	1.54*
	(.47)	(1.13)	(.67)
Party identification	.90**	.74	1.07
	(.33)	(.84)	(.66)
Attitudes regarding minorities	1.48**	1.74	.89
	(.41)	(1.14)	(.77)
Attitudes regarding illegal immigrants	.41	.06	2.79**
	(.38)	(.89)	(.59)
Number of cases	377	126	72
Percent correctly predicted	85	88	75

Source: Los Angeles Times Pre-election Poll, 1993.

Note: Cell entries represent unstandardized regression coefficients; standard errors are in parentheses. All of the independent variables are scaled from zero to one. All of the variables are scaled from liberal to conservative or, with regard to income, from low to high.

*p < .05   **p < .001

TABLE A4.2. Logistic Regression Results for White Moderate Voters, Los Angeles

	Moderate White Voters
Income	1.29
	(.99)
Bradley approval	.42
	(.69)
Party identification	.23
	(.46)
Attitudes regarding minorities	2.83**
	(.79)
Attitudes regarding illegal immigrants	.96
	(.62)
Constant	–.54
	(.88)
Number of cases	114
Percent correctly predicted	75

Source: Los Angeles Times Pre-election Poll, May 1993.

Note: Cell entries represent unstandardized regression coefficients; standard errors are in parentheses. All of the independent variables are scaled from zero to one, from liberal to conservative or, with regard to income, from low to high.

$**p < .001$

Chapter 5

TABLE A5.1.   Logistic Regression Results for New York City Mayoral Voting, 1989

	All Whites	White Democrats	White Moderates
Party identification	.99*	—	.98
	(.41)		(.53)
Ideology	.58	.78	—
	(.55)	(.63)	
Status of race relations	1.94*	1.69*	1.83*
	(.62)	(.82)	(.81)
Attitudes regarding a black mayor	2.53*	3.29*	2.74*
	(.87)	(1.20)	(1.19)
Education	−1.47*	−1.58*	−1.65*
	(.54)	(.71)	(.67)
Constant	−.92*	−1.06*	−.75
Number of cases	256	130	122
Percent correctly predicted	76	72	75

Source: WCBSTV/*New York Times,* New York City Pre-election Poll, June 1989.

Note: Dependent variable is vote choice (Dinkins = 0, Giuliani = 1). Entries represent unstandardized logistic regression coefficients. Standard errors are in parentheses. All independent variables are scaled from zero to one. Attitudes regarding the status of race relations are scaled from bad to good. Attitudes regarding the impact of a black mayor and ideology are scaled from liberal to conservative. Party identification is scaled from Democrat to Republican.

*p < .05

TABLE A5.2. Logistic Regression Results for New York City Mayoral Voting, 1993

	All Whites	White Democrats	White Moderates
Party identification	1.04*	—	.28
	(.52)		(.87)
Ideology	1.40*	1.18	—
	(.55)	(.63)	
Attitudes regarding race relations	3.87**	3.78**	7.43**
	(.76)	(.82)	(1.96)
Crime/safety attitudes	2.05**	2.57**	2.59*
	(.58)	(.68)	(1.28)
Attitudes regarding immigrants	1.13*	1.05*	2.28*
	(.49)	(.53)	(1.03)
Dinkins's handling of the economy	4.04**	3.70**	5.36*
	(1.03)	(1.07)	(1.95)
Constant	−5.90**	−5.97**	−8.33**
Number of cases	281	191	117
Percent correctly predicted	87	84	91

Source: WCBSTV/*New York Times,* New York City pre-election survey, May 1993.

Note: Dependent variable is vote choice (Dinkins = 0, Giuliani = 1). Entries represent unstandardized logistic regression coefficients. Standard errors are in parentheses. All independent variables are scaled from zero to one. Attitudes regarding race relations and immigrant attitudes are scaled from liberal to conservative. Party identification is scaled from Democrat to Republican. Crime/safety attitudes and attitudes regarding Dinkins and the local economy are scaled from good to bad.

*$p < .01$ **$p < .05$

Chapter 6

TABLE A6.1.   Logistic Regression Results: Mayoral Voting in New York City, 1997

	All Voters
Party identification	.72**
	(.13)
Ideology	.46**
	(.12)
Condition of the city economy	.77**
	(.13)
Police brutality less likely under Giuliani	1.06**
	(.11)
City safer than four years ago	.77
	(.14)
Schools better than four years ago	.71**
	(.12)
Household income	.05
	(.06)
Black vs. white	−2.00**
	(.22)
Latino vs. white	−1.20**
	(.20)
Constant	1.59**
	(.54)
Percent correctly predicted	84

Source: Voter News Service Exit Poll, New York City, November 4, 1997.

Note: Cell entries represent unstandardized regression coefficients. Standard errors are in parentheses. The dependent variable is vote for Giuliani. All independent variables are scaled from zero to one. Party identification is scaled from Democrat to Republican. Ideology runs from liberal to conservative. Economic evaluations are scaled from bad to good. Likelihood of police brutality is scaled from more to less. Safety and schools are scaled from worse to better. Household income is scaled from low to high.

$**p < .01$

Bibliography

Abbott, Carl. 1981. *The New Urban America: Growth and Politics in Sunbelt Cities*. Chapel Hill: University of North Carolina Press.

Aberbach, Joel D., and Jack L. Walker. 1973. *Race in the City: Political Trust and Public Policy in the New Urban System*. Boston: Little, Brown.

Acock, Alan C., and Robert M. Halley. 1975. "Ethnic Politics and Issues Reconsidered: Comments on an Earlier Study." *Western Political Quarterly* 28 (1): 737–38.

Adrian, Charles. 1959. "A Typology of Nonpartisan Elections." *Western Political Quarterly* 12:449–58.

Ainsworth, E. 1966. *Maverick Mayor: A Biography of Sam Yorty of Los Angeles*. Garden City, NY: Doubleday.

Alderman, Jeffrey. 1994. "Leading the Public: The Media's Focus on Crime Shaped Sentiment." *Public Perspective* 5 (3): 26–27.

Allport, Gordon. 1954. *The Nature of Prejudice*. Garden City, NY: Doubleday.

Alvarez, R. Michael, and Tara Butterfield. 2000. "The Resurgence of Nativism in California? The Case of Proposition 187 and Illegal Immigration." *Social Science Quarterly* 81:167–79.

Amir, Y. 1969. "Contact Hypothesis in Ethnic Relations." *Psychological Bulletin* 71:319–42.

Arian, A., A. S. Goldberg, J. H. Mollenkopf, and E. T. Rogowsky. 1991. *Changing New York City Politics*. New York: Routledge.

Arrington, Theodore S. 1978. "Partisan Campaigns, Ballots and Voting Patterns: The Case of Charlotte." *Urban Affairs Quarterly* 14:253–61.

Banfield, Edward C., and James Q. Wilson. 1963. *City Politics*. Cambridge, MA: Harvard University Press.

Baldassare, Mark. 2000. *California in the New Millennium: The Changing Social and Political Landscape*. Berkeley: University of California Press.

Barker, Lucius J., and Mack H. Jones. 1994. *African Americans and the American Political System*. 3d ed. Englewood Cliffs, NJ: Prentice Hall.

Barnes, Fred. 1989. "The Mayor's Race." *New Republic,* October 9, 9–10.

Bartels, Larry M. 2000. "Partisanship and Voting Behavior, 1952 to 1996." *American Journal of Political Science* 44 (1): 35–50.

Bell, Derrick. 1992. *Faces at the Bottom of the Well: The Permanence of Racism.* New York: Basic Books.

Berelson, Bernard R., Paul F. Lazarsfeld, and William N. McPhee. 1954. *Voting.* Chicago: University of Chicago Press.

Blalock, Hubert. 1967. *Toward a Theory of Minority Group Relations.* New York: Wiley.

Bledsoe, Timothy, and Susan Welch. 1986. "The Partisan Consequences of Non-partisan Elections and the Changing Nature of Urban Politics." *American Journal of Political Science* 30:128–39.

Blumer, Herbert. 1958. "Race Prejudice as a Sense of Group Position." *Pacific Sociological Review* 1:3–7.

Bobo, Lawrence. 1983. "Whites' Opposition to School Busing: Symbolic Racism or Realistic Group Conflict?" *Journal of Personality and Social Psychology* 45:1196–1210.

———. 1988. "Group Conflict, Prejudice, and the Paradox of Contemporary Racial Attitudes." In Phyllis A. Katz and Dalmas A. Taylor, eds., *Eliminating Racism: Profiles in Controversy.* New York: Plenum Press.

———. 2000. "Race and Beliefs about Affirmative Action." In David O. Sears, Jim Sidanius, and Lawrence Bobo, eds., *Racialized Politics: The Debate about Racism.* Chicago: University of Chicago Press.

Bobo, Lawrence, and Franklin D. Gilliam Jr. 1990. "Race, Sociopolitical Participation, and Black Empowerment." *Journal of Personality and Social Psychology* 84 (2): 377–93.

Bobo, Lawrence, and Vincent L. Hutchings. 1996. "Perceptions of Racial Group Competition: Extending Blumer's Theory of Group Position to a Multiracial Social Context." *American Sociological Review* 61:951–72.

Bobo, Lawrence, and Devon Johnson. 2000. "Racial Attitudes in a Prismatic Metropolis: Mapping Identity, Stereotypes, Competition, and Views on Affirmative Action." In Lawrence D. Bobo, Melvin L. Oliver, James H. Johnson Jr., and Abel Valenzuela, eds., *Prismatic Metropolis: Inequality in Los Angeles.* New York: Russell Sage Foundation.

Bobo, Lawrence, and James R. Kluegel. 1993. "Opposition to Race Targeting: Self-Interest, Stratification Ideology, or Racial Attitudes?" *American Sociological Review* 58:443–64.

Bobo, Lawrence D., Melvin L. Oliver, James H. Johnson Jr., and Abel Valenzuela, eds. 2000. *Prismatic Metropolis: Inequality in Los Angeles.* New York: Russell Sage Foundation.

Bobo, Lawrence, Camille L. Zubrinsky, James H. Johnson Jr., and Melvin L. Oliver. 1994. "Public Opinion before and after a Spring of Discontent." In

Mark Baldassare, ed., *The Los Angeles Riots: Lessons for the Urban Future*. Boulder: Westview Press.

Bovasso, G. 1993. "Self, Group, and Public Interests Motivating Racial Politics." *Political Psychology* 14 (3): 3–20.

Bridges, Amy. 1997. *Morning Glories: Municipal Reform in the Southwest*. Princeton: Princeton University Press.

Brink, William, and Louis Harris. 1967. *Black and White*. New York: Simon and Schuster.

Browning, Rufus, Dale Marshall, and David Tabb. 1979. "Minorities and Urban Electoral Change: A Longitudinal Study. *Urban Affairs Quarterly* 15 (2): 206–27.

———. 1984. *Protest Is Not Enough: The Struggle of Blacks and Hispanics for Equality in City Politics*. Berkeley: University of California Press.

———. 1990. *Racial Politics in American Cities*. New York: Longman.

———. 1997. *Racial Politics in American Cities*. 2d ed. New York: Longman.

———. 2003. *Racial Politics in American Cities*. 3d ed. New York: Longman.

Bullock, Charles S., III. 1984. "Racial Crossover Voting and the Election of Black Officials." *Journal of Politics* 46:238–51.

Bullock, Charles S., III, and Bruce A. Campbell. 1984. "Racist or Racial Voting in the 1981 Atlanta Municipal Elections." *Urban Affairs Quarterly* 20:149–64.

Cain, Bruce, Roderick Kiewiet, and Carole Uhlaner. 1991. "The Acquisition of Partisanship by Latinos and Asian-Americans." *American Journal of Political Science* 35:390–422.

Campbell, Angus, Philip Converse, Warren Miller, and Donald Stokes. 1960. *The American Voter*. Chicago: University of Chicago Press.

Carmichael, Stokely, and Charles Hamilton. 1967. *Black Power: The Politics of Liberation in America*. New York: Random House.

Carmines, Edward G., and Richard A. Champagne Jr. 1990. "The Changing Content of American Racial Attitudes." In Samuel Long, ed., *Research in Micropolitics*, vol. 3. Greenwich, CT: JAI.

Carmines, E. G., R. Huckfeldt, and C. McCurley. 1995. "Mobilization, Counter-Mobilization, and the Politics of Race." *Political Geography* 14 (6–7): 601–19.

Carmines, E. G., and J. A. Stimson. 1980. "The Two Faces of Issue Voting" *American Political Science Review* 74:78–91.

———. 1982. "Racial Issues and the Structure of Mass Belief Systems." *Journal of Politics* 44:2–20.

———. 1989. *Issue Evolution: Race and the Transformation of American Politics*. Princeton: Princeton University Press.

Carsey, Thomas M. 1995. "The Contextual Effects of Race on White Voter Behavior: The 1989 New York City Mayoral Election." *Journal of Politics* 57 (1): 221–28.

Cataldo, Everett F., and John D. Holm. 1983. "Voting on School Finances: A Test of Competing Theories." *Western Political Quarterly* 36:619–31.

Cavanagh, Thomas E. 1991. "When Turnout Matters: Mobilization and Conversion as Determinants of Election Outcomes." In William Crotty, ed., *Political Participation and American Democracy*. New York: Greenwood Press.

Charles, Camille Zubrinsky. 2000. "Residential Segregation in Los Angeles." In Lawrence D. Bobo, Melvin L. Oliver, James H. Johnson Jr., and Abel Valenzuela Jr., eds., *Prismatic Metropolis: Inequality in Los Angeles*. New York: Russell Sage Foundation.

Citrin, Jack, and Donald Green. 1990. "The Self-Interest Motive in American Public Opinion." *Research in Micropolitics* 3:1–28.

Citrin, Jack, Donald Green, Christopher Muste, and Cara Wong. 1997. "Public Opinion toward Immigration Reform: The Role of Economic Motivations." *Journal of Politics* 59 (3): 858–81.

Citrin, Jack, Donald P. Green, and David O. Sears. 1990. "White Reactions to Black Candidates: When Does Race Matter?" *Public Opinion Quarterly* 54:74–96.

Citrin, Jack, Beth Reingold, and Donald P. Green. 1990. "The 'Official English' Movement and the Symbolic Politics of Language in the United States." *Western Political Quarterly* 43:535–59.

Citrin, Jack, D. O. Sears, Christopher Muste, and Cara Wong. 1995. "Liberalism and Multiculturalism: The New Ethnic Agenda in Mass Opinion." Paper delivered at the annual meeting of the American Political Science Association, Chicago.

Clark, T. N. 1996. "Cultural Realignments in American City Politics—Less Class, More Race, and a New Political Culture." *Urban Affairs Review* 31 (3): 367–403.

Cole, Leonard. 1974. "Electing Blacks to Municipal Office: Structural and Social Determinants." *Urban Affairs Quarterly* 10:17–39.

Condran, J. G. 1979. "Changes in Attitudes toward Blacks, 1969–1977." *Public Opinion Quarterly* 43:463–76.

Converse, Philip E. 1964. "The Nature of Belief Systems in Mass Publics." In David E. Apter, ed., *Ideology and Discontent*. New York: Free Press.

Cruz, Jose E. 2000. "Interminority Relations in Urban Settings: Lessons from the Black-Puerto Rican Experience." In Yvette Alex-Assensoh and Lawrence J. Hanks, eds., *Black and Multiracial Politics in America*. New York: New York University Press.

Dahl, Robert A. 1961. *Who Governs? Democracy and Power in an American City*. New Haven: Yale University Press.

Davidson, Chandler. 1972. *Biracial Politics: Conflict and Coalition in the Metropolitan South*. Baton Rouge: Louisiana State University Press.

Davis, Mike. 1991. *City of Quartz: Excavating the Future in Los Angeles.* London: Haymarket Press.

Dawson, Michael C. 1994. *Behind the Mule: Race and Class in African-American Politics.* Princeton: Princeton University Press.

DeSipio, Louis. 1996. "More than the Sum of Its Parts: The Building Blocks of Pan-Ethnic Latino Identity." In Wilbur C. Rich, ed., *The Politics of Minority Coalitions,* 176–89. Westport, CT: Praeger.

———. 2000. "The Dynamo of Urban Growth: Immigration, Naturalization, and the Restructuring of Urban Politics." In Richard A. Keiser and Katherine Underwood, eds., *Minority Politics at the Millennium.* New York: Garland.

Downs, Anthony. 1957. *An Economic Theory of Democracy.* New York: Harper and Row.

Edelman, Murray J. 1964. *The Symbolic Uses of Politics.* Urbana: University of Illinois Press.

Edsall, Thomas B. 2001. "L.A. Politics Being Turned Inside Out: Council Redistricting Symbolizes Transfer of Power to Latinos." *Washington Post,* November 24, A4.

Edsall, Thomas B., and Mary D. Edsall. 1991. *Chain Reaction: The Impact of Race, Rights, and Taxes on American Politics.* New York: W. W. Norton.

Ehrenhalt, Alan. 1991. *The United States of Ambition: Politicians, Power, and the Pursuit of Office.* New York: Times Books.

Eisinger, Peter K. 1976. *Patterns of Interracial Politics: Conflict or Cooperation in the City?* New York: Academic Press.

———. 1980. *The Politics of Displacement: Racial and Ethnic Transition in Three American Cities.* New York: Academic Press.

———. 1982. "Black Employment in Municipal Jobs: The Impact of Black Political Power." *American Political Science Review* 76:330–92.

Ellison, C. G., and D. A. Powers. 1994. "The Contact Hypothesis and Racial Attitudes among Black Americans." *Social Science Quarterly* 75:385–400.

Entmann, Robert M. 1990. "Modern Racism and Images of Modern Blacks in Local Television News." *Critical Studies in Mass Communication* 7 (4): 332–46.

Erie, Steven P. 1988. *Rainbow's End: Irish-Americans and the Dilemmas of Urban Machine Politics, 1840–1985.* Berkeley: University of California Press.

Estrada, Richard. 1995. "Immigration Buries Blacks." *Social Contract* 5:262–63.

Evans, H., and F. Rose. 1993. "GOP's New York Win Echoing Los Angeles Vote, Gives Party Chance to Provide Cures for Urban Ills." *Wall Street Journal,* November 4, A16.

Feldman, Stanley. 1982. "Economic Self-Interest and Political Behavior." *American Journal of Political Science* 26 (3): 446–65.

———. 1988. "Structure and Consistence in Public Opinion: The Role of Core Beliefs and Values." *American Journal of Political Science* 32:416–40.

Feldman, Stanley, and Karen Stenner. 1997. "Perceived Threat and Authoritarianism." *Political Psychology* 18:741–70.

Feldman, Stanley, and John Zaller. 1992. "The Political Culture of Ambivalence: Ideological Responses to the Welfare State." *American Journal of Political Science* 36:268–307.

Fiorina, Morris. 1981. *Retrospective Voting in American National Elections.* New Haven: Yale University Press.

Fiske, Susan T. 1998. "Stereotyping, Prejudice, and Discrimination." In Susan T. Fiske, Daniel Gilbert, and Gardner Lindsey, eds., *The Handbook of Social Psychology.* Boston: McGraw-Hill.

Forbes, H. D. 1997. *Ethnic Conflict.* New Haven: Yale University Press.

Fossett, Mark, and Jill Kiecolt. 1989. "The Relative Size of Minority Populations and White Racial Attitudes." *Social Science Quarterly* 70:820–35.

Frederickson, George M. 1999. "Models of American Ethnic Relations: A Historical Perspective." In Deborah A. Prentice and Dale T. Miller, eds., *Cultural Divides: Understanding and Overcoming Group Conflict.* New York: Russell Sage Foundation.

Gabriel, Richard A. 1972. "A New Theory of Ethnic Voting." *Polity* 4:405–28.

Giles, Michael. 1977. "Percent Black and Racial Hostility: An Old Assumption Reexamined." *Social Science Quarterly* 58:412–17.

Giles, Michael, and Melissa Buckner. 1993. "David Duke and Black Threat: An Old Hypothesis Revisited." *Journal of Politics* 55:702–13.

Giles, Michael, and Arthur Evans. 1986. "The Power Approach to Intergroup Hostility." *Journal of Conflict Resolution* 30:469–86.

Giles, Michael, and Douglas Gatlin. 1980. "Mass Level Compliance with Public Policy: The Case of School Desegregation." *Journal of Politics* 42:722–46.

Gilliam, Franklin D., Jr. 1996. "Exploring Minority Empowerment: Symbolic Politics, Governing Coalitions, and Traces of Political Style in Los Angeles." *American Journal of Political Science* 40 (1): 56–81.

Gilliam, Franklin D., Jr., Shanto Iyengar, Adam Simon, and Oliver Wright. 1996. "Crime in Black and White: The Violent, Scary World of Local News." *Harvard International Journal of Press/Politics* 1 (3): 6–23.

Gilliam, Franklin D., Jr., and Karen M. Kaufmann. 1998. "Is There an Empowerment Lifecycle? Long-term African-American Empowerment and Its Influence on Voter Participation." *Urban Affairs Review* 33 (6): 741–66.

Glanty, Oscar. 1960. "The Negro Voter in Northern Industrial Cities." *Western Political Quarterly* 13:999–1010.

Glaser, James. 1994. "Back to the Black Belt: Racial Environment and the White Racial Attitudes in the South." *Journal of Politics* 56 (1): 21–41.

Glazer, Nathan, and Daniel Patrick Moynihan. 1970. *Beyond the Melting Pot.* 2d ed. Cambridge, MA: MIT Press.

Green, Donald, and Jonathan Cowden. 1992. "Who Protests: Self-Interest and White Opposition to Busing." *Journal of Politics* 54:471–96.

Grimshaw, W. J. 1993. *Bitter Fruit: Black Politics and the Chicago Machine, 1931–1991.* Chicago: University of Chicago Press.

Grogan, Paul S., and Tony Proscio. 2000. *Comeback Cities.* Boulder, CO: Westview Press.

Gurin, Patricia, Shirley Hatchett, and James S. Jackson. 1989. *Hope and Independence: Blacks' Response to Electoral and Party Politics.* New York: Russell Sage Foundation.

Gurin, Patricia, Timothy Peng, Gretchen Lopez, and Biren A. Nagda. 1999. "Context, Identity, and Intergroup Relations." In Deborah A. Prentice and Dale T. Miller, eds., *Cultural Divides: Understanding and Overcoming Group Conflict.* New York: Russell Sage Foundation.

Gurr, Ted. 1968. "Psychological Factors in Civil Violence." *World Politics* 20: 245–78.

Hadden, Jeffrey, Louis Masotti, and Victor Thiessen. 1968. "The Making of Negro Mayors." *Trans-Action* 5:21–30.

Hagensick, A. Clarke. 1964. "Influences of Partisanship and Incumbency on a Nonpartisan Election." *Western Political Quarterly* 17:117–24.

Hahn, Harlan. 1975. "The American Mayor: Retrospect and Prospect." *Urban Affairs Quarterly* 11 (2): 276–88.

Hahn, Harlan, and Timothy Almy. 1971. "Ethnic Politics and Racial Issues: Voting in Los Angeles." *Western Political Quarterly* 24:719–30.

Hahn, Harlan, David Klingman, and Harry Pachon. 1976. "Cleavage, Coalitions, and the Black Candidate: The Los Angeles Mayoralty Elections of 1969 and 1973." *Western Political Quarterly* 19 (1): 507–20.

Haider, Donald. 1989. "Race in the 1989 Mayoral Races." *Public Opinion* 11:16–18.

Hajnal, Zoltan L. 2001. "White Residents, Black Incumbents, and a Declining Racial Divide." *American Political Science Review* 95 (3): 603–17.

Halley, Robert M., Alan C. Acock, and Thomas Greene. 1976. "Ethnicity and Social Class: Voting in the 1973 Los Angeles Municipal Elections." *Western Political Quarterly* 29 (1): 521–30.

Henry, Charles P. 1980. "Black-Chicano Coalitions: Possibilities and Problems." *Western Journal of Black Studies* 4:202–32.

Hero, Rodney. 1992. *Latinos and the U. S. Political System: Two Tiered Pluralism.* Philadelphia: Temple University Press.

———. 1998. *Faces of Inequality: Social Diversity in American Politics.* New York: Oxford University Press.

Hero, Rodney, and K. Beatty. 1989. "The Election of Federico Peña as Mayor of Denver: Analysis and Implications." *Western Political Quarterly* 29 (1): 521–30.

Hero, Rodney, and Caroline Tolbert. 1996. "A Racial/Ethnic Diversity Interpretation of Politics and Policy in the States of the U.S." *American Journal of Political Science* 40:851–71.

Herring, Cedric, James S. House, and Richard P. Mero. 1991. "Racially Based Changes in Political Alienation in America." *Social Science Quarterly* 72 (1): 123–34.

Holloway, Harry. 1968. "Negro Political Strategy: Coalition or Independent Power Politics?" *Social Science Quarterly* 49:534–47.

Hood, M. V., and Irwin L. Morris. 1997. "Amigo or Enemigo? Context, Attitudes, and Anglo Public Opinion toward Immigration." *Social Science Quarterly* 78:301–23.

———. 1998. "Give Us Your Tired and Your Poor . . . But Make Sure They Have a Green Card: The Effects of Documented and Undocumented Migrant Context on Anglo Opinion toward Immigration." *Political Behavior* 20:1–15.

Horowitz, Donald. 1985. *Ethnic Violence.* Cambridge, MA: Harvard University Press.

Howell, Susan. 2000. "Racial Polarization, Reaction to Urban Conditions, and the Approval of Black Mayors." In Yvette M. Alex-Assensoh and Lawrence J. Hanks, eds., *Black and Multiracial Politics in America.* New York: New York University Press.

Howell, Susan, and William Oiler. 1981. "Campaign Activities and Local Election Outcomes." *Social Science Quarterly* 62:152–60.

Huckfeldt, Robert. 1986. *Politics in Context: Assimilation and Conflict in Urban Neighborhoods.* New York: Agathon Press.

Huckfeldt, Robert, and Carol W. Kohfeld. 1989. *Race and the Decline of Class in American Politics.* Urbana: University of Illinois Press.

Huckfeldt, Robert, and John Sprague. 1993. "Citizens, Contexts, and Politics." In Ada Finifter, ed., *Political Science: The State of the Discipline II.* Washington, DC: American Political Science Association.

———. 1995. *Citizens, Politics, and Social Communication: Information Influence in an Election Campaign.* New York: Cambridge University Press.

Hurwitz, Jon, and Mark Peffley. 1998. *Prejudice and Politics: Race and Politics in the United States.* New Haven: Yale University Press.

Iyengar, Shanto. 1990. "Shortcuts to Political Knowledge: The Role of Selective Attention and Accessibility." In John A. Ferejohn and James H. Kuklinski, eds., *Information and Democratic Processes,* 160–85. Urbana: University of Illinois Press.

———. 1991. *Is Anyone Responsible? How Television Frames Political Issues.* Chicago: University of Chicago Press.

Jackson, Byron O., and Michael Preston. 1994. "Race and Ethnicity in Los Angeles Politics." In George E. Peterson, *Big-City Politics, Governance, and Fiscal Constraints.* Washington, DC: Urban Institute Press.

————, eds. 1991. *Racial and Ethnic Politics in California*. Berkeley: IGS Press.

Jackson, John E. 1975. "Issues, Party Choices, and Presidential Votes." *American Journal of Political Science* 19 (2): 161–85.

Jacobson, Gary C. 2001. *The Politics of Congressional Elections*. 5th ed. New York: Longman.

Jeffries, Vincent, and H. E. Ransford. 1972. "Ideology, Social Structure, and the Yorty-Bradley Mayoral Election." *Social Problems* 19:358–72.

Jennings, James. 1994. "Racial Hierarchy and Ethnic Conflict in the United States." In James Jennings, ed., *Blacks, Latinos, and Asians in Urban America: Status and Prospects for Politics and Activism,* 142–57. Westport, CT: Praeger.

Jennings, M. Kent, and Harmon Zeigler. 1966. "Class, Party, and Race in Four Types of Elections: The Case of Atlanta." *Journal of Politics* 28:391–407.

Johnson, James H., Jr., Walter C. Farrell Jr., and Chandra Guinn. 1999. "Immigration Reform and the Browning of America: Tensions, Conflicts, and Community Instability in Metropolitan Los Angeles." In Charles Hirschman, Philip Kasinitz, and Josh DeWind, eds., *The Handbook of International Migration: The American Experience*. New York: Russell Sage Foundation.

Johnson, James H., Jr., Walter C. Farrell Jr., and Melvin L. Oliver. 1993. "Seeds of the Los Angeles Rebellion of 1992." *International Journal of Urban and Regional Research* 17:115–19.

Jones, Bryan D. 1994. *Reconceiving Decision-Making in Democratic Politics: Attention, Choice, and Public Policy*. Chicago: University of Chicago Press.

Jones-Correa, Michael. 2001a. "Structural Shifts and Institutional Capacity: Possibilities for Ethnic Cooperation and Conflict in Urban Settings." In Michael Jones-Correa, ed., *Governing American Cities: Inter-Ethnic Coalitions, Competition, and Conflict*. New York: Russell Sage Foundation.

Jones-Correa, Michael, ed. 2001b. *Governing American Cities: Inter-Ethnic Coalitions, Competition, and Conflict*. New York: Russell Sage Foundation.

Jones-Correa, Michael, and David L. Leal. 1996. "Becoming 'Hispanic': Secondary Panethnic Identification among Latin American-Origin Populations in the United States." *Hispanic Journal of Behavioral Sciences* 18 (2): 214–54.

Judd, Dennis R. 1979. *The Politics of American Cities*. New York: Harper Collins.

Judd, Dennis R., and Todd Swanstrom. 1994. *City Politics: Private Power and Public Policy*. New York: Harper Collins.

Kahn, Kim Fridkin, and Patrick J. Kenney. 1999. *The Spectacle of U.S. Senate Campaigns*. Princeton: Princeton University Press.

Karnig, Albert. 1976. "The Impact of Local Election Systems on Black Political Representation." *Urban Affairs Quarterly* 12:223–42.

Kaufmann, Karen M. 1996. "Riots and Rebellion: The Impact of Civil Unrest on the Voting Behavior of Whites." Paper presented at the annual meeting of the Midwest Political Science Association, Chicago.

————. 1998a. "Voting in American Cities: The Group Interest Theory of Local Voting Behavior." Ph.D. diss., University of California, Los Angeles.

————. 1998b. "Racial Conflict and Political Choice: A Study of Mayoral Voting Behavior in Los Angeles and New York." *Urban Affairs Review* 33 (5): 655–85.

————. 2002. "Divided We Stand, Together We Fall? Mass Attitudes and the Prospects for Black/Latino Urban Political Coalitions." Paper presented at the annual meeting of the American Political Science Association, Boston.

————. 2003a. "Black and Latino Voters in Denver: Responses to Each Other's Political Leadership." *Political Science Quarterly* 118 (1): 107–25.

————. 2003b. "Cracks in the Rainbow: Perceived Commonality as a Basis for Latino and African-American Political Coalitions." *Political Research Quarterly* 56 (2): 199–210.

Keiser, Richard A. 1997. *Subordination or Empowerment? African-American Leadership and the Struggle for Urban Power.* New York: Oxford University Press.

————. 2000. "Analyzing Urban Regime Change: Black Power, White Backlash, and Shades of Gray." In Richard A. Keiser and Katherine Underwood, eds., *Minority Politics at the Millennium.* New York: Garland.

————. 2003. "Philadelphia's Evolving Biracial Coalition." In Rufus P. Browning, Dale Rogers Marshall, and David H. Tabb, eds., *Racial Politics in American Cities.* 3d ed. New York: Longman.

Keiser, Richard A., and Katherine Underwood, eds. 2000. *Minority Politics at the Millennium.* New York: Garland.

Keller, Edmond. 1978. "The Impact of Black Mayors on Urban Policy." *Annals of the American Academy of Political and Social Science* 439:40–52.

Kelley, Robert. 1979. *The Cultural Pattern of American Politics.* New York: Alfred A. Knopf.

Kemp, Kathleen. 1986. "Race, Ethnicity, Class, and Urban Spatial Conflict: Chicago as a Crucial Test Case." *Urban Studies* 23:197–208.

Key, V. O., Jr. 1949. *Southern Politics in State and Nation.* New York: Alfred A. Knopf.

————. 1966. *The Responsible Electorate: Rationality in Presidential Voting, 1936–1960.* Cambridge, MA: Belknap Press of Harvard University Press.

Key, V. O., Jr., and Frank Munger. 1959. "Social Determinism and Electoral Decision: The Case of Indiana." In Eugene Burdick and Arthur J. Brodbeck, eds., *American Voting Behavior.* Glencoe, Ill.: Free Press.

Killian, Lewis M. 1968. *The Impossible Revolution, Phase II: Black Power and the American Dream.* New York: Random House.

Kinder, Donald, and Roderick Kiewiet. 1981. "Sociotropic Politics: The American Case." *British Journal of Political Science* 11:129–61.

Kinder, Donald R., and Tali Mendelberg. 1995. "Cracks in the American

Apartheid: The Political Impact of Prejudice among Desegregated Whites." *Journal of Politics* 57:402–24.

Kinder, Donald R., and Lynn Sanders. 1996. *Divided by Color: Racial Politics and Democratic Ideals.* Chicago: University of Chicago Press.

Kinder, Donald R., and David O. Sears. 1981. "Prejudice and Politics: Symbolic Racism versus Racial Threats to the Good Life." *Journal of Personality and Social Psychology* 40 (3): 414–31.

Klein, Joe. 1989. "Rudy's Fall from Grace: Can Ailes Put Giuliani's Campaign Back Together Again?" *New York Magazine,* August 21, 40–43.

Kleppner, Paul. 1985. *Chicago Divided: The Making of a Black Mayor.* DeKalb: Northern Illinois University Press.

Kohfeld, Carol W. 1995. "Racial Context and Voting Behavior in One-Party Urban Political Systems." *Political Geography* 14 (6–7): 571–99.

Lazarsfeld, P., B. Berelson, and H. Gaudet. 1948. *The People's Choice.* New York: Columbia University Press.

Lee, Eugene C. 1960. *The Politics of Nonpartisanship: A Study of California City Elections.* Berkeley: University of California Press.

Leighley, Jan E. 2001. *Strength in Numbers? The Political Mobilization of Racial and Ethnic Minorities.* Princeton: Princeton University Press.

Levine, Charles H. 1974. *Racial Conflict and the American Mayor.* Lexington, MA: Lexington Books.

Levine, R. A., and D. T. Campbell. 1972. *Ethnocentrism: Theories of Conflict, Ethnic Attitudes, and Group Behavior.* New York: Wiley.

Lieske, Joel. 1989. "The Political Dynamics of Urban Voting." *American Journal of Political Science* 33:150–74.

Lieske, Joel, and Jan Hillard. 1984. "The Racial Factor in Urban Elections." *Western Political Quarterly* 37:545–63.

Lopez, David, and Yen Espiritu. 1990. "Panethnicity in the United States: A Theoretical Framework." In Darrell Y. Hamamoto and Rodolfo D. Torres, eds., *New American Destinies: A Reader in Contemporary Asian and Latino Immigration,* 195–217. New York: Routledge.

Lorinskas, Robert, Brett Hawkins, and Stephen Edwards. 1969. "The Persistence of Ethnic Voting in Urban and Rural Areas: Results for the Controlled Election Method." *Social Science Quarterly* 49 (4): 891–99.

Lovrich, N. P., and O. Marenin. 1974. "Differing Priorities in an Urban Electorate: Service Preferences and Anglo, Black, and Mexican American Voters." *Social Science Quarterly* 55:534–47.

Lublin, David I. 1995. "Race, Representation, and Redistricting." In Paul E. Peterson, ed., *Classifying by Race.* Princeton: Princeton University Press.

Lublin, David, and Katherine Tate. 1995. "Racial Group Competition in Urban Elections." In Paul E. Peterson, ed., *Classifying by Race.* Princeton: Princeton University Press.

Mandery, Evan J. 1999. *The Campaign: Rudy Giuliani, Ruth Messinger, Al Sharpton, and the Race to Be Mayor of New York City.* Boulder: Westview Press.

Marable, Manning. 1994. "Building Coalitions among Communities of Color: Beyond Racial Identity Politics." In James Jennings, ed., *Blacks, Latinos, and Asians in Urban America: Status and Prospects for Politics and Activism,* 29–43. Westport, CT: Praeger.

Markus, Gregory B., and Philip E. Converse. 1979. "A Dynamic Simultaneous Equation Model of Electoral Choice." *American Political Science Review* 73 (4): 1055–70.

Masotti, Louis H., and Don R. Bowen, eds. 1968. *Riots and Rebellion: Civil Violence in the Urban Community.* Beverly Hills, CA: Sage.

Massey, Douglas S., and Nancy A. Denton. 1993. *American Apartheid.* Cambridge, MA: Harvard University Press.

Maullin, Richard. 1971. "Los Angeles Liberalism." *Trans-Action* 8:40–50.

McAdam, Doug. 1982. *Political Process and the Development of Black Insurgency, 1930–1970.* Chicago: University of Chicago Press.

McClain, Paula D. 1993. "The Changing Dynamics of Urban Politics: Black and Hispanic Municipal Employment—Is There Competition?" *Journal of Politics* 55:339–414.

McClain, Paula D., and Albert K. Karnig. 1990. "Black and Hispanic Socioeconomic and Political Competition." *American Political Science Review* 84: 535–45.

McClain, Paula D., and Joseph Stewart Jr. 1999. *Can't We All Get Along? Racial and Ethnic Minorities in American Politics.* 2d ed. update. Boulder: Westview Press.

McClain, Paula D., and Steven C. Tauber. 1998. "Black and Latino Socioeconomic Competition: Has a Decade Made a Difference?" *American Politics Quarterly* 26:237–52.

———. 2001. "Racial Minority Group Relations in a Multiracial Society." In Michael Jones-Correa, ed., *Governing American Cities: Inter-Ethnic Coalitions, Competition, and Conflict.* New York: Russell Sage Foundation.

McConahay, J. B., and J. C. Hough Jr. 1976. "Symbolic Racism." *Journal of Social Issues* 32:23–45.

McDermott, Monica. 1994. "Race Class Interactions in the Formation of Political Ideology." *Sociological Quarterly* 35 (2): 347–66.

McGuire, William J. 1968. "Personality and Susceptibility to Social Influence." In E. F. Borgatta and W. W. Lambert, eds., *Handbook of Personality Theory and Research.* Chicago: Rand McNally.

Meier, Kenneth J., and Joseph Stewart Jr. 1991. "Cooperation and Conflict in Multiracial School Districts." *Journal of Politics* 53 (4): 1123–33.

Mendelberg, Tali. 1997. "Executing Hortons: Racial Crime in the 1988 Presidential Campaign." *Public Opinion Quarterly* 61 (spring): 134–57.

———. 2001. *The Race Card: Campaign Strategy, Implicit Messages, and the Norm of Equality.* Princeton: Princeton University Press.

Metz, David Haywood, and Katherine Tate. 1995. "The Color of Urban Campaigns." In Paul E. Peterson, ed., *Classifying by Race.* Princeton: Princeton University Press.

Meyerson, Harold. 2001. "A City Hesitates at Political Change." *New York Times,* June 8, A25.

Miller, Abraham. 1971. "Ethnicity and Political Behavior: A Review of Theories and an Attempt at Reformulation." *Western Political Quarterly* 24:483–500.

Miller, Arthur, Patricia Gurin, Gerald Gurin, and Oksana Malanchuk. 1981. "Group Consciousness and Political Participation." *American Journal of Political Science* 25:494–511.

Mladenka, Kenneth D. 1989. "Blacks and Hispanics in Urban Politics." *American Political Science Review* 83 (1): 165–92.

Mollenkopf, John H. 1990. "New York: The Great Anomaly," In Rufus P. Browning, Dale Rogers Marshall, and David H. Tabb, eds. *Racial Politics in American Cities.* New York: Longman.

———. 1994. *A Phoenix in the Ashes: The Rise and Fall of the Koch Coalition in New York City Politics.* Princeton: Princeton University Press.

———. 1997. "New York: The Great Anomaly." In Rufus P. Browning, Dale Rogers Marshall, and David H. Tabb, eds., *Racial Politics in American Cities.* New York: Longman.

———. 1999. "Urban Political Conflicts and Alliances: New York and Los Angeles Compared." In Charles Hirschman, Philip Kasinitz, and Josh DeWind, eds., *The Handbook of International Migration: The American Experience.* New York: Russell Sage Foundation.

———. 2003. "New York: Still the Great Anomaly." In Rufus P. Browning, Dale Rogers Marshall, and David H. Tabb, eds., *Racial Politics in American Cities.* 3d ed. New York: Longman.

Mollenkopf, John, David Olson, and Timothy Ross. 2001. "Immigrant Participation in New York and Los Angeles." In Michael Jones-Correa, ed., *Governing American Cities: Inter-Ethnic Coalitions, Competition, and Conflict.* New York: Russell Sage Foundation.

Morris, Richard T., and Vincent Jeffries. 1970. "The White Reaction Study." In Nathan Cohen, ed., *The Los Angeles Riots: A Socio-psychological Study.* New York: Praeger.

Morrison, Minion K. C. 1987. *Black Political Mobilization: Leadership, Power, and Mass Behavior.* Albany: State University of New York Press.

Munoz, Carlos, Jr., and Charles P. Henry. 1986. "Rainbow Coalitions in Four Big Cities." *PS* 19:598–609.

———. 1990. "Coalition Politics in San Antonio and Denver: The Cisneros and Peña Mayoral Campaigns." In Rufus Browning, Dale Rogers Marshall, and

David Tabb, eds., *Racial Politics in American Cities,* 179–92. New York: Longman.

Murray, Richard, and Arthur Vedlitz. 1978. "Racial Voting Patterns in the South: An Analysis of Major Elections from 1960 to 1977 in Five Cities." *American Academy of Political and Social Science Annals* 439:29–39.

Myrdal, Gunnar. 1944. *An American Dilemma.* New York: Harper and Row.

Nelson, William E., Jr. 1982. "Cleveland: The Rise and Fall of the New Black Politics." In Michael B. Preston, Lenneal J. Henderson Jr., and Paul Puryear, eds., *The New Black Politics.* New York: Longman.

———. 1987. "Cleveland: The Evolution of Black Political Power." In *The New Black Politics: The Search for Political Power,* 2d ed. New York: Longman.

———. 1995. "Cleveland: The Evolution of Black Political Power." In Dennis Keating, Norman Krumholz, and David Perry, eds., *Cleveland: A Metropolitan Reader.* Kent, OH: Kent State University Press.

Nelson, William E., Jr., and Philip J. Meranto. 1977. *Electing Black Mayors.* Columbus: Ohio State University Press.

Newfield, Jack, and Wayne Barrett. 1988. *City for Sale: Ed Koch and the Betrayal of New York.* New York: Perennial.

Nie, Norman, and Sidney Verba. 1972. *Participation in America: Political Democracy and Social Equality.* New York: Harper and Row.

Nie, Norman, Sidney Verba, and John Petrocik. 1976. *The Changing American Voter.* Cambridge, MA: Harvard University Press.

Noel, Peter. 2001. "Take It or Leave It, Mark Green." *Village Voice,* November 6, 28.

O'Connor, Alice, Chris Tilly, and Lawrence D. Bobo, eds. 2001. *Urban Inequality: Evidence from Four Cities.* New York: Russell Sage Foundation.

Ojito, Mirita. 2001. "The 2001 Elections: The Voters: City's Hispanics Shift, Moving Toward G.O.P." *New York Times,* November 8, D5.

Oliver, J. Eric. 2001. *Democracy in Suburbia.* Princeton: Princeton University Press.

Oliver, J. Eric, and T. Mendelberg. 2000. "Reconsidering the Environmental Determinants of White Racial Attitudes." *American Journal of Political Science* 44:574–89.

Olzak, Susan. 1992. *The Dynamics of Ethnic Competition and Conflict.* Stanford: Stanford University Press.

Orr, Marion. 2003. "The Struggle for Black Empowerment in Baltimore." In Rufus P. Browning, Dale Rogers Marshall, and David H. Tabb, eds., *Racial Politics in American Cities,* 3d ed., 227–54. New York: Longman.

Page, Benjamin I., and Calvin C. Jones. 1979. "Reciprocal Effects of Policy Preferences, Party Loyalties, and the Vote." *American Political Science Review* 73 (4): 1071–89.

Page, Benjamin I., and Robert Y. Shapiro. 1992. *The Rational Public: Fifty Years of Trends in American's Policy Preferences.* Chicago: University of Chicago Press.

Parenti, Michael. 1967. "Ethnic Politics and the Persistence of Ethnic Identification." *American Political Science Review* 61:717–26.

Peterson, Paul E. 1981. *City Limits.* Chicago: University of Chicago Press.

Petrocik, John R., and Daron Shaw. 1991. "Nonvoting in America: Attitudes in Context." In William Crotty, ed., *Political Participation and American Democracy.* New York: Greenwood Press.

Pettigrew, Thomas F. 1971. "When a Black Candidate Runs for Mayor: Race and Voting Behavior." In Harlan Hahn, ed., *People and Politics in Urban Society,* 90–105. Beverly Hills, CA: Sage.

Pettigrew, Thomas F., and Denise Alston. 1988. *Tom Bradley's Campaigns for Governor: The Dilemmas of Race and Political Strategies.* Washington, DC: Joint Center for Political Studies.

Pinderhughes, Diane. 1987. *Race and Ethnicity in Chicago Politics.* Urbana: University of Illinois Press.

———. 1994. "Racial and Ethnic Politics in Chicago Mayoral Elections." In George E. Peterson, ed., *Big City Politics, Governance, and Fiscal Constraints.* Washington, DC: Urban Institute Press.

———. 2003. "Chicago Politics: Political Incorporation and Restoration." In Rufus P. Browning, Dale Rogers Marshall, and David H. Tabb, eds., *Racial Politics in American Cities.* 3d ed. New York: Longman.

Piven, Frances, and Richard Cloward. 1979. *Poor People's Movements: Why They Succeed, How They Fail.* New York: Vintage Books.

Pohlmann, Marcus. 1978. "The Electoral Impact of Partisanship and Incumbency Reconsidered: An Extension to Low Salience Elections." *Urban Affairs Quarterly* 13:495–503.

Pomper, Gerald. 1966. "Ethnic and Group Voting in Non-Partisan Municipal Elections." *Public Opinion Quarterly* 30:79–97.

Prentice, Deborah A., and Dale T. Miller, eds. 1999. *Cultural Divides: Understanding and Overcoming Group Conflict.* New York: Russell Sage Foundation.

Preston, Michael. 1976. "Limitations of Black Urban Power: The Case of Black Mayors." In Louis H. Masotti and Robert L. Lineberry, eds., *The New Urban Politics.* Cambridge, MA: Ballinger.

Preston, M. B., B. Cain, and S. Bass, eds. 1997. *Racial and Ethnic Politics in California.* Vol. 2. Berkeley: University of California Press.

Preston, Michael, Lenneal Henderson Jr., and Paul L. Puryear. 1987. *The New Black Politics: The Search for Political Power.* New York: Longman.

Przeworski, Adam, and Henry Teune. 1970. *The Logic of Comparative Social Inquiry.* New York: Wiley.

Purdum, Todd S. 2001. "New Electoral Math changing the script in Los Angeles Duel." *Los Angeles Times,* June 4, A1.

Quillian, Lincoln. 1995. "Prejudice as a Response to Perceived Group Threat: Population Composition and Anti-Immigrant and Racial Prejudice in Europe." *American Sociological Review* 60:586–611.

———. 1996. "Group Threat and Regional Change in Attitudes toward African Americans." *American Journal of Sociology* 102 (3): 816–60.

Quinnipiac University Polling Institute. 2001. "Green Leads 51–35 Percent in Mayoral Race; Bloomberg Seen Better to Rebuild NYC." Press release, October 24. <http:www.quinnipiac.edu/polls/nycpolls.html>.

Ransom, Bruce. 1987. "Black Independent Electoral Politics in Philadelphia: The Election of Mayor W. Wilson Goode." In Michael Preston, Lenneal Henderson Jr., and Paul L. Puryear, eds., *The New Black Politics: The Search for Political Power*, 256–90. New York: Longman.

Reed, Adolph, Jr. 1986. "The Black Urban Regime: Structural Origins and Constraints." *Comparative Urban and Community Research*, 138–89.

Reeves, Keith. 1997. *Voting Hopes or Fears? White Voters, Black Candidates, and Racial Politics in America*. New York: Oxford.

Reibstein, Regina. 1969. "Mayoralty Elections in New York City." *City Almanac* (bimonthly publication by the Center for New York City Affairs of the New School for Social Research), 4, no. 3 (October).

Rich, Wilbur C., ed. 1996. *The Politics of Minority Coalitions: Race, Ethnicity, and Shared Uncertainties*. Westport, CT: Praeger.

Riley, Robert T., and Thomas Pettigrew. 1976. "Dramatic Events and Attitude Change." *Journal of Personality and Social Psychology* 34:1004–15.

Rodriguez, Nestor. 1999. "U.S. Immigration and Changing Relations between African Americans and Latinos." In Charles Hirschman, Philip Kasinitz, and Josh DeWind, eds., *The Handbook of International Migration: The American Experience*. New York: Russell Sage Foundation.

Rogowsky, Edward T., Louis H. Gold, and David W. Abbott. 1971. "The Civilian Review Board Controversy." In Jewell Bellush and Steven M. David, eds., *Race and Politics in New York City: Five Cases in Policy-Making*. New York: Praeger.

Rose, Joseph B. 1989. "Mayor Culpa." *New Republic*, May 8, 18–21.

Rosenstone, Steven J., and John Mark Hansen. 1993. *Mobilization, Participation, and Democracy in America*. New York: MacMillan.

Ross, Bernard H., and Myron A. Levine. 2000. *Urban Politics: Power in Metropolitan America*. 6th ed. Itasca, IL: F. E. Peacock.

Salisbury, Robert H., and Gordon Black. 1963. "Class and Party in Partisan and Nonpartisan Elections: The Case of Des Moines." *American Political Science Review* 57:584–92.

Schuman, Howard, Charlotte Steeh, and Lawrence Bobo. 1997. *Racial Attitudes in America: Trends and Interpretations*. Rev. ed. Cambridge, MA: Harvard University Press.

Sears, David O. 1988. "Symbolic Racism." In P. A. Katz and D. A. Taylor, eds., *Eliminating Racism: Profiles in Controversy.* New York: Plenum Press.

———. 1993. "Symbolic Politics: A Social-Psychological Theory." In Shanto Iyengar and William J. McGuire, eds., *Explorations in Political Psychology.* Durham, NC: Duke University Press.

Sears, David O., and H. M. Allen Jr. 1984. "The Trajectory of Local Desegregation Controversies and Whites' Opposition to Busing." In N. Miller and M. B. Brewer, eds., *Groups in Contact: The Psychology of Desegregation.* New York: Academic Press.

Sears, David O., Jack Citrin, Sharmaine V. Cheleden, and Colette van Laar. 1994. "Urban Rioting in Los Angeles: A Comparison of 1965 with 1992." In Mark Baldassare, ed., *The Los Angeles Riots: Lessons for the Urban Future.* Boulder: Westview Press.

———. 1999. "Cultural Diversity and Multicultural Politics: Is Ethnic Balkanization Psychologically Inevitable?" In Deborah A. Prentice and Dale T. Miller, eds., *Cultural Divides: Understanding and Overcoming Group Conflict.* New York: Russell Sage Foundation.

Sears, David O., Jack Citrin, and Collette van Laar. 1995. "Black Exceptionalism in a Multicultural Society." Paper presented at the annual meeting of the American Political Science Association, Chicago.

Sears, David O., and Carolyn Funk. 1991. "The Role of Self-Interest in Social and Political Attitudes." *Advances in Experimental Social Psychology* 24:1–91.

Sears, D. O., C. P. Hensler, and L. K. Speer. 1979. "Whites' Opposition to Busing: Self-interest or Symbolic Politics." *American Political Science Review* 74:369–84.

Sears, David O., and Donald R. Kinder. 1971. "Racial Tensions and Voting in Los Angeles." In W. Z. Hirsch, ed., *Los Angeles: Viability and Prospects for Metropolitan Leadership.* New York: Praeger.

Sears, David O., and J. B. McConahay. 1973. *The Politics of Violence: The New Urban Blacks and the Watts Riot.* Boston: Houghton Mifflin.

Sears, David O., Jim Sidanius, and Lawrence Bobo. 2000. *Racialized Politics: The Debate about Racism.* Chicago: University of Chicago Press.

Sheffield, James F., and Charles D. Hadley. 1984. "Racial Voting in a Biracial City." *American Politics Quarterly* 12:449–63.

Shefter, Martin. 1985. *Political Crisis, Fiscal Crisis: The Collapse and Revival of New York City.* New York: Basic Books.

Sidanius, Jim, and Felicia Pratto. 1999. *Social Dominance: An Intergroup Theory of Social Hierarchy and Oppression.* New York: Cambridge University Press.

Siegel, Joel. 2001. "A Bruising Dem Showdown Reflected Ethnic, Racial Rift." *New York Daily News,* October 12, A7.

Simon, Herbert. 1985. "Human Nature in Politics: The Dialogue of Psychology with Political Science." *American Political Science Review* 79:293–304.

Skolnick, Jerome H. 1969. *The Politics of Protest*. New York: Simon and Schuster.

Sleeper, Jim. 1990. *The Closest of Strangers: Liberalism and the Politics of Race in New York*. New York: W. W. Norton.

———. 1993. "The End of the Rainbow? The Changing Politics of America's Cities." *New Republic,* November 1, 20–25.

Sniderman, P., and E. Carmines. 1997. *Reaching beyond Race*. Cambridge, MA: Harvard University Press.

Sniderman, Paul, and Thomas Piazza. 1993. *The Scar of Race*. Cambridge, MA: Harvard University Press.

Sniderman, Paul, and P. E. Tetlock. 1986. "Symbolic Racism: Problems of Motive Attribution in Political Analysis." *Journal of Social Issues* 42:129–50.

Sniderman, Paul, P. E. Tetlock, and E. Carmines. 1993. *Prejudice, Politics, and the American Dilemma*. Stanford: Stanford University Press.

Sonenshein, Raphael J. 1993a. *Politics in Black and White: Race and Power in Los Angeles*. Princeton: Princeton University Press.

———. 1993b. "Is This the End? Biracial Coalition in the 1993 Los Angeles Mayoral Election." Paper delivered at the annual meeting of the American Political Science Association, Washington, DC.

Sonenshein, R., and N. Valentino. 1995. "Minority Politics at the Crossroads: Voting Patterns in the 1993 Los Angeles Mayoral Election." Paper delivered at the annual meeting of the Western Political Science Association, Pasadena, CA, March.

Starks, Robert T. 1991. "A Commentary and Response to 'Exploring the Meaning and Implication of Deracialization in African-American Urban Politics.'" *Urban Affairs Quarterly* 27 (2): 216–22.

Stein, Robert M. 1990. "Economic Voting for Governor and U.S. Senator: The Electoral Consequences of Federalism." *Journal of Politics* 52 (February): 29–53.

Stein, Robert M., Stephanie Shirley Post, and Allison L. Rinden. 2000. "Reconciling Context and Contact Effects on Racial Attitudes." *Political Research Quarterly* 53 (2): 285–304.

Stone, Clarence N. 1989. *Regime Politics: Governing Atlanta, 1946–1988*. Lawrence: University Press of Kansas.

———. 1993. "Urban Regimes and the Capacity to Govern: A Political Economy Approach." *Journal of Urban Affairs* 15 (1): 1–28.

Stowers, G., and R. Vogel. 1994. "Racial and Ethnic Voting Patterns in Miami." In G. E. Peterson, ed., *Big City Politics, Governance, and Fiscal Constraints*. Washington, DC: Urban Institute Press.

Swanstrom, Todd. 1985. *The Crisis of Growth Politics: Cleveland, Kucinich, and the Challenge of Urban Populism*. Philadelphia: Temple University Press.

Tate, Katherine. 1989. "Black Political Participation in the 1984 and 1988 Presidential Elections." *American Political Science Review* 85 (4): 1159–76.

———. 1993. *From Protest to Politics: The New Black Voters in American Elections.* Cambridge, MA: Russell Sage, Harvard University Press.

Taylor, Marylee C. 1998. "How White Attitudes Vary with the Racial Composition of Local Populations: Numbers Count." *American Sociological Review* 63:512–35.

Tedin, K. L. 1994. "Self-interest, Symbolic Values, and the Financial Equalization of the Public Schools." *Journal of Politics* 56 (3): 628–49.

Terkildsen, Nadia. 1993. "When White Voters Evaluate Black Candidates: The Processing Implications of Candidate Skin Color, Prejudice, and Self-Monitoring." *American Journal of Political Science* 37:1032–53.

Tierney, Kathleen J. 1994. "Property Damage and Violence: A Collective Behavior Analysis." In Mark Balassare, ed., *The Los Angeles Riots: Lessons for the Urban Future.* Boulder: Westview Press.

Tolbert, Caroline J., and Rodney E. Hero. 1996. "Race/Ethnicity and Direct Democracy: An Analysis of California's Illegal Immigration Initiative." *Journal of Politics* 58 (3): 806–18.

———. 2001. "Dealing with Diversity: Racial/Ethnic Context and Social Policy Change." *Political Research Quarterly* 54 (3): 571–604.

Turner, John C. 1987. *Rediscovering the Social Group: A Self-categorization Theory.* Oxford: Basil Blackwell.

Uhlaner, Carole. 1989. "Rational Turnout: The Neglected Role of Groups." *American Journal of Political Science* 33 (2): 390–422.

———. 1991. "Perceived Discrimination and Prejudice and the Coalition Prospects of Blacks, Latinos, and Asian Americans." In Byron O. Jackson and Michael Preston, eds., *Racial and Ethnic Politics in California.* Berkeley: IGS Press.

Uhlaner, Carole, Bruce Cain, and Roderick Kiewiet. 1989. "Political Participation of Ethnic Minorities in the 1980s." *Political Behavior* 11:195–231.

Valle, Victor M., and Rodolfo D. Torres. 2000. *Latino Metropolis.* Minneapolis: University of Minnesota Press.

Vanderleeuw, James M. 1990. "A City in Transition: The Impact of Changing Racial Composition on Voting Behavior." *Social Science Quarterly* 71:326–38.

Waldinger, Roger. 1995. "When the Melting Pot Boils Over: The Irish, Jews, Blacks, and Koreans of New York." In Michael Peter Smith and Joe R. Feagin, eds., *The Bubbling Cauldron: Race, Ethnicity, and the Urban Crisis.* Minneapolis: University of Minnesota Press.

———. 1996. *Still the Promised City: African-Americans and New Immigrants in Post-Industrial New York.* Cambridge, MA: Harvard University Press.

Wattenberg, Martin P. 1991. *The Rise of Candidate-Centered Politics: Presidential Elections of the 1980s.* Cambridge, MA: Harvard University Press.

White, J. E. 1993. "Bright City Lights." *Time,* November 1, 28–32.

Williams, Oliver P. 1967. "Life-style Values and Political Decentralization in Metropolitan Areas." *Social Science Quarterly* 48:299–310.

Winn, Mylon. 1990. "The Election of Norman Rice as Mayor of Seattle" (part of a symposium of black electoral success in 1989). *PS* 23:158–59.

Wolfinger, Raymond. 1965. "The Development and Persistence of Ethnic Voting." *American Political Science Review* 59:896–908.

———. 1974. *The Politics of Progress*. Englewood Cliffs, NJ: Prentice Hall.

Wolfinger, Raymond, and Fred Greenstein. 1968. "The Repeal of Fair Housing in California: An Analysis of Referendum Voting." *American Political Science Review* 62:753–59.

Wolfinger, Raymond E., and Steven J. Rosenstone. 1980. *Who Votes?* New Haven: Yale University Press.

Wright, Gerald. 1977. "Contextual Models of Electoral Behavior: The Southern Wallace Vote." *American Political Science Review* 71:497–508.

Zaller, John R. 1992. *The Nature and Origins of Mass Opinion*. New York: Cambridge University Press.

Index

Note: *Page numbers in italics refer to tables.*